A Theory of Content

and Other Essays

A Theory of Content

and Other Essays

Jerry A. Fodor

A Bradford Book
The MIT Press
Cambridge, Massachusetts
London, England

This book was set in Palatino
by DEKR Corporation
and printed and bound
in the United States of America.

Library of Congress Cataloging-in-Publication Data

Fodor, Jerry A.
  A theory of content and other essays / by Jerry A. Fodor.
     p.   cm.

  "A Bradford book."
  Includes bibliographical references.
  ISBN 0-262-06130-9
  1. Mind, Philosophy of. 2. Content (Psychology) 3. Functionalism
(Psychology) 4. Semantics (Philosophy) I. Title.
BD418.3.F63   1990
128'.2—dc20   89-28523
                                                                           CIP

Contents

vi   Contents

Preface and Acknowledgments

Except for the eponymous essay, all the pieces collected here have been published previously. Though I've corrected some minor errors, typos and the like, I've otherwise left them intact. In some cases, the later essays reject ideas toward which the earlier ones were partial. (An egregious example is the treatment of teleological approaches to the naturalization of semantical relations; these are viewed with optimism in "Fodor's Guide" and "Semantics, Wisconsin Style" but denounced in "A Theory of Content I.") I think there's nevertheless a substantial consistency from chapter to chapter; a fairly fixed sense of what needs to be done comports with an evolving account of how to do it. Since, anyhow, I don't write for posterity, I don't feel bad about changing my mind in public. Posterity will, no doubt, have problems of its own; I am glad to settle for a slightly better story to tell than the one I had last week.

"Fodor's Guide to Mental Representation" is reprinted from *Mind*, Spring 1985, pp. 55–97, by the kind permission of the Oxford University Press. "Semantics, Wisconsin Style" is reprinted from *Synthese* 59, 1984, pp. 231–250, copyright Kluwer Academic Publishers, by the kind permission of the publisher. "Making Mind Matter More" is reprinted from *Philosophical Topics* LXVII, 1, pp. 59–79, by the kind permission of *Philosophical Topics*. "Substitution Arguments and the Individuation of Belief" is reprinted from G. Boolos, ed., 1989, *Method, Reason and Language*, Cambridge: the Cambridge University Press, by the kind permission of the publisher. "Review of Stephen Schiffer's *Remnants of Meaning*" is reprinted from *Philosophy and Phenomenological Research* 50, 2, by the kind permission of *Philosophy and Phenomenological Research*. "Précis of *Modularity of Mind*" is reprinted from *The Behavioral and Brain Sciences* 8, 1985, 1–42 by the kind permission of the publisher, Cambridge University Press. "Why Should the Mind Be Modular?" is reprinted from A. George, ed., *Reflections on Chomsky*, 1989, by the kind permission of Basil Blackwell, Ltd. "Observation Reconsidered" is reprinted from *Philosophy of Science*

51, 1984, pp. 23–43, and "A Reply to Churchland's 'Perceptual Plasticity and Theoretical Neutrality'" is reprinted from *Philosophy of Science* 55, 1988, pp. 188–198. Both are reprinted by the kind permission of *Philosophy of Science*.

I should like to thank Mr. Martin Schisselman for his help in assembling the manuscript.

Introduction

With the exception of two enjoyable, but essentially digressive, interludes of Connectionist bashing (see Fodor and Pylyshyn, 1988; Fodor and McLaughlin, 1989) the essays included here represent my major professional preoccupations for the last five or six years. As the reader will see at a glance, they divide in two. On the one hand, there's a batch of more or less philosophical pieces on mental representation and the foundations of intentionality; and, on the other hand, there's a batch of more or less psychological pieces on cognitive architecture. You may wonder whether these topics have anything in common other than my recent interest in both. I thought that a brief introductory note on that might be appropriate.

Here is one way that the two topics might be taken to connect: a goal that theories of cognitive architecture pursue is to say whatever there is that's general about the character of the causal interactions that can occur among cognitive states. You might think of such theories as trying to provide a taxonomy of the nomologically possible mental processes, where a "nomologically possible" mental process is one that's compatible with psychological law. Now, among the views of intentional content that have, from time to time, found favor in the philosophical community, there is this familiar "functionalist" one: the intentional contents of mental states are constituted—or, anyhow, constrained—by their causal interrelations. So, according to such views, part (or maybe all) of what it is for your current mental state to be a thought that *some cats have whiskers* is its being a state that has a disposition to cause you to think the thought that some animals do. It is thus intrinsic to cat thoughts that they tend to cause animal thoughts; so this sort of story goes. Suppose, for the moment, that this is true. Then a theory that says what kinds of causal relations among mental states are possible would, ipso facto, be a theory of the (or of one of the) determinants of content. Functionalism proposes a bridge from cognitive architecture to semantics, to put the point in a nutshell. Given functionalism, what mental processes there can be partly determines what thoughts you can have.

I say you might suppose this, but I don't. Finding alternatives to functionalist accounts of mental content is a major concern in these studies. Here's why:

I take it very seriously that there is no principled distinction between matters of meaning and matters of fact. Quine was right; you can't have an analytic/synthetic distinction. In the present context, this means that you can't have a principled distinction between the kinds of causal relations among mental states that determine content and the kind of causal relations among mental states that don't. The immediate consequence is that you can't have functionalism without holism; if *any* of the function of a mental state bears on its content, then *all* of its function bears on its content. But if all of function bears on content, then no two mental state tokens ever have the same content and there can be no such thing as psychological explanation by subsumption under intentional law.

So the story is that if you take it seriously that there is no analytic/ synthetic distinction, then there's a prima facie inference from functionalism to holism and from holism to skepticism; and the question is what to do about it. As far as I can tell, there are two main camps: either you accept the inference and live with the skepticism, or you try to block the inference by taking it less than absolutely seriously that there is no analytic/synthetic distinction. The first kind of philosopher says: "Well, *very strictly speaking*—in a first-class conceptual system, and like that—it really isn't true that people act out of their beliefs and desires. *Very strictly speaking* there can't be a scientific intentional psychology, however much belief-desire explanation may be a *human* necessity and however well it may work in practice." The other kind of philosopher says: "I know, of course, that you can't have a *full-blown* analytic synthetic distinction; but perhaps you can have a graded, or relativized, or localized, or otherwise denatured analytic/synthetic distinction. In which case, functionalism doesn't imply holism and is compatible with intentional realism after all."

But it seems to me that none of this will do. If it follows from your semantics that *very strictly speaking* nobody has ever thought that perhaps it was going to rain, then there is something wrong with your semantics. (Cf. G. E. Moore on epistemologies from which it follows that *very strictly speaking* you don't know whether you have hands.) And the arguments that there is no analytic/synthetic distinction are arguments that there is *no* analytic/synthetic distinction; not even a little one. Quine's point (utterly convincing, in my view) is that what pass for intuitions of analyticity are in fact intuitions of centrality; and centrality is an *epistemic* relation, not a semantical one. That is to say: a functional analysis which would account for intuitions of analyticity, wouldn't determine *content*. It wouldn't be a *semantic* theory (even if we had one—which we don't).

The semantical parts of this book are largely about how to square intentional realism with Quine's being right about analytic/synthetic. The way to do it is to be relentlessly atomistic about meaning (which means, of course not being a functionalist about meaning; see above). What's nice about informational theories of meaning is precisely that they point the way to relentless semantic atomism. In the general case, the information that a symbol carries is independent of it causal relations to other symbols; a symbol can satisfy the constraints for carrying information *even if it doesn't belong to a language*. Informational theories of meaning have their problems, to be sure, many of which raise their heads in the chapters that follow. But holism is not among the problems that they have. Informational semanticists can therefore be robustly realist about content; something that no other kind of semanticist has thus far figured out how to be.

So much, then, for what the two parts of this book *don't* have in common; they aren't linked by a semantics that makes cognitive architecture a determinant of intentional content.

In fact, the unity is thematic. Just as an informational view of semantics, of the sort developed in part I, offers the possibility of atomism about meaning, so a modular view of cognitive architecture, of the sort developed in part II, offers the possibility of atomism about perception. Semantic atomism is the idea that what you mean is largely independent of what you believe; perceptual atomism is the idea that so too is what you see.

These ideas come together in epistemology in a way that the last essays in this volume only begin to explore. It is, perhaps, the characteristic strategy of (serious) philosophers in our time to appeal to semantic and psychological holism to support epistemic relativism. (Our frivolous philosophers arrive at much the same conclusion, though by worse arguments, or by none).

Thus, if what you mean depends on what you believe, it must be a fallacy of equivocation to suppose that Jones' theory could assert what Smith's theory denies. So the theory Jones believes must be compatible with the theory Smith believes. Between compatible theories there is, however, nothing to choose. Thus semantic holism leads to incommensurability and incommensurability leads to relativism. Or again, if what you see is determined by what you believe, then scientists with different theories see different things *even when they are in the same experimental environment*. So experimental observations are theoretically biased, not just from time to time but in the nature of the case. So unbiased experimental observation isn't what decides scientific controversies. So maybe nothing that's unbiased does. Thus holism about perception leads to skepticism about observation, and skepticism about observation leads to relativism about confirmation. This is all very rough, to be sure; but I suppose that the geography is familiar.

I hate relativism. I think it affronts intellectual dignity. I am appalled that it is thought to be respectable. But, alas, neither my hating it nor its affronting intellectual dignity nor my being appalled that it is thought to be respectable shows that relativism is false. What's needed to show that it is false is to take away the arguments that purport to show that it is true. The argument, par excellence, that purports to show that relativism is true is holism. So this book is an attempt to take away holism. Hate me, hate my dog.

I do not think that this book is a *successful* attempt to take away holism. But I don't think it's an outright failure either. Quite generally, I don't think of philosophy as a kind of enterprise in which the sole options are outright failure or success. What I hope for, rather, is this: I would like to convince you that the arguments for (semantic and psychological) holism really aren't very substantial; that there are serious atomistic alternatives to each; that the possibilities for further development of such alternatives look sufficiently bright to merit our careful and detailed attention. Everybody takes holism for granted these days, but not, I think, for any very good reasons; certainly not for any very good reasons that they've managed to make explicit. I'd like to change all that.

That's what I'd like. What I'll settle for is just convincing you that *holism might not be true* (and therefore must not be assumed in arguments for relativism). Then, maybe, my next book will convince you that holism *really* might not be true. And so on. You've got to start somewhere, I suppose; and everybody tells me it's the first million that's the hard one.

PART I

Intentionality

If the fool would persist in his folly, he would become wise.
—William Blake

Chapter 1

Fodor' Guide to Mental Representation: The Intelligent Auntie's Vade-Mecum

It rained for weeks and we were all *so* tired of ontology, but there didn't seem to be much else to do. Some of the children started to sulk and pull the cat's tail. It was going to be an *awful* afternoon until Uncle Wilifred thought of Mental Representations (which was a game that we hadn't played for *years*) and everybody got *very* excited and we jumped up and down and waved our hands and all talked at once and had a perfectly *lovely* romp. But Auntie said that she couldn't stand the noise and there would be tears before bedtime if we didn't please calm down.

Auntie rather disapproves of what is going on in the Playroom, and you can't entirely blame her. Ten or fifteen years of philosophical discussion of mental representation has produced a considerable appearance of disorder. Every conceivable position seems to have been occupied, along with some whose conceivability it is permissible to doubt. And every view that anyone has mooted, someone else has undertaken to refute. This does *not* strike Auntie as constructive play. She sighs for the days when well-brought-up philosophers of mind kept themselves occupied for hours on end analyzing their behavioral dispositions.

But the chaotic appearances are actually misleading. A rather surprising amount of agreement has emerged, if not about who's winning, at least about how the game has to be played. In fact, everybody involved concurs, pretty much, on what the options are. They differ in their hunches about which of the options it would be profitable to exercise. The resulting noise is of these intuitions clashing. In this paper, I want to make as much of the consensus as I can explicit; both by way of reassuring Auntie and in order to provide new participants with a quick guide to the game: Who's where and how did they get there? Since it's very nearly true that you can locate all the players by their answers to quite a small number of diagnostic questions, I shall organize the discussion along those lines. What follows is a short projective test of the sort that self-absorbed persons use to reveal their hitherto unrecognized proclivities. I hope for a great success in California.

First Question: How Do You Feel about Propositional Attitudes?

The contemporary discussion about mental representation is intimately and intricately involved with the question of Realism about propositional attitudes. Since a goal of this essay is to locate the issues about mental representation with respect to other questions in the philosophy of mind, we commence by setting out this relation in several of its aspects.

The natural home of the propositional attitudes is in "commonsense" (or "belief/desire") psychological explanation. If you ask the Man on the Clapham Omnibus what precisely he is doing there, he will tell you a story along the following lines: "I wanted to get home (to work, to Auntie's) and I have reason to believe that there—or somewhere near it—is where this omnibus is going." It is, in short, untendentious that people regularly account for their voluntary behavior by citing beliefs and desires that they entertain; and that, if their behavior is challenged, they regularly defend it by maintaining the rationality of the beliefs ("Because it *says* it's going to Clapham") and the probity of the desires ("Because it's *nice* visiting Auntie"). That, however, is probably as far as the Clapham Omnibus will take us. What comes next is a philosophical gloss—and, eventually, a philosophical theory.

First Philosophical Gloss: When the ordinary chap says that he's doing what he is because he has the beliefs and desires that he does, it is reasonable to read the 'because' as a *causal* 'because'—whatever, exactly, a causal 'because' may be. At a minimum, common sense seems to require belief/desire explanations to support counterfactuals in ways that are familiar in causal explanation at large: if, for example, it is true that Psmith did A because he believed B and desired C, then it must be that Psmith would *not* have done A if either he had not believed B or he had not desired C. (Ceteris paribus, it goes without saying.) Common sense also probably takes it that if Psmith did A because he believed B and desired C, then—ceteris paribus again—believing B and desiring C is causally sufficient for doing A. (However, common sense does get confused about this since—though believing B and desiring C was what caused Psmith to do A—still it is common sense that Psmith could have believed B and desired C and *not* done A had he so decided. It is a question of some interest whether common sense can have it both ways.) Anyhow, to a first approximation the commonsense view is that there is mental causation, and that mental causes are subsumed by counterfactual—supporting generalizations of which the practical syllogism is perhaps the paradigm.

Closely connected is the following: Everyman's view seems to be that propositional attitudes cause (not only behavior but also) other propositional attitudes. Thoughts cause desires (so that thinking about visiting Auntie makes one want to) and—perhaps a little more tendentiously—the other way around as well (so that the wish is often father to the thought, according to the commonsense view of mental genealogy). In the paradigm mental process—viz. thinking—thoughts give rise to one another and eventuate in the fixation of beliefs. That is what Sherlock Holmes was supposed to be so good at.

Second Philosophical Gloss: Common sense has it that beliefs and desires are semantically evaluable; that they have *satisfaction-conditions*. Roughly, the satisfaction-condition for a belief is the state of affairs in virtue of which that belief is true or false and the satisfaction-condition for a desire is the state of affairs in virtue of which that desire is fulfilled or frustrated. Thus, 'that it continues to rain' makes true the belief that it is raining and frustrates the desire that the rain should stop. This could stand a lot more sharpening, but it will do for the purposes at hand.

It will have occurred to the reader that there are other ways of glossing commonsense belief/desire psychology. And that, even if this way of glossing it is right, commonsense belief/desire psychology may be in need of emendation. Or cancellation. Quite so, but my purpose isn't to defend or criticize; I just want to establish a point of reference. I propose to say that someone is a *Realist* about propositional attitudes if (a) he holds that there are mental states whose occurrences and interactions cause behavior and do so, moreover, in ways that respect (at least to an approximation) the generalizations of commonsense belief/desire psychology; and (b) he holds that these same causally efficacious mental states are also semantically evaluable.

So much for commonsense psychological explanation. The connection with our topic is this: the full-blown Representational Theory of Mind (hereinafter RTM, about which a great deal presently) purports to explain how there *could be* states that have the semantical and causal properties that propositional attitudes are commonsensically supposed to have. In effect, RTM proposes an account of what the propositional attitudes *are*. So, the further you are from Realism about propositional attitudes, the dimmer the view of RTM that you are likely to take.

Quite a lot of the philosophical discussion that's relevant to RTM, therefore, concerns the status and prospects of commonsense intentional psychology. More, perhaps, than is generally realized. For example, we'll see presently that some of the philosophical worries about RTM derive from scepticism about the semantical properties of mental representations. Putnam, in particular, has been explicit in questioning whether coherent sense could be made of such properties. (See Putnam, 1986, 1983.) I have my doubts about the seriousness of these worries (see Fodor, 1985); but the present point is that they are, in any event, misdirected as arguments against RTM. If there is something wrong with meaning, what that shows is something *very* radical, viz. that there is something wrong with propositional attitudes (a moral, by the way, that Quine, Davidson, and Stich, among others, have drawn explicitly). That, and *not* RTM, is surely the ground on which this action should be fought.

If, in short, you think that common sense is just plain *wrong* about the aetiology of behavior—i.e., that there is *nothing* that has the causal and semantic properties that common sense attributes to the attitudes—then the questions that RTM purports to answer don't so much as arise for you. You won't care much what the attitudes are if you take the view that there aren't any. Many philosophers do take this view and are thus united in their indifference to RTM. Among these Anti-Realists there are, however, interesting differences in motivation and tone of voice. Here, then, are some ways of not being a Realist about beliefs and desires.

First Anti-Realist Option: You could taken an *instrumentalist* view of intentional explanation. You could hold that though there are, *strictly speaking*, no such things as belief and desires, still talking as though there were some often leads to confirmed behavioral predictions. Everyman is therefore licensed to talk that way—to adopt, as one says, the intentional stance—so long as he doesn't take the ontological commitments of belief/desire psychology literally. (Navigators talk geocentric astronomy for convenience, and nobody holds it against them; it gets them where they want to go.) The great virtue of instrumentalism—here as elsewhere—is that you get all the goodness and suffer none of the pain: you get to use propositional-attitude psychology to make behavioral predictions; you get to 'accept' all the intentional explanations that it is convenient to accept; but you don't have to answer hard questions about what the attitudes *are*.

There is, however, a standard objection to instrumentalism (again, here as elsewhere): it's hard to explain why belief/desire psychology works so well if belief/desire psychology is, as a matter of fact, not true. I propose to steer clear, throughout this essay, of general issues in the philosophy of science; in particular of issues about the status of scientific theories at large. But—as Putnam, Boyd and others have emphasized—there is surely a presumptive inference from the predictive successes of a theory to its truth; still more so when (unlike geocentric astronomy) it is the *only* predictively successful theory in the field. It's not, to put it mildly, obvious why this presumption shouldn't militate in favor of a Realist—as against an instrumentalist—construal of belief/desire explanations.

The most extensively worked-out version of instrumentalism about the attitudes in the recent literature is surely owing to D. C. Dennett. (See the papers in Dennett (1978a), especially the essay "Intentional Systems.") Dennett confronts the 'if it isn't true, why does it work?' problem (Dennett, 1981), but I find his position obscure. Here's how I *think* it goes: (a) belief/desire explanations rest on very comprehensive rationality assumptions; it's only fully rational systems that such explanations could be literally true of. These rationality assumptions are, however, generally contrary to fact; *that's* why intentional explanations can't be better than instrumental. On the other hand, (b) intentional explanations *work* because we apply them only to evolutionary successful (or other "designed") systems; and if the behavior of a system didn't at least *approximate* rationality it wouldn't *be* evolutionarily successful; what it would be is extinct.

There is a lot about this that's problematic. To begin with, it's unclear whether there really is a rationality assumption implicit in intentional explanation and whether, it there is, the rationality assumption that's required is so strong as to be certainly false. Dennett says in "Intentional Systems" (Dennett, 1978c) that unless we assume rationality, we get no behavioral predictions out of belief/desire psychology since without rationality any behavior is compatible with any beliefs and desires. Clearly, however, you don't need to assume *much* rationality if all you want is *some* predictivity; perhaps you don't need to assume more rationality than organisms actually have.

Perhaps, in short, the rationality that Dennett says that natural selection guarantees is enough to support *literal* (not just instrumental) intentional ascription. At a minimum, there seems to be a clash between Dennett's principles (a) and (b) since if it *follows from* evolutionary theory that successful organisms are pretty rational, then it's hard to see how attributions of rationality to successful organisms can be construed purely instrumentally (as merely a 'stance' that we adopt towards systems whose behavior we seek to predict).

Finally, if you admit that it's a matter of fact that some agents are rational to some degree, then you have to face the hard question of how they *can* be. After all, not *everything* that's "designed" is rational even to a degree. Bricks aren't, for example; they have the wrong kind of structure. The question what sort of structure is required for rationality does, therefore, rather suggest itself and it's very unclear that that question can be answered without talking about structures of beliefs and desires; intentional psychology is the only candidate we have so far for a theory of how rationality is achieved. This suggests—what I think is true but won't argue for here—that the rational systems are a species of the intentional ones rather than the other way around. If that is so, then it is misguided to appeal to rationality in the analysis of intentionality since, in the order of explanation, the latter is the more fundamental notion. With what one thing and another, it does seem possible to doubt that a coherent instrumentalism about the attitudes is going to be forthcoming.

Second Anti-Realist Option: You could take the view that belief/desire psychology is just plain false and skip the instrumentalist trimmings. On this way of telling the Anti-Realist story, belief/desire psychology is in competition with alternative accounts of the aetiology of behavior and should be judged in the same way that the alternatives are; by its predictive successes, by the plausibility of its ontological commitments, and by its coherence with the rest of the scientific enterprise. No doubt the predictive successes of belief/desire explanations are pretty impressive—especially when they are allowed to make free use of ceteris paribus clauses. But when judged by the second and third criteria, commonsense psychology proves to be a *bad* theory; 'stagnant science' is the preferred epithet (see Paul Churchland, 1981; Stich, 1983). What we ought therefore to do is get rid of it and find something better.

There is, however, some disagreement as to what something better would be like. What matters here is how you feel about Functionalism. So let's have that be our next diagnostic question.

(Is everybody still with us? In case you're not, see the decision tree in figure 1.1 for the discussion so far. Auntie's motto: a place for every person; every person in his place.)

Second Question: How Do You Feel about Functionalism?

(This is a twice-told tale, so I'll be quick. For a longer review, see Fodor, 1981; Fodor, 1981C.)

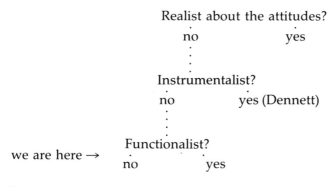

Figure 1.1.
Decision Tree, stage 1.

It looked, in the early 1960s, as though anybody who wanted psychology to be compatible with a physicalistic ontology had a choice between some or other kind of *behaviorism* and some or other kind of *property-identity theory*. For a variety of reasons, neither of these options seemed very satisfactory (in fact, they still don't) so a small tempest brewed in the philosophical teapot.

What came of it was a new account of the type/token relation for psychological states: psychological-state tokens were to be assigned to psychological-state types *solely* by reference to their causal relations to proximal stimuli ('inputs'), to proximal responses ('outputs'), and to one another. The advertising claimed two notable virtues for this theory: first, it was *compatible* with physicalism in that it permitted tokenings of psychological states to be identical to tokenings of physical states (and thus to enjoy whatever causal properties physical states are supposed to have). Second, it permitted tokens of one and the same psychological-state type to differ arbitrarily in their physical kind. This comforted the emerging intuition that the natural domain for psychological theory might be physically heterogeneous, including a motley of people, animals, Martians (always, in the philosophical literature, assumed to be silicon based), and computing machines.

Functionalism, so construed, was greeted with audible joy by the new breed of 'Cognitive Scientists' and has clearly become the received ontological doctrine in that discipline. For, if Functionalism is true, then there is plausibly a *level of explanation* between common-sense belief/desire psychology, on the one hand, and neurological (circuit-theoretic; generally 'hard-science') explanation on the other. 'Cognitive Scientists' could plausibly formulate their enterprise as the construction of theories pitched at that level. Moreover, it was possible to tell a reasonable and aesthetically gratifying story about the relations *between* the levels: commonsense belief/desire explanations *reduce* to explanations articulated in terms of functional states (at least the true ones do) because, according to Functionalism, beliefs and desires *are* functional states. And, for each (true) psychological explanation, there will be a corresponding story, to be told in hard-science terms, about how the functional states that it postulates are "realized" in the system under study. Many different hard-science stories may correspond to one and the same functional explanation since, as we saw, the criteria for the tokening of functional states abstract from the physical character of the tokens. (The most careful and convincing Functionalist manifestos I know are Block, 1980; and Cummins, 1983; q.v.)

Enthusiasm for Functionalism was (is) not, however, universal. For example, viewed from a neuroscientist's perspective (or from the perspective of a hard-line "type-physicalist") Functionalism may appear to be merely a rationale for making do with bad psychology. A picture many neuroscientists have is that, if there really are beliefs and desires (or memories, or percepts, or mental images or whatever else the psychologist may have in his grab bag), it ought to be possible to "find" them in the brain; where what *that* requires is that two tokens of the same *psychological* kind (today's desire to visit Auntie, say, and yesterday's) should correspond to two tokens of the same *neurological* kind (today's firing of neuron #535, say, and yesterday's). Patently, Functionalism relaxes that requirement; relaxes it, indeed, to the point of invisibility. Functionalism just *is* the doctrine that the psychologist's theoretical taxonomy doesn't need to look "natural" from the point of view of any lower-level science. This seems to some neuroscientists, and to some of their philosopher friends, like letting psychologists get away with murder. (See, for example, Churchland, 1981, which argues that Functionalism could have "saved" alchemy if only the alchemists had been devious enough to devise it.) There is, for once, something tangible at issue here: who has the right theoretical vocabulary for explaining behavior determines who should get the grants.

So much for Functionalism except to add that one can, of course, combine *accepting* the Functionalist ontology with *rejecting* the reduction of belief/desire explanations to functional ones (for example, because you think that, though *some* Functionalist psychological explanations are true, no commonsense belief/desire psychological explanations are). Bearing this proviso in mind, we can put some more people in their places: if you are Anti-Realist (and anti-instrumentalist) about belief/desire psychology *and* you think there is no Functional level of explanation, then probably you think that behavioral science is (or, anyhow, ought to be) neuroscience.[1] (A fortiori, you will be no partisan of RTM, which is, of course, way over on the other side of the decision tree.) The Churchlands are the paradigm inhabitants of this niche. On the other hand, if you combine eliminativist sentiments about propositional attitudes with enthusiasm for the functional individuation of mental states, then you anticipate the eventual *replacement* of commonsense belief/desire explanations by theories couched in the vocabulary of a Functionalist psychology; replacement rather than *reduction*. You are thus led to write books with such titles as *From Folk Psychology to Cognitive Science* and are almost certainly identical to Steven Stich.

One more word about Anti-Realism. It may strike you as odd that, whereas instrumentalists hold that belief/desire psychology works so well that we can't do anything without it, eliminativists hold that it works so badly ("stagnant science" and all that) that we can't do anything *with* it. Why, you may ask, don't these Anti-Realists get their acts together?

This is not, however, a real paradox. Instrumentalists can agree with elminativists that *for the purposes of scientific/serious explanation* the attitudes have to be dispensed with. And eliminativists can agree with instrumentalists that for *practical* purposes, the attitudes do seem quite indispensable. In fact—and here's the point I want to stress just now—what largely motivates Anti-Realism is something deeper than the empirical speculation that belief/desire explanations won't pan out as science; it's the sense that there is something intrinsically wrong with the intentional. This is so important that I propose to leave it to the very end.

Now for the other side of the decision tree. (Presently we'll get to RTM.)

If you are a Realist about propositional attitudes, then of course you think that there are beliefs and desires. Now, on this side of the tree too you get to decide whether to be a Functionalist or not. If you are not, then you are probably John Searle, and you drop off the edge of this paper. My own view is that RTM, construed as a species of Functionalist psychology, offers the best Realist account of the attitudes that is currently available; but this view is—to put it mildly—not universally shared. There are philosophers (many of whom like Searle, Dreyfus, and Haugeland are more or less heavily invested in Phenomenology) who are hyper-Realist about the attitudes but deeply unenthusiastic about both Functionalism and RTM. It is not unusual for such theorists to hold (a) that there *is* no currently available, satisfactory answer to the question 'how could there be things that satisfy the constraints that common sense places upon the attitudes?'; and (b) that finding an answer to this question is, in any event, not the philosopher's job. (Maybe it is the psychologist's job, or the neuroscientist's. See Dreyfus, 1979; Haugeland, 1971; Searle, 1981.)

For how the decision tree looks now, see figure 1-2.

If you think that there are beliefs and desires, and you think that they are functional states, then you get to answer the following diagnostic question:

Third Question: Are Propositional Attitudes Monadic Functional States?

This may strike you as a *silly* question. For, you may say, since propositional attitudes are by definition relations to propositions, it follows that propositional attitudes are by definition not monadic. A propositional attitude is, to a first approximation, a *pair* of a proposition and a set of intentional systems, viz., the set of intentional systems which bear that attitude to that proposition.

That would seem to be reasonable enough. But the current (Naturalistic) consensus is that if you've gone this far you will have to go further. Something has to be said about the place of the semantic and the intentional in the natural order; it won't do to have unexplicated "relations to propositions" at the foundations of the philosophy of mind.

Just *why* it won't do—precisely what physicalist or Naturalist scruples it would outrage—is, to be sure, not very clear. Presumably the issue isn't Nominalism, for why raise that issue *here*; if physicists have numbers to play with, why shouldn't psychologists have propositions? And it can't be worries about individuation since distinguishing propositions is surely no harder than distinguishing

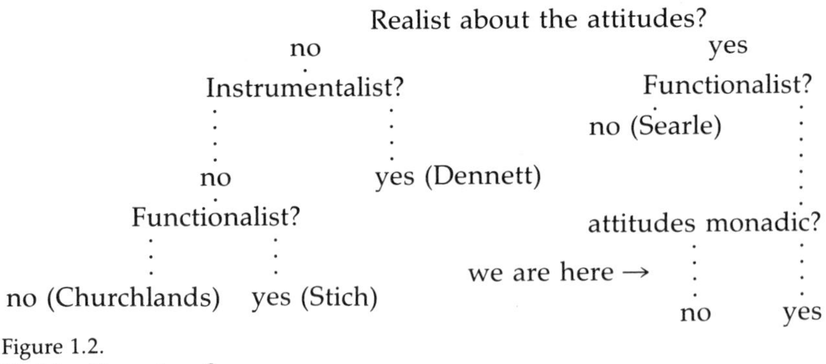

Realist about the attitudes?

             no   yes

Instrumentalist?   Functionalist?

                           no (Searle)

   no   yes (Dennett)

Functionalist?   attitudes monadic?

                   we are here →

no (Churchlands)   yes (Stich)   no   yes

Figure 1.2.
Decision Tree, stage 2.

propositional attitudes and, for better or worse, we're committed to the latter on this side of the decision tree. A more plausible scruple—one I am inclined to take seriously—objects to unreduced *epistemic* relations like *grasping* propositions. One really doesn't want psychology to presuppose any of *those*; first because epistemic relations are preeminently what psychology is supposed to *explain*, and second for fear of "ontological danglers." It's not that there aren't propositions, and it's not that there aren't graspings of them; it's rather that graspings of propositions aren't plausible candidates for ultimate stuff. If they're real, they must be really something else.

Anyhow, one might as well sing the songs one knows. There *is* a reductive story to tell about *what it is* for an attitude to have a proposition as its object. So, metaphysical issues to one side, why not tell it?

The story goes as follows. Propositional attitudes are monadic, functional states of organisms. Functional states, you will recall, are type-individuated by reference to their (actual and potential) causal relations; you know everything that is essential about a functional state when you know which causal generalizations subsume it. Since, in the psychological case, the generalizations that count for type individuation are the ones that relate mental states to one another, a census of mental states would imply a network of causal interrelations. To specify such a network would be to constrain the nomologically possible mental histories of an organism; the network for a given organism would exhibit the possible patterns of causal interaction among its mental states (insofar, as least, as such patterns of interaction are relevant to the type individuation of the states). Of necessity, the actual life of the organism would appear as a path through this network.

Given the Functionalist assurance of individuation by causal role, we can assume that each mental state can be identified with a node in such a network: for each mental state there is a corresponding causal role and for each causal role there is a corresponding node. (To put the same point slightly differently, each mental state can be associated with a formula—e.g., a Ramsey sentence, see Block, 1980—that uniquely determines its location in the network by specifying its potentialities for causal interaction with each of the other mental states.) Notice, however, that while this gives a Functionalist sense to the individuation of propositional attitudes, it does not, in and of itself, say what it is for a propositional attitude to have the propositional content that it has. The present proposal is to remedy this defect by reducing the notion of propositional content to the notion of causal role.

So far, we have a network of mental states defined by their causal interrelations. But notice that there is also a network generated by the *inferential* relations that hold among *propositions*; and it is plausible that its inferential relations are among the properties that each proposition has essentially. Thus, it is presumably a noncontingent property of the proposition that Auntie is shorter than Uncle Wilifred that it entails the proposition that Uncle Wilifred is taller than Auntie. And it is surely a noncontingent property of the proposition that *P & Q* that it entails the proposition that *P* and the proposition that *Q*. It may also be that there are evidential relations that are, in the relevant sense, noncontingent; for example, it may be constitutive of the proposition that many of the *G*'s are *F* that it is, ceteris paribus, evidence for the proposition that all of the *G*'s are *F*. If it be so, then so be it.

The basic idea is that, given the two networks—the causal and the inferential—we can establish partial isomorphisms between them. Under such an isomorphism, *the causal role of a propositional attitude mirrors the semantic role of the proposition that is its object*. So, for example, there is the proposition that John left and Mary wept; and it is partially constitutive of this proposition that it has the following semantic relations: it entails the proposition that John left; it entails the proposition that Mary wept; it is entailed by the pair of propositions {John left, Mary wept}; it entails the proposition that somebody did something; it entails the proposition that John did something; it entails the proposition that either it's raining or John left and Mary wept . . . and so forth. Likewise there are, among the potential episodes in an organism's mental life, states which we may wish to construe as: (S^1) having the belief that John left and Mary wept; (S^2) having the belief that John left; (S^3) having the belief that Mary wept; (S^4) having the belief that somebody did something; (S^5) having the belief that either it's raining or John left and Mary wept . . . and so forth. The crucial point is that it constrains the assignment of propositional contents to these mental states that the latter exhibit an appropriate pattern of causal relations. In particular, it must be true (if only under idealization) that being in S^1 tends to cause the organism to be in S^2 and S^3; that being in S^1 tends to cause the organism to be in S^4; that being (simultaneously) in states (S^2, S^3) tends—very strongly, one supposes—to cause the organism to be in state S^1, that being in state S^1 tends to cause the organism to be in state S^5 (as does being in state S^6, viz. the state of believing that it's raining). And so forth.

In short, we can make nonarbitrary assignments of propositions as the objects of propositional attitudes because there is this isomorphism between the network generated by the semantic relations among propositions and the network generated by the causal relations among mental states. The assignment is nonarbitrary precisely in that it is constrained to preserve the isomorphism. And because the isomorphism is perfectly objective (which is not, however, to say that it is perfectly unique; see below), knowing what proposition gets assigned to a mental state—what the object of an attitude is—is knowing something useful. For, within the limits of the operative idealization, *you can deduce the causal consequences of being in a mental state from the semantic relations of its propositional object.* To know that John thinks that Mary wept is to know that it's highly probable that he thinks that somebody wept. To know that Sam thinks that it is raining is to know that it's highly probable that he thinks that either it is raining or that John left and Mary wept. To know that Sam thinks that it's raining and that Sam thinks that if it's raining it is well to carry an umbrella is to be far along the way to predicting a piece of Sam's behavior.

It may be, according to the present story, that preserving isomorphism between the causal and the semantic networks is *all* that there is to the assignment of contents to mental states; that nothing constrains the attribution of propositional objects to propositional attitudes *except* the requirement that isomorphism be preserved. But one need not hold that that is so. On the contrary, many—perhaps most—philosophers who like the isomorphism story are attracted by so-called 'two-factor' theories, according to which what determines the semantics of an attitude is not just its functional role but also its causal connections to objects 'in the world'. (This is, notice, still a species of functionalism since it's still causal role alone that counts for the type individuation of mental states; but two-factor theories acknowledge as semantically relevant 'external' causal relations, relations between, for example, states of the organism and *distal* stimuli. It is these mind-to-world causal relations that are supposed to determine the denotational semantics of an attitude: what it's about and what its truth-conditions are.) There are serious issues in this area, but for our purposes—we are, after all, just sightseeing—we can group the two-factor theorists with the pure functional-role semanticists.

The story I've just told you is, I think, the standard current construal of Realism about propositional attitudes.[2] I propose, therefore, to call it Standard Realism (SR for convenience). As must be apparent, SR is a compound of two doctrines: a claim about the 'internal' structure of attitudes (viz., that they are *monadic* functional states) and a claim about the source of their semantic properties (viz., that some or all of such properties arise from isomorphisms between the causal role of mental states and the implicational structure of propositions). Now, though they are usually held together, it seems clear that these claims are orthogonal. One could opt for monadic mental states without functional-role semantics; or one could opt for functional-role semantics together with some nonmonadic account of the polyadicity of the attitudes. My own view is that SR should be rejected wholesale: that it is wrong about both the structure *and* the semantics of the attitudes. But—such is the confusion and perversity of my colleagues—this view is widely thought to be eccentric. The standard Realistic alternative to Standard Realism holds that SR is right about functional semantics but wrong about monadicity. I propose to divide these issues: monadicity first, semantics at the end.

If, in the present intellectual atmosphere, you are Realist and Functionalist about the attitudes, but you don't think that the attitudes are *monadic* functional states, then probably you think that to have a belief or a desire—or whatever—is to be related in a certain way to a Mental Representation. According to the canonical formulation of this view: for any organism O and for any proposition P, there is a relation R and a mental representation MP such that: MP means that (expresses the proposition that) P; and O believes that P iff O bears R to MP. (And similarly, R desires that P iff O bears some *different* relation, R', to MP. And so forth. For elaboration, see Fodor, 1975, 1978; Field, 1978.) This is, of course, the doctrine I've been calling full-blown RTM. So we come, at last, to the bottom of the decision tree. (See figure 1.3.)

As compared with SR, RTM assumes the heavier burden of ontological commitment. It quantifies not just over such mental states as believing that P and desiring that Q but also over mental representations; symbols in a "language of thought." The burden of proof is thus on RTM. (Auntie holds that it doesn't matter who has the burden of proof because the choice between SR and RTM isn't a *philosophical* issue. But I don't know how she tells. Or why she cares.) There are two sorts of considerations that, in my view, argue persuasively for RTM. I think they are the implicit sources of the Cognitive Science community's commitment to the mental representation construct.

First Argument for RTM: Productivity and Constituency

The collection of states of mind is productive: for example, the thoughts that one actually entertains in the course of a mental life comprise a relatively unsystematic subset drawn from a vastly larger

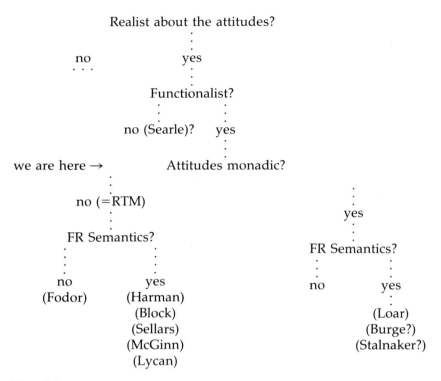

Figure 1.3.
Decision Tree, stage 3.

variety of thoughts that one could have entertained had an occasion for them arisen. For example, it has probably never occurred to you before that no grass grows on kangaroos. But, once your attention is drawn to the point, it's an idea that you are quite capable of entertaining, one which, in fact, you are probably inclined to endorse. A theory of the attitudes ought to account for this productivity; it ought to make clear what it is about beliefs and desires in virtue of which they constitute open-ended families.

Notice that Naturalism precludes saying 'there are arbitrarily many propositional attitudes because there are infinitely many propositions' and leaving it at that. The problem about productivity is that there are arbitrarily many propositional attitudes that one can *have*. Since relations between organisms and propositions aren't to be taken as primitive, one is going to have to say what it is about organic states like believing and desiring that allows them to be (roughly) as differentiated as the propositions are. If, for example, you think that attitudes are mapped to propositions in virtue of their causal roles (see above), then you have to say what it is about the attitudes that accounts for the productivity *of the set of causal roles.*

A natural suggestion is that the productivity of thoughts is like the productivity of natural languages, i.e., that there are indefinitely many thoughts to entertain for much the same reason that there are indefinitely many sentences to utter. Fine, but how do natural languages manage to be productive? Here the outlines of an answer are familiar. To a first approximation, each sentence can be identified with a certain sequence of subsentential constituents. Different sentences correspond to different ways of arranging these subsentential constituents; new sentences correspond to new ways of arranging them. And the meaning of a sentence—the proposition it expresses—is determined, in a regular way, by its constituent structure.

The constituents of sentences are, say, words and phrases. What are the constituents of propositional attitudes? A natural answer would be: other propositional attitudes. Since, for example. you can't believe that *P* and *Q* without believing that *P* and believing that *Q*, we could take the former state to be a complex of which the latter are the relatively (or perhaps absolutely) simple parts. But a moment's consideration makes it clear that this won't work with any generality: believing that *P* or *Q* doesn't require either believing that *P* or believing that *Q*, and neither does believing that if *P* then *Q*. It looks as though we want propositional attitudes to be built out of *something*, but not out of other propositional attitudes.

There's an interesting analogy to the case of speech-acts (one of many such; see Vendler, 1972). There are indefinitely many distinct assertions (i.e., there are indefinitely many propositions that one can assert); and though you can't assert that *P* and *Q* without asserting that *P* and asserting that *Q*, the disjunctive assertion, *P* or *Q*, does not imply the assertion of either of the disjuncts, and the hypothetical assertion, if *P* then *Q*, does not imply the assertion of its antecedent or its consequent. So how do you work the constituency relation for *assertions*?

Answer: you take advantage of the fact that making an assertion involves using symbols (typically it involves *uttering* symbols); the constituency relation is defined for the symbols that assertions are made by using. So, in particular, the standard (English-language) vehicle for making the assertion that either John left or Mary wept is the form of words 'either John left or Mary wept'; and, notice, this complex linguistic expression *is*, literally, a construct out of the simpler linguistic expressions 'John left' and 'Mary wept'. You can assert that *P* or *Q* without asserting that *P* or asserting that *Q*, but you can't utter the form of words '*P* or *Q*' without uttering the form of words '*P*' and the form of words '*Q*'.

The moral for treatments of the attitudes would seem to be straightforward: solve the *productivity* problem for the attitudes by appealing to constituency. Solve the *constituency* problem for the attitudes in the same way that you solve it for speech-acts: tokening an attitude involves tokening a symbol, just as tokening an assertion does. What kind of symbol do you have to token to token an attitude? A mental representation, of course. Hence RTM. (Auntie says that it is crude and preposterous and *unbiological* to suppose that people have sentences in their heads. Auntie always talks like that when she hasn't got any arguments.)

Second Argument for RTM: Mental Processes

It is possible to doubt whether, as functional-role theories of meaning would have it, the propositional contents of mental states are reducible to, or determined by, or epiphenomena of, their causal roles. But what *can't* be doubted is this: the causal roles of mental states typically closely parallel the implicational structures of their propositional objects; and the predictive successes of propositional-attitude psychology routinely exploit the symmetries thus engendered. If we know that Psmith believes that *P* → *Q* and we know that he believes that *P*, then we generally expect him to infer that *Q* and to act according to his inference. Why do we expect this? Well, because we believe the business about Psmith to be an instance of a true and counterfactual-supporting generalization according to which believing *P* and believing *P* → *Q* is causally sufficient for inferring *Q*, ceteris paribus. But then, *what is it about the mechanisms of thinking in virtue of which such generalizations hold*? What, in particular, could believing and inferring be, such that thinking the premises of a valid inference leads, so often and so reliably, to thinking its conclusion?

It was a scandal of midcentury Anglo-American philosophy of mind that though it worried a lot about the nature of mental states (like the attitudes) it quite generally didn't worry much about the nature of mental *processes* (like thinking). This isn't, in retrospect, very surprising given the behaviorism that was widely prevalent. Mental processes are causal sequences of mental states; if you're eliminativist about the attitudes you're hardly likely to be Realist about their causal consequences. In particular, you're hardly likely to be Realist about their *causal interactions*. It now seems clear enough, however, that our theory of the structure of the attitudes *must* accommodate a theory of thinking; and that it is a preeminent constraint on the latter that it provide a mechanism for symmetry between the inferential roles of thoughts and their causal roles.

This isn't, by any means, all that easy for a theory of thinking to do. Notice, for example, that the philosophy of mind assumed in traditional British Empiricism was Realist about the attitudes and accepted a form of RTM. (Very roughly, the attitudes were construed as relations to mental images, the latter being endowed with semantic properties in virtue of what they resembled and with causal properties in virtue of their associations. Mental states were productive because complex images can be constructed out of simple ones.) But precisely because the mechanisms of mental causation were assumed to be associationistic (and the conditions for association to involve preeminently spatio-temporal propinquity), the Empiricists had no good way of connecting the *contents* of a thought with the effects of entertaining it. They therefore never got close to a plausible theory of thinking, and neither did the associationistic psychology that followed in their footsteps.

What associationism missed—to put it more exactly—was the similarity between trains of thoughts and *arguments*. Here, for an example, is Sherlock Holmes doing his thing at the end of "The Speckled Band":

> I instantly reconsidered my position when . . . it became clear to me that whatever danger threatened an occupant of the room could not come either from the window or the door. My attention was speedily drawn, as I have already remarked to you, to this ventilator, and to the bell-rope which hung down to the bed. The discovery that this was a dummy, and that the bed was clamped to the floor, instantly gave rise to the suspicion that the rope was there as a bridge for something passing through the hole, and coming to the bed. The idea of a snake instantly occurred to me, and when I coupled it with my knowledge that the Doctor was furnished with a supply of the creatures from India I felt that I was probably on the right track . . .

The passage purports to be a bit of reconstructive psychology, a capsule history of the sequence of mental episodes which brought Holmes first to suspect, then to believe, that the Doctor did it with his pet snake. Now, back when Auntie was a girl and reasons weren't allowed to be causes, philosophers were unable to believe that such an aetiology could be literally true. I assume, however, that liberation has set in by now; we have no philosophically impressive reason to doubt that Holmes's train of thoughts went pretty much the way that he says it did.

What is therefore interesting, for our purposes, is that Holmes's story isn't *just* reconstructive psychology. It does a double duty since it also serves to assemble *premises* for a plausible inference to the *conclusion* that the doctor did it with the snake. ("A snake could have crawled through the ventilator and slithered down the bell-rope," "the Doctor was known to keep a supply of snakes in his snuff box," and so forth.) Because this train of thoughts is tantamount to an argument, Holmes expects Watson to be *convinced* by the considerations that, when they occurred to him, caused Holmes's own conviction. (Compare the sort of mental history that goes, "Well, I went to bed and slept on it, and when I woke up in the morning I found that the problem had solved itself." Or the sort that goes, "Bell-ropes always make me think of snakes, and snakes make me think of snake oil, and snake oil makes me think of doctors; so when I saw the bell-rope it popped into my head that the Doctor and a snake might have done it between them." That's mental causation perhaps; but it's not *thinking*.)

What connects the causal-history aspect of Holmes's story with its plausible-inference aspect is precisely the parallelism between trains of thought and arguments: the thoughts that effect the fixation of the belief that P provide, often enough, good *grounds* for believing that P. (As Holmes puts it in another story, "one true inference invariably suggests others.") Were this not the case—were there not this general harmony between the semantical and the causal properties of thoughts—there wouldn't, after all, be much profit in thinking.

What you want to make thinking worth the while is that trains of thoughts should be generated by mechanisms that are generally truth-preserving (so that "a true inference [generally] suggests other inferences *that are also true*"). Argument is generally truth-preserving; that, surely, is the teleological basis of the similarity between trains of thoughts and arguments. The associationists noticed hardly any of this; and even if they had noticed it, they wouldn't have known what to do with it. In this respect, Conan Doyle was a far deeper psychologist—far closer to what is essential about the mental life—than, say, James Joyce (or William James, for that matter).

When, therefore, Rationalist critics (including, notably, Kant) pointed out that thought—like argument—involves judging and inferring, the cat was out of the bag. Associationism was the best available form of Realism about the attitudes, and associationism failed to produce a credible mechanism for thinking. Which is to say that it failed to produce a credible theory of the attitudes. No wonder everybody gave up and turned into a behaviorist.

Cognitive Science is the art of getting the cat back in. The trick is to abandon associationism and combine RTM with the "computer metaphor." In this respect I think there really has been something like an intellectual breakthrough. Technical details to one side, this is—in my view—the *only* respect in which contemporary Cognitive Science represents a major advance over the versions of RTM that were its eighteenth- and nineteenth-century predecesors.

Computers show us how to connect semantical with causal properties *for symbols*. So, if the tokening of an attitude involves the tokening of a symbol, then we can get some leverage on connecting semantical with causal properties *for thoughts*. Here, in roughest outline, is how the story is supposed to go.

You connect the causal properties of a symbol with its semantic properties via its syntax. The syntax of a symbol is one of its second-order physical properties. To a first approximation, we can think of its syntactic structure as an abstract feature of its (geometric or acoustic) *shape*. Because, to all intents and purposes, syntax reduces to shape, and because the shape of a symbol is a potential determinant of its causal role, it is fairly easy to see how there could be environments in which the causal role of a symbol correlates with its syntax. It's easy, that is to say, to imagine symbol tokens interacting causally *in virtue of* their syntactic structures. The syntax of a symbol might determine the causes and effects of its tokenings in much the way that the geometry of a key determines which locks it will open.

But, now, we know from formal logic that certain of the semantic relations among symbols can be, as it were, "mimicked" by their syntactic relations; that, when seen from a very great distance, is what proof-theory is about. So, within certain famous limits, the semantic relation that holds between two symbols when the proposition expressed by the one is implied by the proposition expressed by the other can be mimicked by syntactic relations in virtue of which one of the symbols is derivable from the other. We can therefore build machines which have, again within famous limits, the following property: the operations of such a machine consist entirely of transformations of symbols; in the course of performing these operations, the machine is sensitive solely to syntactic properties of the symbols; and the operations that the machine performs on the symbols are entirely confined to alterations of their shapes. Yet the machine is so devised that it will transform one symbol into another if and only if the symbols so transformed stand in certain *semantic* relations; e.g., the relation that the premises bear to the conclusion in a valid argument. Such machines—computers, of course—just *are* environments in which the causal role of a symbol token is made to parallel the inferential role of the proposition that it expresses.[3]

I expect it's clear how this is all supposed to provide an argument for quantifying over mental representations. Computers are a solution to the problem of mediating between the causal properties of symbols and their semantic properties. So *if* the mind is a sort of computer, we begin to see how you can have a theory of mental processes that succeeds where associationism (to say nothing of behaviorism) abjectly failed; a theory which explains how there could regularly be nonarbitrary content relations among causally related thoughts.

But, patently, there are going to have to be mental representations if this proposal is going to work. In computer design, causal role is brought into phase with content by exploiting parallelisms between the syntax of a symbol and its semantics. But that idea won't do the theory of *mind* any good unless there are *mental* symbols; mental particulars possessed of semantic *and syntactic* properties. There must be mental symbols because, in a nutshell, only symbols have syntax, and our best available theory of mental processes—indeed, the *only* available theory of mental processes that isn't *known* to be false— needs the picture of the mind as a syntax-driven machine.[4]

A brief addendum before we end this section: the question of the extent to which RTM must be committed to the 'explicitness' of mental representation is one that keeps getting raised in the philosophical literature (and elsewhere; see Dennett, 1978b; Stabler, 1983). The issue becomes clear if we consider real computers as deployed in Artificial Intelligence research. So, to borrow an example of Dennett's, there are chess machines that play as though they 'believe' that it's a good idea to get one's Queen out early. But there needn't be—in fact, there probably wouldn't be—anywhere in the system of heuristics that constitutes the program of such a machine a symbol that *means* '(try and) get your Queen out early'; rather the machine's obedience to that rule of play is, as it were, an epiphenomenon of its following many *other* rules, much more detailed, whose joint effect is that, ceteris paribus, the Queen gets out as soon as it can. The moral is supposed to be that though the contents of *some* of the attitudes it would be natural to attribute to the machine *may* be explicitly represented, none of them *have* to be, *even assuming the sort of story about how computational processes work that is supposed to motivate RTM*. So, then, what exactly *is* RTM minimally committed to by way of explicit mental representation?

The answer should be clear in light of the previous discussion. According to RTM, mental processes are transformations of mental

representations. The rules which determine the course of such transformations may, but needn't, be themselves explicitly represented.
But the mental contents (the 'thoughts', as it were) that get transformed *must be* explicitly represented or the theory is simply false.
To put it another way: if the occurrence of a thought is an episode
in a mental process, then RTM is committed to the explicit representation of the content of the thought. Or, to put it still a third way—
the way they like to put it in AI—according to RTM, programs may
be explicitly represented and data structures have to be.

For the sake of a simple example, let's pretend that associationism
is true; we imagine that there is a principle of Association by Proximity in virtue of which thoughts of salt get associated with thoughts
of pepper. The point is that even on the assumption that it subsumes
mental processes, the rule 'associate by proximity' need not itself be
explicitly represented; association by proximity may emerge from
dynamical properties of ideas (as in Hume) or from dynamical properties of neural stuff (as in contemporary connectionism). But what
must be explicit is the Ideas—of pepper and salt, as it might be—that
get associated. For, according to the theory, mental processes are
actually *causal sequences of tokenings of such Ideas;* so, no Ideas, no
mental processes.

Similarly, mutatis mutandis, for the chess case. The rule 'get it out
early' may be emergent out of its own implementation; out of lower-
level heuristics, that is, any one of which may or may not itself be
explicitly represented. But the representation of the board—of actual
or possible states of play—over which such heuristics are defined
must be explicit or the representational theory of chess playing is
simply false. The theory says that a train of chess thoughts is a causal
sequence of tokenings of chess representations. If, therefore, there
are trains of chess thoughts but no tokenings of chess representations, it *follows* that something is not well with the theory.

So much, then, for RTM and the polyadicity of the attitudes. What
about their semanticity? We proceed to our final diagnostic question:

Fourth Question: How Do You Feel about Truth-Conditions?

I remarked above that the two characteristic tenets of SR—that the
attitudes are monadic and that the semanticity of the attitudes arises
from isomorphisms between the causal network of mental states and
the inferential network of propositions—are mutually independent.
Similarly for RTM; it's not mandatory, but you are at liberty to combine RTM with functional-role (FR) semantics if you choose. Thus,
you could perfectly well say: 'Believing, desiring, and so forth are

relations between intentional systems and mental representations that get tokened (in their heads, as it might be). Tokening a mental representation has causal consequences. The totality of such consequences implies a network of causal interrelations among the attitudes . . .' and so on to a functional-role semantics. In any event, it's important to see that RTM needs *some* semantic story to tell if, as we have supposed, RTM is going to be Realist about the attitudes and the attitudes have their propositional objects essentially.

Which semantic story to tell is, in my view, going to be *the* issue in mental representation theory for the foreseeable future. The questions here are so difficult, and the answers so contentious, that they really fall outside the scope of this paper; I had advertised a tour of an intellectual landscape about whose topography there exists some working consensus. Still, I want to say a little about the semantic issues by way of closing. They are the piece of Cognitive Science where philosophers feel most at home; and they're where the 'philosophy of psychology' (a discipline over which Auntie is disinclined to quantify) joins the philosophy of language (which, I notice, Auntie allows me to spell without quotes).

There are a number of reasons for doubting that a functional-role semantic theory of the sort that SR proposes is tenable. This fact is currently causing something of a crisis among people who would like to be Realists about the attitudes.

In the first place—almost, by now, too obvious to mention—functional-role theories make it seem that empirical constraints must underdetermine the semantics of the attitudes. What I've got in mind here isn't the collection of worries that cluster around the 'indeterminacy of translation' thesis; if that sort of indeterminacy is to be taken seriously at all—which I doubt—then it is equally a problem for *every* Realist semantics. There are, however, certain sources of underdetermination that appear to be built into functional-role semantics as such; considerations which suggest either that there is no unique best mapping of the causal roles of mental states on to the inferential network of propositions or that, even if there is, such a mapping would nevertheless underdetermine assignments of contents to the attitudes. I'll mention two such considerations, but no doubt there are others; things are always worse than one supposes.

Idealization.   The pattern of causal dispositions actually accruing to a given mental state must surely diverge very greatly from the pattern of inferences characteristic of its propositional object. We don't, for example, believe all the consequences of our beliefs; not just because we haven't got time to, and not just because everybody is at least a little irrational, but also because we surely have some false beliefs about what the consequences of our beliefs are. This amounts to saying that some substantial idealization is required if we're to get from the causal dispositions that mental states actually exhibit to the sort of causal network that we would like to have: a causal network whose structure is closely isomorphic to the inferential network of propositions. And now the problem is to provide a noncircular justification—one which does not itself appeal to semantical or intentional considerations—for preferring *that* idealization to an infinity or so of others that ingenuity might devise. (It won't do, of course, to say that we prefer that idealization because it's the one which allows mental states to be assigned the intuitively plausible propositional objects; for the present question is precisely whether anything besides prejudice underwrites our common-sense psychological intuitions.) Probably the idealization problem arises, in some form or other, for any account of the attitudes which proposes to reduce their semantic properties to their causal ones. That, alas, is no reason to assume that the problem can be solved.

Equivalence.   Functionalism guarantees that mental states are individuated by their causal roles; hence by their position in the putative causal network. But *nothing* guarantees that *propositions* are individuated by their *inferential* roles. Prima facie, it surely seems that they are not, since equivalent propositions are ipso facto identical in their inferential liaisons. Are we therefore to say that equivalent propositions are identical? Not, at least, for the psychologist's purposes, since attitudes whose propositional objects are equivalent may nevertheless differ in their causal roles. We need to distinguish, as it might be, the belief that P from the belief that P and $(Q \text{ v}-Q)$, hence we need to distinguish the *proposition* that P from the proposition that P and $(Q \text{ v}-Q)$. But surely what distinguishes these propositions is not their inferential roles, assuming that the inferential role of a proposition is something like the set of propositions it entails and is entailed by. It seems to follow that propositions are not individuated by their position in the inferential network, hence that assignments of propositional objects to mental states, if constrained only to preserve isomorphism between the networks, ispo facto underdetermine the contents of such states. There are, perhaps, ways out of such equivalence problems; 'situation semantics' (see Barwise and Perry, 1983) has recently been advertising some. But all the ways out that I've heard of violate the assumptions of FR semantics; specifically, they don't identify propositions with nodes in a network of inferential roles.

In the second place, FR semantics isn't, after all, much of a panacea for Naturalistic scruples. Though it has a Naturalistic story to tell about how mental states might be paired with their propositional objects, the semantic properties of the propositions themselves are assumed, not explained. It is, for example, an intrinsic property of the proposition that Psmith is seated that it is true or false in virtue of Psmith's posture. FR semantics simply takes this sort of fact for granted. From the Naturalist's point of view, therefore, it merely displaces the main worry from: 'What's the connection between an attitude and its propositional object?' to 'What's the connection between the propositional object of an attitude and whatever state of affairs it is that makes the proposition true or false?' Or, to put much the same point slightly differently, FR semantics has a lot to say about the mind-to-proposition problem but nothing at all to say about the mind-to-world problem. In effect FR semantics is content to hold that the attitudes inherit their satisfaction-conditions from their propositional objects and that propositions have *their* satisfaction-conditions *by stipulation*.

And, in the third place, to embrace FR semantics is to raise a variety of (approximately Quinean) issues about the individuation of the attitudes; and these, as Putnam and Stich have recently emphasized, when once conjured up are not easily put down. The argument goes like this: according to FR semantic theories, each attitude has its propositional object in virtue of its position in the causal network: 'different objects iff different loci' holds to a first approximation. Since a propositional attitude has its propositional object essentially, this makes an attitude's identity depend on the identity of its causal role. The problem is, however, that we have no criteria for the individuation of causal roles.

The usual sceptical tactic at this point is to introduce some or other form of slippery-slope argument to show—or at least to suggest—that there *couldn't be* a criterion for the individuation of causal roles that is other than arbitrary. Stich, for example, has the case of an increasingly senile woman who eventually is able to remember about President McKinley only that he was assassinated. Given that she has no *other* beliefs about McKinley—given, let's suppose, that the *only* causal consequence of her believing that McKinley was assassinated is to prompt her to produce and assent to occasional utterances of 'McKinley was assassinated' and immediate logical consequences thereof—is it clear that she in fact has *any* beliefs about McKinley at all? But if she *doesn't* have, *when, precisely, did she cease to do so*? How much causal role does the belief that McKinley was assassinated have to have to be the belief that McKinley was assassinated? And what reason is there to suppose that this question has an answer? (See Stich, 1983; and also Putnam, 1983.) Auntie considers slippery-slope arguments to be in dubious taste and there is much to be said for her view. Still, it looks as though FR semantics has brought us to the edge of a morass and I, for one, am not an enthusiast for wading in it.

Well then, to summarize: the syntactic theory of mental operations promises a reductive account of the *intelligence* of thought. We can now imagine—though, to be sure, only dimly and in a glass darkly— a psychology that exhibits quite complex cognitive processes as being constructed from elementary manipulations of symbols. This is what RTM, together with the computer metaphor, has brought us; and it is, in my view, no small matter. But a theory of the *intelligence* of thought does not, in and of itself, constitute a theory of thought's *intentionality*. (Compare such early papers as Dennett, 1978c, where these issues are more or less comprehensively run together, with such second thoughts as Fodor, 1981, and Cummins, 1983, where they more or less aren't.) If RTM is true, the problem of the intentionality of the mental is largely—perhaps exhaustively—the problem of the semanticity of mental representations. But of the semanticity of mental representations we have, as things now stand, no adequate account.

Here ends the tour. Beyond this point there be monsters. It may be that what one descries, just there on the farthest horizon, is a glimpse of a causal/teleological theory of meaning (Stampe 1977; Dretske, 1981; Fodor, unpublished, and 1984); and it may be that the development of such a theory would provide a way out of the current mess. At best, however, it's a long way off. I mention it only to encourage such of the passengers as may be feeling queasy.

"Are you finished playing now?"
"Yes, Auntie."
"Well, don't forget to put the toys away."
"No, Auntie."

Notes

1. Unless you are an eliminativist behaviorist (say, Watson) which puts you, for present purposes, beyond the pale.

   While we're at it, it rather messes up my nice taxonomy that there are philosophers who accept a Functionalist view of psychological explanation and are Realist about belief/desire psychology, but who reject the reduction of the latter to the former. In particular, they do not accept the identification of any of the entities that Functionalist psychologists posit with the propositional attitudes that common sense holds dear. (A version of this view says that functional states "realize" propositional attitudes in much the way that the physical states are supposed to realize functional ones. See, for example, Matthews, 1984.)

2. This account of the attitudes seems to be in the air these days, and, as with most doctrines that are in the air, it's a little hard to be sure exactly who holds it. Far the most detailed version is in Loar, 1981, though I have seen variants in unpublished papers by Tyler Burge, Robert Stalnaker, and Hartry Field.

3. Since the methods of computational psychology tend to be those of proof theory, its limitations tend to be those of formalization. Patently, this raises the well-known issues about completeness; less obviously, it connects the Cognitive Science enterprise with the Positivist program for the formalization of inductive (and, generally, nondemonstrative) styles of argument. On the second point, see Glymour, 1987.)

4. It is possible to combine enthusiasm for a syntactical account of mental processes with any degree of agnosticism about the attitudes—or, for that matter, about semantic evaluability itself. To claim that the mind is a "syntax-driven machine" is precisely to hold that the theory of mental processes can be set out in its entirety without reference to any of the semantic properties of mental states (see Fodor, 1981b), hence without assuming that mental states *have* any semantic properties. Steven Stich is famous for having espoused this option (Stich, 1983). My way of laying out the field has put the big divide between Realism about the attitudes and its denial. This seems to me justifiable, but admittedly it underestimates the substantial affinities between Stich and the RTM crowd. Stich's account of what a good science of behavior would look like is far closer to RTM than it is to, for example, the eliminative materialism of the Churchlands.

Chapter 2
Semantics, Wisconsin Style

There are, of course, two kinds of philosophers. One kind of philosopher takes it as a working hypothesis that belief/desire psychology
(or, anyhow, *some* variety of propositional attitude psychology) is the
best theory of the cognitive mind that we can now envision; hence
that the appropriate direction for psychological research is the construction of a belief/desire theory that is empirically supported and
methodologically sound. The other kind of philosopher takes it that
the entire apparatus of propositional attitude psychology is conceptually flawed in irremediable ways; hence that the appropriate direction for psychological research is the construction of alternatives to
the framework of belief/desire explanation. This way of collecting
philosophers into philosopher-kinds cuts across a number of more
traditional, but relatively superficial, typologies. For example, eliminativist behaviorists like Quine and neurophiles like the Churchlands
turn up in the same basket as philosophers like Steve Stich, who
think that psychological states are computational and functional all
right, but not intentional. Dennett is probably in the basket too,
along with Putnam and other (how should one put it?) dogmatic
relativists. Whereas, among philosophers of the other kind one finds
a motley that includes, very much inter alia, reductionist behaviorists
like Ryle and (from time to time) Skinner, radical individualists like
Searle and Fodor, mildly radical anti-individualists like Burge, and,
of course, all cognitive psychologists except Gibsonians.

Philosophers of the first kind disagree with philosophers of the
second kind about many things besides the main issue. For example,
they tend to disagree vehemently about who has the burden of the
argument. However—an encouraging sign—recent discussion has
increasingly focused upon one issue as the crux par excellence on
which the resolution of the dispute must turn. The point about
propositional attitudes is that they are *representational* states. What-

Reprinted with permission from *Synthese* 59, 1984, 231–250.

ever else a belief is, it is a kind of thing of which semantic evaluation is appropriate. Indeed, the very individuation of beliefs proceeds via (oblique) reference to the states of affairs that determine their semantic value; the belief that it is raining is essentially the belief whose truth or falsity depends on whether it is raining. Willy-nilly, then, the friends of propositional attitudes include only philosophers who think that serious sense can be made of the notion of representation (de facto, they tend to include *all* and only philosophers who think this). I emphasize that the notion of representation is crucial for every friend of propositional attitudes, not just the ones (like, say, Field, Harman, and Fodor) whose views commit them to quantification over symbols in a mental language. Realists about propositional attitudes are ipso facto Realists about representational states. They must therefore have *some* view about what it is for a state to *be* representational even if (like, say, Loar and Stainaker) they are agnostic about, or hostile toward, identifying beliefs and desires with sentences in the language of thought.

Well, what would it be like to have a serious theory of representation? Here, too, there is some consensus to work from. The worry about representation is above all that the semantic (and/or the intentional) will prove permanently recalcitrant to integration in the natural order; for example, that the semantic/intentional properties of things will fail to supervene upon their physical properties. What is required to relieve the worry is therefore, at a minimum, the framing of *naturalistic* conditions for representation. That is, what we want at a minimum is something of the form 'R *represents* S' is true *iff* C where the vocabulary in which condition C is couched contains neither intentional nor semantic expressions.[1]

I haven't said anything, so far, about what R and S are supposed to range over. I propose to say as little about this as I can get away with, both because the issues are hard and disputatious and because it doesn't, for the purposes of this paper, matter much how they are resolved. First, then, I propose to leave it open which things *are* representations and how many of the things that qualify a naturalistic theory should cover. I assume only that we must have a naturalistic treatment of the representational properties of the propositional attitudes; if propositional attitudes are relations to mental representations, then we must have a naturalistic treatment of the representational properties of the latter.[2]

In like spirit, I propose to leave open the ontological issues about the possible values of S. The paradigmatic representation relation I have in mind holds between things of the sorts that have truth values and things of the sorts by which truth values are determined. I shall usually refer to the latter as 'states of affairs', and I'll use '-ing nominals' as canonical forms for expressing them (e.g., 'John's going to the store'; 'Mary's kissing Bill'; 'Sam's being twelve years' old next Tuesday'). Since the theories we'll discuss hold that the relations between a representation and what it represents are typical causal, I shall assume further that S ranges over kinds of things that can be causes.

Last in this list of things that I'm not going to worry about is type token ambiguities. A paradigm of the relation we're trying to provide a theory for is the one that holds between my present, occurrent belief that Reagan is president and the state of affairs consisting of Reagan's being President. I assume that this is a relation between tokens; between an individual belief and an individual state of affairs. But I shall also allow talk of relations between representation *types* and state of affairs *types*; the most important such relation is the one that holds when tokens of a situation type cause, or typically cause, tokenings of a representation type. Here again there are ontological deep waters; but I don't propose to stir them up unless I have to.

OK, let's go. There are, so far as I know, only two sorts of naturalistic theories of the representation relation that have ever been proposed. And at least one of these is certainly wrong. The two theories are as follows: that C specifies some sort of *resemblance* relation between R and S: and that C specifies some sort of *causal relation* between R and S.[3] The one of this pair that is certainly wrong is the resemblance theory. For one thing, as everybody points out, resemblance is a symmetical relation and representation isn't; so resemblance can't *be* representation. And, for another, resemblance theories have troubles with the *singularity* of representation. The concept *tiger* represents *all tigers*; but the concept *this tiger* represents only this one. There must be (possible) tigers that resemble this tiger to any extent you like, and if resemblance is sufficient for representation, you'd think the concept *this tiger* should represent those tigers too. But it doesn't, so again resemblance can't be sufficient for representation.

All this is old news. I mention it only to indicate some of the ways in which the idea of a causal theory of representation is prima facie attractive and succeeds where resemblance theories fail. (1) Causal relations are natural relations if *anything* is. You might wonder whether resemblance is part of the natural order (or whether it's only, as it were, in the eye of the beholder). But to wonder that about causation is to wonder whether there *is* a natural order. (2) Causation, unlike resemblance, is nonsymmetric. (3) Causation is, par excellence, a relation among *particulars*. Tiger a can resemble tiger b as much as you like, and it can still be tiger *a* and not tiger *b* that caused this set of tiger prints. Indeed, if it was tiger *a* that caused them, it *follows* that tiger *b* didn't (assuming, of course, that tiger *a* is distinct from tiger *b*).

Well, in light of all this, several philosophers who are sympathetic towards propositional attitudes have recently been playing with the idea of a causal account of representation (see, particularly, Stampe 1975, 1977; Dretske 1981; and Fodor, unpublished. Much of this has been going on at the University of Wisconsin, hence the title of this essay.) My present purpose is to explore some consequences of this idea. Roughly, here's how the argument will go: causal theories have trouble distinguishing the conditions for *representation* from the conditions for *truth*. This trouble is intrinsic; the conditions that causal theories impose on representation are such that, when they're satisfied, *mis*representation cannot, by that very fact, occur. Hence, causal theories about how propositional attitudes represent have Plato's problem to face: how is false belief possible? I'll suggest that the answer turns out to be that, in a certain sense, it's not, and that this conclusion may be more acceptable than at first appears.

I said I would argue for all of that; in fact I'm going to do less. I propose to look at the way the problem of misrepresentation is handled in the causal theories that Stampe and Dretske have advanced; and I really *will* argue that their treatments of misrepresentation don't work. This exercise should make it reasonably clear why misrepresentation is so hard to handle in causal theories generally. I'll then close with some discussion of what we'll have to swallow if we choose to bite the bullet. The point of all this, I emphasize, is *not* to argue against causal accounts of representation. I think, in fact, that something along the causal line is the best hope we have for saving intentionalist theorizing, both in psychology and in semantics. But I think too that causal theories have some pretty kinky consequences, and it's these that I want to make explicit.

To start with, there are, strictly speaking, *two* Wisconsin theories about representation; one that's causal and one that's epistemic. I propose to give the second pretty short shrift, but we'd better have a paragraph or two.

The basic idea of (what I shall call) an epistemic access theory is that R represents S if you can find out about S from R.[4] So, for example, Dretske says (1983, p. 10), "A message . . . carries information about X to the extent to which one could learn (come to know) something about X from the message." And Stampe says (1975, p. 223), "An object will represent or misrepresent the situation

. . . only if it is such as to enable one to come to know the situation, i.e., what the situation is, should it be a faithful representation."

Now, generally speaking, if representation requires that S cause R, then it will of course be possible to learn about R by learning about S; inferring from their effects is a standard way of coming to know about causes. So, depending on the details, it's likely that an epistemic account of representation will be satisfied whenever a causal one is. But there is no reason to suppose that the reverse inference holds, and we're about to see that epistemic accounts have problems to which the causal ones are immune.

1. The epistemic story (like the resemblance story) has trouble with the nonsymmetry of representation. You can find out about the weather from the barometer, but you can also find out about the barometer from the weather since, if it's storming, the barometer is likely to be low. Surely the weather doesn't represent the barometer, so epistemic access can't be sufficient for representation.

2. The epistemic story (again like the one about resemblance) has trouble with the singularity of representation. What shows this is a kind of case that Stampe (1977) discusses extensively. Imagine a portrait of, say, Chairman Mao. If the portrait is faithful, then we can infer from properties of the picture to properties of the Chairman (e.g., if the portrait is faithful, then if it shows Mao as bald, then we can learn *from* the portrait *that* Mao is bald). The trouble is, however, that if Mao has a doppelgänger and we know he does, then we can *also* learn from the portrait that Mao's doppelgänger is bald. But the portrait is of Mao and not of his doppelgänger for all that.

Dretske has a restriction on his version of the epistemic access theory that is, I expect, intended to cope with the singularity problem; he allows that a message carries information about X only if a "suitably equipped but *otherwise ignorant* receiver" could learn about X from the message (1983, p. 10, my emphasis). I imagine the idea is that, though we could learn about Mao's doppelgänger from Mao's portrait, we couldn't do so *just from the portrait alone*; we'd also have to use our knowledge that Mao has a doppelgänger. I doubt, however, that this further condition can really be enforced. What Dretske has to face is, in effect, the Dreaded Collateral Information Problem; i.e., the problem of how to decide when the knowledge that we use to interpret a symbol counts as knowledge about the symbol, and when it counts as collateral knowledge. This problem may seem self-solving in the case of *pictures* since we have a pretty good pretheoretical notion of which properties of a picture count as the pictorial ones. But in the case of, e.g., linguistic symbols, it's very far from evident how, or even whether, the corresponding distinction can be drawn. If I say to you 'John is thirty-two,' you can learn something reliable about John's age from what I said. But, of course, you can also learn something reliable about John's *weight* (e.g., that he weighs more than a gram). It may be possible to discipline the intuition that what you learn about John's age you learn just from the symbol and what you learn about his weight you learn from the symbol plus background information. But drawing that distinction is notoriously hard and, if the construal of representation depends on our doing so, we are in serious trouble.

3. Epistemic theories have their own sorts of problems about misrepresentation. Stampe says,

> An object will represent or misrepresent the situation . . . only if it is such as to enable one to come to know the situation, i.e., what the situation is, should it be a faithful representation. If it is not faithful, it will misrepresent the situation. That is, one *may* not be able to tell from it what the situation is, despite the fact that it is a representation of the situation. In either case, it represents the same thing, just as a faithful and an unrecognizable portrait may portray the same person.

But, to begin with, the example is perhaps a little question-begging, since it's not clear that the bad portrait represents its sitter *in virtue of* the fact that if it were accurate it would be possible to learn from it how the sitter looks. How, one wonders, could this bare counterfactual determine representation? Isn't it, rather, the other way around; i.e., not that it's a portrait of Mao because (if it's faithful) you can find out about Mao from it, but rather that you can find out about Mao from it (if it's faithful) because it's Mao that it's a portrait of.

To put the same point slightly differently: we'll see that causal theories have trouble saying how a symbol could be tokened and still be false. The corresponding problem with epistemic access theories is that they make it hard to see how a symbol could be *intelligible* and false. Stampe says: "An object will represent or misrepresent the situation . . . only if it is such as to enable one to come to know the situation, i.e., what the situation is, should it be a faithful representation." (1975, p. 223). Now, there is a nasty scope ambiguity in this; viz., between:

(a) if R is faithful (you can tell what the case is); vs.
(b) you can tell (what the case is if R is faithful).

It's clear that it is (a) that Stampe intends; ((b) leads in the direction of a possible world semantics, which is where Stampe explicitly doesn't want to go; see especially 1975, circa p. 224). So, consider the symbol 'Tom is Armenian,' and let's suppose the fact—viz., the fact in virtue of which that symbol has its truth value—is that Tom is Swiss. Then Stampe wants it to be that what the symbol represents (i.e., *mis*represents) is Tom's being Swiss; *that's* the fact to which, if it were faithful, the symbol would provide epistemic access.

Now, to begin with, this counterfactual seems a little queer. What, precisely would it be *like* for 'Tom is Armenian' to be faithful to the fact it (mis)represents—viz., to the fact that Tom is Swiss? Roughly speaking, you can make a false sentence faithful either by changing the world or by changing the sentence; but neither will do the job that Stampe apparently wants done.

1. Change the world: make it be that Tom is Armenian. The sentence is now faithful, but to the wrong fact. That is, the fact that it's now faithful to isn't the one that it (mis)represented back when it used to be untrue; that, remember, was the fact that Tom is Swiss.

2. Change the sentence: make it *mean* that Tom is Swiss. The sentence is now faithful to the fact that it used to (mis)represent. But is the counterfactual intelligible? Can we make sense of talk about what a sentence would represent if it—the very same sentence—meant something different? And, if meaning can change while what is represented stays the same, in what sense does a theory of representation constitute a theory of meaning?

Problems, problems. Anyhow, the main upshot is clear enough, and it's one that Stampe accepts. According to the epistemic access story, when a symbol *mis*represents, 'one *may* not be able to tell from it what the situation is, despite the fact that it is a representation of the situation'. Here not being 'able to tell what the situation is' doesn't mean not being able to tell what it is that's *true* in the situation; it means not being able to tell *what situation it is that the symbol represents*. You can't tell, for example, that the symbol 'Tom is Armenian' represents Tom's being French unless you happen to know Tom's nationality.

It may be supposed that Stampe could disapprove of this along the following lines: you *can*, in one sense, tell what 'Tom is Armenian' represents even if you don't know that Tom is Swiss. For, you can know that 'Tom is Armenian' represents Tom's nationality (i.e., that if it's faithful it provides epistemic access to his nationality) even if you don't know what Tom's nationality is. I think this is OK, but you buy it at a price: on this account, knowing what a symbol *represents* (what it provides epistemic access to) can't be equated with knowing what the symbol *means*. Notice that though 'Tom is Armenian' has the property that if it's faithful it provides epistemic access to Tom's nationality, so too do a scillion other, nonsynonymous sentences like 'Tom is Dutch,' 'Tom is Norwegian,' 'Tom is Swiss,' and so forth. To put the same point another way, on the present construal of Stampe's account, what a truth-valuable symbol represents isn't, in general, its truth condition. (The truth condition of a symbol is the state of affairs which, if it obtains, would make the symbol true; and what would make 'Tom is Armenian' true is Tom's being Armenian, not Tom's being Swiss.) Correspondingly, what you can know about 'Tom is Armenian' if you don't know that Tom is Swiss is not what its truth condition is, but only what it represents, viz., that it represents Tom's nationality. This means that Stampe has either to give up on the idea that understanding a symbol is knowing what would make it true, or develop a reconstruction of the notion of truth condition as well as a reconstruction of the notion of representation. Neither of these alternatives seems particularly happy.

There's more to be said about the epistemic approach to representation; but let's, for present purposes, put it to one side. From here on, only causal accounts will be at issue.

The basic problem for causal accounts is easy enough to see. Suppose that S is the truth condition of R in virtue of its being the cause of R. Now, causation is different from resemblance in the following way: a symbol can (I suppose) resemble something merely possible; it's OK for a picture to be a picture of a unicorn. But, surely, no symbol can be an effect of something merely possible. If S causes R, then S obtains. But if S obtains and S is the truth condition of R, it looks as though R has to be true; being true just *is* having truth conditions that obtain. So it looks like this: a theory that numbers *causation* among the relations in virtue of which a representation has its truth conditions is going to allow truth conditions to be assigned only when they're satisfied. I don't say that this argument is decisive; but I do say—and will now proceed to argue—that Wisconsin semantics hasn't thus far found a way around it.

I'll start with Dretske's treatment of the misrepresentation problem in *Knowledge And the Flow of Information*. The crucial passage is on pp. 194–195. Here is what Dretske says:

> In the learning situation special care is taken to see that incoming signals have an intensity, a strength, sufficient unto delivering the required piece of information *to* the learning subject. . . . Such precautions are taken in the learning situation . . . in order to ensure that an internal structure is developed with the information that s is F. . . . But once we have meaning, once the subject has articulated a structure that is selectively sensitive to

information about the *F*-ness of things, instances of this structure, tokens of this type, can be triggered by signals that *lack* the
appropriate piece of information. . . . We (thus) have a case of
misrepresentation—a token of a structure with a false content.
We have, in a word, meaning without truth. [emphasis
Dretske's]

All you need to remember to understand this well enough for present
purposes is (1) that Dretske's notion of information is fundamentally
that of counterfactual supporting correlation (i.e., that objects of type
R carry information about states of affairs of type *S* to the extent that
tokenings of the type *S* are nomically responsible for tokenings of
the type *R*). And (2) that the tokening of a representation carries the
information that *s* is *F* in *digital* form if and only if the information
that *s* is *F* is the most specific information that tokening carries about
s. Roughly speaking, the pretheoretic notion of the *content* of a representation is reconstructed as the information that the representation digitalizes.

Now then: how does *mis*representation get into the picture? There
is, of course, no such thing as mis*information* on Dretske's sort of
story. Information is correlation and though correlations can be better
or worse—more or less reliable—there is no sense to the notion of a
*mis*correlation; hence there is nothing, so far, to build the notion of
misrepresentation out of.

The obvious suggestion would be this: suppose *R*s are nomically
correlated with—hence carry information about—*S*s; then, as we've
seen, given the satisfaction of further (digitization) conditions, we
can treat *R*s as representations of *S*s: *S* is the state of affairs type that
symbols of the *R* type represent. But suppose that, from time to time,
tokenings of *R* are brought about (not by tokenings of *S* but) in some
other way. Then these, as one might say, 'wild' tokenings would
count as *mis*representations: for, on the one hand, they have the
content that *S*; but, on the other hand, since it isn't the fact that *S*
that brings about their tokening the content that they have is false.
Some sort of identification of misrepresentations with etiologically
wild tokenings is at the heart of all causal accounts of
misrepresentation.

However, the crude treatment just sketched clearly won't do; it is
open to an objection that can be put like this: If there are wild
tokenings of *R*, it follows that the nomic dependence of *R* upon *S* is
imperfect; some *R*-tokens—the wild ones—are *not* caused by *S* tokens. Well, but clearly they are caused by *something*; i.e., by something that is, like *S*, sufficient but not necessary for bringing *R*s about.

Call this second sort of sufficient condition the tokening of situations of type T. Here's the problem: R represents the state of affairs with which its tokens are causally correlated. Some representations of type R are causally correlated with states of affairs of type S; some representations of type R are causally correlated with states of affairs of type T. So it looks as though what R represents is not either S or T, but rather the disjunction $(S \lor T)$: The correlation of R with the disjunction is, after all, *better than* its correlation with either of the disjuncts and, ex hypothesis, correlation makes information and information makes representation. If, however, what Rs represent is not S but $(S \lor T)$, then tokenings of R that are caused by T aren't, *after all, wild tokenings* and our account of misrepresentation has gone West.

It is noteworthy that this sort of argument—which, in one form or other, will be with us throughout the remainder of this essay—seems to be one that Dretske himself accepts. The key assumption is that, ceteris paribus, if the correlation of a symbol with a disjunction is better than its correlation with either disjunct, it is the disjunction, rather than either disjunct, that the symbol represents. This is a sort of 'principle of charity' built into causal theories of representation: 'so construe the content of a symbol that what it is taken to represent is what it correlates with *best*'. Dretske apparently subscribes to this. For example, in 1983 (circa p. 17) he argues that, for someone on whose planet there is both XYZ and H_2O but who learns the concept *water* solely from samples of the former, the belief that such and such is water is the belief that it is *either* H_2O *or* XYZ. This seems to be charity in a rather strong form: R represents a disjunction even if all tokenings of R are caused by the satisfaction of the *same* disjunct, so long as satisfaction of the other disjunct *would have caused R tokenings had they happened to occur*. I stress this by way of showing how much the counterfactuals count; Dretske's conditions on representation are intensional (with an '*s*'); they constrain the effects of counterfactual causes.

To return to Dretske's treatment of misrepresentation: his way out of the problem about disjunction is to enforce a strict distinction between what happens in the learning period and what happens after. Roughly, the correlations that the learning period establish determine what R represents; and the function of the Teacher is precisely to ensure that the correlation so established is a correlation of R tokens with S tokens. It may be that *after* the learning period, R tokens are brought about by something *other than* S tokens; if so, these are wild tokenings of R and their contents are false.

This move is ingenious but hopeless. Just for starters, the distinction between what happens in the learning period and what happens thereafter surely isn't principled; there is no time after which one's use of a symbol stops being merely shaped and starts to be, as it were, in earnest. Perhaps idealization will bear some of this burden, but it's hard to believe that it could yield a notion of learning period sufficiently rigorous to underwrite the distinction between truth and falsity; which is, after all, precisely what's at issue. Second, if Dretske does insist upon the learning period gambit, he limits the applicability of his notion of misrepresentation to *learned* symbols. This is bad for me because it leaves us with no way in which innate information could be false; and it's bad for him because it implies a basic dichotomy between *natural* representation (smoke and fire; rings in the tree and the age of the tree) and the intentionality of mental states.

All of that, however, is mere limbering up. The real problem about Dretske's gambit is internal; it just doesn't work. Consider a trainee who comes to produce R tokens in S circumstances during the training period. Suppose, for simplification, that the correlation thus engendered is certainly nomic, and that S tokenings are elicited by *all and only* R tokenings during training: error-free learning. Well, time passes, a whistle blows (or whatever), and the training period comes to an end. At some time later still, the erstwhile trainee encounters a tokening of a T situation (T not equal to S) and produces an R in causal consequence. The idea is, of course, that this T-elicited tokening of R is ipso facto wild and, since it happens after the training period ended, it has the (false) content *that S.*

But, as I say, this won't work: it ignores relevant counterfactuals. Imagine, in particular, what *would have* happened if a token of situation type T *had* occurred during the training period. Presumably what would have happened is that it would have elicited a tokening of R. After all, tokenings of T are assumed to be sufficient to cause R tokenings *after* training; that's the very assumption upon which Dretske's treatment of wild R-tokenings rests. So we can assume—indeed, we can stipulate—that T is a situation that, if it had occurred *during* training, would have been sufficient for R. But that means, of course, that if you include the counterfactuals, the correlation that training established is (not between R and S but) between R and the disjunction (S v T). So now we have the old problem back again. If training established a correlation with (S v T) then the content of a tokening of R is *that* (S v T). So a tokening of R caused by T isn't a wild tokening after all; and since it isn't wild it also isn't false. A token with the content (S v T) is, of course, *true* when it's the case that T.

There is a way out for Dretske. He could say this: "The trouble is, you still haven't taken care of *all* the relevant counterfactuals; in particular, you've ignored the fact that if a *T*-tokening has occurred during training and elicited an *R*-tokening *the Teacher would have corrected the R response*. This distinguishes the counterfactual consequences of *T*-elicited *R*-tokens occurring during training from those of *S*-elicited *R*-tokens occurring during training since the latter would not, of course, have been corrected. In the long run, then, it is *these* counterfactuals—ones about what the teacher *would have corrected*— that are crucial; *R*s represent *S*s (and not *T*s) because the Teacher would have disapproved of *T*-elicited *R*-responses if they had occurred."

But I don't think Dretske would settle for this, and nor will I. It's no good for Dretske because it radically alters the fundamental principle of his theory, which is that the character of symbol-to-situation correlations determines the content of a symbol. On this revised view, the essential determinant is not the actual, or even the counterfactual, correlations that hold between the symbol and the world; rather it's the Teacher's pedagogical intentions; specifically, the Teacher's intention to reward only such *R* tokenings as are brought about by *S*s. And it's no good for me because it fails a prime condition upon *naturalistic* treatment of representations; viz., that appeals to intentional (with a '*t*') states must not figure essentially therein. I shall therefore put this suggestion of Dretske's to one side and see what else may be on offer.

Let's regroup. The basic problem is that we want there to be conditions for the *truth* of a symbol over and above the conditions whose satisfaction determines what the symbol represents. Now, according to causal theories, the latter—representation determining—conditions include whatever is necessary and sufficient to bring about tokenings of the symbol (including nomically possible counterfactual tokenings.) So the problem is, to put it crudely, if we've already used up all that to establish representation, what more could be required to establish truth?

An idea that circulates in all the texts I've been discussing (including my own) goes like this. Instead of thinking of the representation making conditions as whatever is necessary and sufficient for causing tokenings of the symbol, think of them as whatever is necessary and sufficient for causing such tokenings *in normal circumstances*. We can think of the wild tokens as being (or, anyhow, as including) the ones that come about when the 'normal conditions' clause is *not satisfied*. This doesn't, of course, get us out of the woods. At a minimum, we still need to show (what is by no means obvious) that for a theory of representations to appeal to normalcy conditions (over and above causal ones) isn't merely question-begging; for example, that you can characterize what it is for the conditions of a tokening to be normal without invoking intentional and/or semantic notions. Moreover, we'll also have to show that appealing to normalcy conditions is a way of solving the disjunction problem, and that, alas, isn't clear either. We commence with the first of these worries.

It is, I think, no accident that there is a tendency in all the texts I've been discussing (again including mine) to introduce normalcy conditions by appeal to examples where *teleology* is in play. For example, to use a case that Dretske works hard, a voltmeter is a device which, under normal conditions, produces an output which covaries (nomically) with the voltage across its input terminals. 'Normal conditions' include that all sorts of constraints on the internal and external environment of the device should be satisfied (e.g., the terminals must not be corroded) but it seems intuitively clear that what the device registers is the voltage and not the voltage together with the satisfaction of the normalcy conditions. If the device reads zero, that means that there's no current flowing, not that *either* there is no voltage flowing *or* the terminals are corroded.

However, we know this because we know what the device is *for* and we can know what the device is for only because there *is* something that the device is for. The tendency of causal theorists to appeal to teleology for their best cases of the distinction between representation-making causal conditions and mere normalcy conditions is thus unnerving. After all, in the case of artifacts at least, being 'for' something is surely a matter of being *intended* for something. And we had rather hoped to detach the representational from the intentional since, if we can't, our theory of representation ipso facto fails to be naturalistic and the point of the undertaking becomes, to put it mildly, obscure.

There are, it seems, two possibilities. One can either argue that there can be normalcy without teleology (i.e., that there are cases *other than* teleological ones where a distinction between causal conditions and normal conditions can be convincingly drawn); or one can argue that there can be teleology without intentionality (*natural teleology*, as it were) and that the crucial cases of representation rest exclusively upon teleology of this latter kind. Unlike Dretske and Stampe, I am inclined towards the second strategy. It seems to me that our intuitions about the distinction between causal and normal conditions are secure only in the cases where the corresponding intuitions about teleology are secure, and that where we *don't* have intuitions about teleology, the disjunction argument seems persuasive.[5] Let's look at a couple of cases.

Thermometers are OK; given normalcy conditions (e.g., a vacuum in the tube) the nomic covariance between the length of the column and the temperature of the ambient air determines what the device represents. Violate the normalcy conditions and, intuition reports, you get wild readings; i.e., *mis*representations of the temperature. But, of course, thermometers are *for* measuring something, and precisely what they're for measuring (viz., the temperature of the ambient air) is what the present analysis treats as a causal (rather than a normalcy) condition. Compare, by way of contrast, the diameter of the coin in my pocket. Fix my body temperature and it covaries with the temperature of the ambient air; fix the temperature of the ambient air, and it covaries with the temperature of my body. I see *no* grounds for saying that one of these things is what really represents and the other is a normalcy condition (e.g., that the diameters that are affected by body temperature are misrepresentations of the air temperature).[6] In short, where there is no question of teleology it looks as though one's intuitions about which are the normalcy conditions are unstable. Such examples should make one dubious about the chance for a notion of normalcy that applies in *non*teleological cases.

Or, consider an example of Stampe's:

> The number of rings (in a tree stump) represents the age of the tree. . . . The causal conditions, determining the production of this representation, are most saliently the climatic conditions that prevailed during the growth of the tree. If these are normal . . . then one ring will be added each year. Now what *is* that reading . . . It is not, for one thing, infallible. There may have been drought years. . . . It is a *conditional* hypothesis: that *if* certain conditions hold, then something's having such and such properties would cause the representation to have such and such properties. . . . Even under those normal conditions, there may be other things that would produce the rings—an army of some kind of borer, maybe, or an omnipotent evil tree demon. (1977, p. 49)

Stampe's analysis of this case rests on his decision to treat the seasonal climatic variations as the causal component of the conditions on representation and the absence of (e.g.) drought, tree borers, evil demons, and the rest as normalcy conditions. And, of course, given that decision, it's going to follow from the theory that the tree's rings represent the tree's age and that tree-borer-caused tree ring tokens are wild (i.e., that they *mis*represent the tree's age). The worrying question is what, if anything, motivates this decision.

We should do this in several steps. Let's consider a particular case of tree-borer-caused tree ring tokenings. Suppose, for the moment, we agree that the general truth is that a tree's rings represent the tree's age. And suppose we agree that it follows from this general truth that all tree ring tokenings represent the age of the tree that they're tokened in. Well, even given all that it's not obvious what these tree-borer-caused tokenings represent since it's not obvious that they are, in the relevant sense, tree rings.

Perhaps the right way to describe the situation is to say that these things merely *look like* tree rings. Compare the token of 'Look upon my works, oh ye mighty, and despair' that the wind traces in the desert sands. This *looks like* a token of an English sentence type (and, of course, if it *were* a token of that sentence type it would be unfaithful, what with there not being anything to look at and all). But it's not a token of that English sentence since it's not a token of *any* sentence. A fortiori, it's not a wild or unfaithful token. Similarly, mutatis mutandis (maybe) with the putative tree rings; they're not wild (unfaithful) representations of the tree's age because, even if all tree rings are representation of a tree's age, *these aren't tree rings*.

I hope I will be seen not to be merely quibbling. Stampe wants it to come out that tree-borer-caused tree rings are wild; that they're misrepresentations of the tree's age. He needs this a lot since this sort of case is Stampe's paradigm example of a distinction between causal conditions and normalcy conditions that doesn't rest on teleology. But I claim that the case doesn't work *even assuming what's yet to be shown, viz., that tree rings represent tree age rather than tree-age-plus-satisfaction-of-normalcy-conditions*. For Stampe is assuming a non-question-begging—hence naturalistic—criterion for something being a token of a representation type. And there isn't one. (Of course, we do have a criterion which excludes the wind token's being a sentence inscription; but that criterion is *non*naturalistic, hence unavailable to a causal theorist; it invokes the intentions of the agent who produced the token.)

Now let's look at it the other way. Suppose that these tree-borer-caused rings *are* tree rings (by stipulation) and let's ask what they represent. The point here is that even if 'under normal conditions, tree rings represent the tree's age' is true, it *still* doesn't follow that *these* abnormally formed tree rings represent the tree's age. Specifically, it doesn't follow that these rings represent the tree's age rather than the tree borer's depredations. (Look closely and you'll see the marks their little teeth left. Do these represent the tree's age too?)

This is just the disjunction problem over again, though it shows an interesting wrinkle that you get when you complicate things by adding in normalcy conditions. 'If circumstances are normal, *x*s are *F*' doesn't, of course, tell you about the *F*-ness of *x*s when circumstances are *ab*normal. The most you get is a counterfactual, viz., 'if circumstances *had been* normal, this *x* would have been *F*.' Well, in the present case, if etiological circumstances had been normal, these rings would have represented the tree's age (viz., accurately). It doesn't follow that, given the way the etiological circumstances actually were, these rings still represent the tree's age (viz., *in*accurately). What you need is some reason to suppose that etiologically abnormal (hence wild) rings represent the same thing that etiologically normal rings do. This is precisely equivalent to saying that what you need is a solution to the disjunction problem, and that is precisely what I've been arguing all along that we haven't got.

We *would* have it, at least arguably, if this were a teleological case. Suppose that there is some mechanism that (not only produces tree rings but) produces tree rings with an end in view. (Tree rings are, let's suppose, Mother Nature's calendar). Then there is a trichotomous distinction between (a) tree rings produced under normal circumstances; (b) wild tree rings (inscribed, for example, when Mother Nature is a little tipsy); and (c) things that look like tree rings but aren't (tree borer's depredations). This *does* enforce a distinction between representation, misrepresentation and nonrepresentation; not so much because it relativizes representation to *normalcy*, however, but because it relativizes representation to *end-in-view*. The reason that wild tree rings represent the same things as normal ones is that *the wild ones and the normal ones are supposed to serve the same function.* Notice that it's the intensionality of 'supposed to' that's doing all the work.

I'm afraid what all this comes to is that the distinction between normal and wild tokens rests—so far at least—on a pretty strong notion of teleology. It's only in the teleological cases that we have any way of justifying the claim that wild tokens represent the same thing that etiologically normal ones do; and it is, as we've seen, that claim on which the present story about misrepresentation rests. How bad is this? Well, for one thing, it's not as bad as if the distinction had turned out to rest on an *intentional* notion. There are, as I remarked above, plausible cases of nonintentional, natural teleology and a naturalistic theory of representation can legitimately appeal to these. On the other hand, if the line of the argument we have been exploring is right, then the hope for a *general* theory of representation (one that includes tree rings, for example) is going to have to be abandoned. Tree rings will have to represent only at a remove, via the interests of an observer, since only what has natural teleology can represent absolutely. This is, as a matter of fact, OK with me. For I hold that only sentences in the language of thought represent in, as it were, the first instance; and they represent in virtue of the natural teleology of the cognitive mechanisms. Propositional attitudes represent *qua* relations to sentences in the language of thought. All other representation depends upon the propositional attitudes of symbol users.

Even allowing all this, however, it is arguable that we haven't yet got a notion of misrepresentation robust enough to live with. For we still have this connection between the etiology of representations and their truth values: representations generated in teleologically normal circumstances must be true. Specifically, suppose M is a mechanism the function of which is to generate tokens of representation type R in, and only in, tokens of situation type S; M mediates the causal relation between Ss and Rs. Then we can say that M-produced tokens of R are wild when M is functioning abnormally; but when M is functioning normally (i.e., when its tokening of R is causally contingent, in the right way, upon the tokening of S) then not only do the tokens of R have the content *that* S, but also the contents of these tokens are satisfied, and what the tokens say is true.

Well, consider the application to belief fixation. It looks as though (1) only beliefs with abnormal etiologies can be false, and (2) 'abnormal etiology' will have to be defined with respect to the teleology of the belief-fixing (i.e., cognitive) mechanisms. As far as I can see, this is tantamount to: 'beliefs acquired under epistemically optimal circumstances must be true' since, surely, the function of the cognitive mechanisms will itself have to be characterized by reference to the beliefs it *would* cause one to acquire *in* such optimal circumstances. (I take it for granted that we can't, for example, characterize the function of the cognitive mechanisms as the fixation of *true* beliefs because truth is a semantical notion. If our theory of representation is to rest upon the teleology of the cognitive mechanisms, cognitive teleology must itself be describable naturalistically; viz., without recourse to semantic concepts. For an extended discussion of this sort of stuff, see Fodor, unpublished.)

It appears that we have come all this way only in order to rediscover verificationism. For, I take it, verificationism just *is* the doctrine that truth is what we would believe in cognitively optimal circumstances. Is this simply too shameful for words? Can we bear it? I have three very brief remarks to make. They are, you will be pleased to hear, concluding remarks.

First, *all* Naturalistic theories in semantics, assuming that they are reductive rather than eliminative, have got to hold that there are circumstances specifiable without resort to semantical notions like truth, reference, correspondence, or the like, such that, if a belief is formed *in* those circumstances, then it must be true. Verificationism adds to this only the idea that the circumstances are epistemic (they involve, for example, such idealizations as unrestricted access to the evidence) and that wouldn't seem to be the part that hurts. I guess what I'm saying is: if you're going to be a naturalist, there's no obvious reason not to be a verificationist. (And if you're *not* going to be a naturalist, why are you working on a causal theory of representation?)

The second point is this: verificationism isn't an ontological doctrine. It has usually, in the history of philosophy, been held with some sort of idealistic malice aforethought, but that surely is an accident and one we can abstract from. The present sort of verificationism defines truth conditions by reference to the function of the cognitive mechanisms. Plausibly, the function of the cognitive mechanisms is to achieve, for the organism, epistemic access to the world. There is no reason on God's green earth why you shouldn't, in parsing that formula, construe 'the world' Realistically.

Finally, verificationism isn't incompatible with a correspondence theory of truth. The teleology of the nervous system determines what must be the case if R represents S; and it follows from the analysis that if R represents S and the situation is teleologically normal, S must be true. This is because what R represents is its truth condition, and its truth condition is whatever causes its tokening in teleologically normal situations. But this is entirely compatible with holding that what *makes* R true in teleologically normal situations is that its truth condition obtains; that R corresponds, that is to say, to the way that the world is.

I see no way out of this: a causal theory must so characterize representation and normalcy that there is no misrepresentation in normal circumstances. My view is: if that is the price of a workable theory of representation, we ought simply to pay it.

Notes

1. Since we haven't any general and satisfactory way of saying which expressions *are* semantical(/intentional), it's left to intuition to determine when a formulation of C meets this condition. This will not, however, pose problems for the cases we will examine.
2. I said that the formulation of naturalistic conditions for representation is *the least* that the vindication of an intentional psychology requires. What worries some

philosophers is that there may be no *unique* answer to the question what something represents; e.g., that the representational content of a symbol (belief, etc.) may be *indeterminate* given the totality of physical fact. Notice that settling the question about naturalism doesn't automatically settle this question about determinacy. Even if it proves possible to give naturalistic necessary and sufficient conditions for representation, there might be more than one way to satisfy such conditions, hence more than one thing that R could be taken to represent. For purposes of the present paper, however, I propose to put questions about determinacy of representation entirely to one side and focus just on the prospects for naturalism.

3. An example of the former: Propositional attitudes are relations to mental representations; mental representations are Ideas; Ideas are images; and Images represent what they resemble. I take it that Hume held a view not entirely unlike this.

4. In fact, Dretske gives the epistemic analysis as a condition upon 'R *carries information about S*' rather than 'R represents S'. This difference may *make* a difference and I'd have to attend to it if exposition were the goal. In much of what follows, however, I shall be less than sensitive to details of Dretske and Stampe's proposals. What I have in mind to exhibit are certain very pervasive characteristics of causal accounts; ones which I don't *think* can be avoided by tinkering.

5. I should add that, though Stampe clearly thinks that you can, in principle, get representation without teleology, cases which turn on functional analysis loom large among his examples. ". . . one doubts whether statistical normality will get us far in dealing with living systems and with language or generally with matters of teleological natures. Here, I think we shall want to identify fidelity conditions with certain conditions of well functioning, of a functional system." (Stampe 1977, p. 51)

6. Alternatively, you could go the disjunction route and say that the diameter of the coin represents some function of body temperature and air temperature. But this has the familiar consequence of rendering the covariance between R and S perfect and thus depriving us of examples of wild tokenings.

Chapter 3

A Theory of Content, I:

The Problem

Introduction

It counts as conventional wisdom in philosophy that (*i*) the intentional/semantical predicates form a closed circle and (*ii*) intentional states are intrinsically holistic. (*i*) unpacks as: 'It may be possible to formulate sufficient conditions for the satisfaction of some of the intentional/semantic predicates in a vocabulary that includes other of the intentional/semantic predicates; but it is not possible to formulate such conditions in a vocabulary that is exclusively *non*semantic/intentional.' (*ii*) unpacks as: 'Nothing can exhibit any intentional properties unless it exhibits many intentional properties; the metaphysically necessary conditions for a thing's being in any intentional state include its being in many other intentional states.' (*i*) is supposed to rule out the possibility of framing physicalistically sufficient conditions for the truth of intentional ascriptions; (*ii*) is supposed to rule out the possibility of punctate minds.

Working severally and together, (*i*) and (*ii*) have served to ground quite a lot of philosophical skepticism about intentional explanation. For example, (*i*) appears to preclude a physicalistic ontology for psychology since if psychological states were physical then there would surely be physicalistically specifiable sufficient conditions for their instantiation.[1] But it's arguable that if the ontology of psychology is not physicalistic, then there is no such science.

By contrast, (*ii*) could be true consonant with physicalism; why, after all, shouldn't there be properties that are both physicalistic and holistic? But it's nevertheless plausible that (*ii*) would preclude an intentional psychology with scientific status. One important way that psychological laws achieve generality is *by quantifying over all the organisms that are in a specified mental state* (all the organisms that believe that *P*, or intend that *Q*, or whatever). But holism implies that very many mental states must be shared if any of them are. So the more holistic the mind is, the more similar the mental lives of two organisms (or of two time slices of the same organism) have to be in order that the same psychological laws should subsume them both. At the limit of holism, two minds share any of their intentional states only if they share all of them. And since, of course, no two minds ever do share all of their intentional states, the more (*ii*) is true the more the putative generalizations of intentional psychology fail, de facto, to generalize.[2] (It's a question of some interest whether, having once embraced a holistic view of intentional content, there is anywhere to stop short of going the limit. I'm inclined to think that anyone who takes it seriously that there is no analytic/synthetic distinction is obliged to answer this question in the negative. I shan't, however, argue the point here.)

The moral, in short, is that the price of an Intentional Realism that's worth having—at least for scientific purposes—is a physicalist and atomistic account of intentional states. And, as I say, it's the conventional wisdom in philosophy that no such account can be given.

There is, however, an increasingly vociferous minority in dissent from this consensus. In particular, recent developments in "informational" semantics suggest the possibility of a naturalistic and atomistic theory of the relation that holds between a predicate and the property that it expresses. Such as theory would, of course, amount to a good deal less than a complete understanding of intentionality. But it would serve to draw the skeptic's fangs since his line is that irreducibility and holism are *intrinsic* to intentionality and semantic evaluability. Given any suitably atomistic, suitably naturalistic break in the intentional circle, it would be reasonable to claim that the main *philosophical* problem about intentionality had been solved. What remained to do would then be a job of more or less empirical theory construction or a more or less familiar kind.

What follows is in part a review paper; things have recently been moving so fast in work on "naturalized semantics"[3] that it seemed to me that an overview might be useful. Here is how I propose to proceed. In chapter 3, I'll give a sketch of how approaches to the naturalization problem have evolved over the last couple of decades. (Since what I primarily want to do is make clear the current appreciation of the structure of the naturalization problem, my treatment will be dialectical and polemical, and I'll settle for my usual C− in historical accuracy.) In chapter 4, I'll offer what seems to me to be a promising version of an information-based semantic theory: this will have the form of a physicalist, atomistic, and putatively sufficient condition for a predicate to express a property. I will then go through all the proposed counterexamples and counterarguments to this condition that my friends and relations and I have thus far succeeded in dreaming up. I will try to convince you (and me, and Greycat) that none of these counterexamples and counterarguments works. Or, anyhow, that none of them *certainly* works.

Even, however, if I am right that none of them works, someone will surely find one that works tomorrow. So, the proposed moral of the paper isn't really that there is no longer a philosophical problem about intentionality. Rather, the moral I'm inclined to draw—and that I hope I can convince you to take seriously—is that a number of the problems that once made the construction of a naturalistic semantics seem absolutely hopeless now appear rather less utterly intractable than they used to. It might therefore be wise, when one goes about one's business in the philosophy of language and the philosophy of mind, to become cautious about taking intentional irrealism for granted; more cautious, at a minimum, than has been the philosophical fashion for the last forty years or so.

1. The Background

Skinner

Our story starts with, of all things, Chomsky's (1959) review of Skinner's *Verbal Behavior*.[4] Skinner, you'll remember, had a theory about meaning. A slightly cleaned-up version of Skinner's theory might go like this:

The English word "dog" expresses the property of *being a dog* (and hence applies to all, and only, dogs). This semantical fact about English reduces to a certain fact about the behavioral dispositions of English speaker; viz., that their verbal response "dog" is 'under the control of' a certain type of discriminative stimuli; viz., that it's under the control of dogs. Roughly, a response is under the control of a certain type of discriminative stimulus if it is counterfactual supporting that the probability of an emission of the response increases 'in the presence of' a stimulus of that type.

There is also a Skinnerian story about how English speakers come to have these sorts of behavioral dispositions. Roughly, an operant response (including an operant linguistic response) comes under the control of a type of discriminative stimulus as a function of the frequency with which the response elicits reinforcement when produced in the presence of stimuli of that type. So tokens of "dog" express the property *dog* because speakers have been reinforced for uttering "dog" when there are dogs around.

Notice that—prima facie—this theory is naturalistic by the present criteria: The condition in virtue of the satisfaction of which "dog" means *dog* is specified in the prima facie *non* intentional/semantic vocabulary of response frequency and stimulus control; and the theory is atomistic since there is, in general, no internal connection between having any one response disposition and having any other. It is, for example, conceptually possible that there should be a speaker whose response "dog" is under the control of dogs but who has no verbal response (including, a fortiori, "cat") that is under the control of cats. Indeed, Skinner's semantics allows the possibility of a speaker who has *no* discriminated verbal operants other than the disposition to respond "dog" to dogs. That could be, as Wittgenstein (1953) says in a related context, "the *whole* language . . .; even the whole language of a tribe."

As everybody knows, Chomsky rolled all over this theory; no term was left unstoned. Nor, I think, could anyone reasonable deny that his having done so was a Very Good Thing. Behaviorism had become an incubus; Chomsky's critique effected a liberation of theoretical imagination in psychology and was a critical episode on the way to developing a serious cognitive science. But for all that—as people like MacCorquadale (1970) correctly pointed out—the theory of language we were left with when Chomsky got finished with Skinner was embarrassingly lacking in answers to questions about meaning. It still is, and something needs to be done about it.

Now that the dust has settled, it's worth trying to get clear on exactly what Chomsky showed that Skinner was wrong about. I want to suggest that there is an only somewhat quixotic sense in which Chomsky's criticism, though devastatingly effective against Skinner's behaviorism and against his attempt to apply learning theory to explain language acquisition, nevertheless left the *semantical* proposal per se pretty much untouched. It is, I think, the implicit recognition of this that grounds the recent interest in informational semantics.

For example, one of Chomsky's best lines of attack is directed against the idea—required by Skinner's learning theory—that the characteristic effect of linguistic apprenticeship is to alter the strength of an operant response. (Before you learn English, the probability of your uttering "dog" when there is a dog around is presumed to be very small; after you learn English it is presumed to be appreciably bigger). Chomsky argues, to begin with, that the technical sense of response strength, according to which it is measured by, for example, frequency, intensity, and resistance to extinction, doesn't have any serious application to the use of language. One does not, qua English speaker in the presence of a dog, utter "dog" repeatedly, tirelessly, and in a loud voice. Unless, perhaps, one is bonkers.

More important, Chomsky points out, in the usual case utterances aren't *responses* at all; they're *actions*. This is to say, at a minimum, that the character of one's verbal behavior is sensitive to the content of one's beliefs and utilities. Verbal behavior is 'cognitively penetrable', as one says these days: whether one utters "dog" in the presence of a dog depends on things like whether one thinks one's auditors would be interested to hear that there's a dog about, and whether one is desirous of telling them what one thinks they would be interested to hear, and so forth. To say nothing of its depending on whether one happens to notice the dog. To put the same point slightly differently: as Skinner uses it (at least when he's outside the laboratory) "response" is really a crypto-intentional term. So the idea that Skinner has achieved the naturalization of a semantical concept by the (putative) reduction of linguistic meaning to verbal responding turns out to be a sham.

And finally, Chomsky remarks, it appears just not to be true that language learning depends on the application of carefully scheduled socially mediated reinforcement. Language seems to be learned without being taught, and Skinner's story doesn't explain how this could be so.

This is, I think, all perfectly correct and brilliantly observed. But just how much damage does it do, and just which doctrines does it do the damage to? Notice, in the first place, that in principle Skinner's semantics can perfectly well dispense with his learning theory. Skinner could—though, of course, he wouldn't want to—tell the story that goes '"dog" expresses the property *dog* because tokenings of the former are under the control of instantiations of the latter' without saying *anything* about how discriminated responses *come to be* under the control of discriminative stimuli. He could therefore simply jettison the stuff about language learning reducing to social reinforcements mediating alterations in the strength of verbal operants; which would be a very good thing for him to do since it's hopeless.

The objection that notions like 'response' are crypto-intentional when applied to the use of language is fatal to Skinner's behaviorism but, once again, not to his semantics. For, although *talking* is a form of voluntary behavior, and hence a kind of acting, *thinking* presumably isn't. Someone who is an Intentional Realist but not a behaviorist could thus embrace a Skinnerian semantics *for thoughts* while entirely rejecting Skinner's account of language. Here's how the revised story might go: There is a mental state—of entertaining the concept DOG, say—of which the intentional object is the property *dog*. (Or, as I shall sometimes say for brevity, there is a mental state that *expresses* the property *dog*). The fact that this state expresses this property reduces to the fact that tokenings of the state are, in the relevant sense, discriminated responses to instances of the property; i.e., instancings of the state covary with (they are 'under the control of') instancings of the property, and this covariation is lawful, hence counterfactual supporting.

This account isn't behavioristic since it's unabashed about the postulation of intentional mental states. And it isn't learning-theoretic since it doesn't care about the ontogeny of the covariance in terms of which the semantic relation between dog-thoughts and dogs is explicated. But it is atomistic since it is presumably conceptually possible for dog-thoughts to covary with dog instances even in a mind none of whose other states are intentional; the conditions for meaning can thus be satisfied by symbols that don't belong to symbol *systems*.

It's also atomistic in a further sense; one that I want to emphasize for later reference. The basic idea of Skinnerian semantics is that *all* that matters for meaning is "functional" relations (relations of nomic covariance) between symbols and their denotations. In particular, it doesn't matter *how that covariation is mediated*; it doesn't matter what mechanisms (neurological, intentional, spiritual, psychological, or whatever) sustain the covariation. This makes Skinnerian semantics atomistic in a way that Quineian semantics, for instance, isn't. It's a typically Quineian move to argue that since the semantical relations between, as it might be, 'proton's and protons is *theory mediated* (since, in particular, theoretical inferences mediate our applications of 'proton' to protons), it must be that *what one means by 'proton' is partly determined by the theories about protons that one endorses.* And since, for Quine, the observation vocabulary/theory vocabulary distinction isn't principled, it comes out that what one means by *any* 'X' is partly determined by what one believes about Xs.[5]

But Quine is not a good Skinnerian in holding this. A good Skinnerian says that what 'proton' means is determined *just by its functional relation to* (its causal covariance with) *protons*; given that this covariation holds, the theoretical inferences by which it's mediated are *semantically irrelevant*. In particular, two individuals whose 'proton' tokens exhibit the *same* functional relation to protons ipso facto mean the same thing by 'proton', *whatever theories of protons they may happen to hold*. The conditions for meaning constrain the functional relation between a symbol and its referent, but they *quantify over* the mechanisms (theoretical commitments, as it might be) that sustain these functional relations.[6] For Skinner, then, though not for Quine, content is radically detached from ideology. Quine's affection for

Skinner is merely sentimental after all; given his semantic holism, Quine *can't* be a Skinnerian.

Well, finally, this updated Skinnerian semantics is physicalistic on the assumption that token states of entertaining a concept can be picked out by reference to their nonsemantical properties (e.g., by reference to their neurological, or functional, or 'syntactic' properties). Which perhaps they can; who knows?[7] The point is that this highly reconstructed Skinnerianism—from which, to be sure, practically everything that Skinner cares about has been removed—would satisfy the naturalism requirement; and, as far as I can tell, it is not touched by the arguments that Chomsky mounted against *Verbal Behavior*.

In fact, if you take the behaviorism and the learning theory away from the theory of meaning in *Verbal Behavior*, what you're left with is a doctrine that looks quite a lot like the informational semantics of Dretske's *Knowledge And The Flow of Information*. Which brings us to the next stage of our story.

Dretske
F1 gives what I take to be the basic idea of Dretske's theory.

> F1. *S-events (e.g., tokenings of symbols) express the property P if the generalization 'Ps cause Ss' is counterfactual supporting.*

For example, tokenings of "dog" express the property *dog* because the generalization, 'Dogs cause "dog"-tokens' is counterfactual supporting.

I like this way of putting Dretske's proposal because it makes clear the continuity of his program with Skinner's. In Dretske's own formulation, however, the fundamental semantic relation is 'carrying information' (rather than 'expressing a property'). A first-blush account of carrying information is given by F2.

> F2. *S-events carry information about P-events if 'Ps cause Ss' is a law.*[8]

However, F2 would also not be acceptable to Dretske. For example, according to his theory, Ss carry information about Ps only if the probability that an arbitrary S is P-caused is always one; in effect, Dretske requires that 'Ps and only Ps cause Ss' be a law.

His main argument for this very strong condition is this:[9] suppose we allow that Ss carry information about Ps even when the probability that Ss are P-caused is some *p* less than one. Then we could get a situation where Ss carry information about Ps, Rs carry information about *Q*s, but *S&R*s don't carry information about *P&Q*s (viz., because the probability that *P&Q* given *S&R* is less than *p*).

But I think this argument is ill advised. There is no reason why a semantical theory should assign informational content *independently* to each expression in a symbol system. It will do if contents are assigned only to the *atomic* expressions, the semantics for molecular symbols being built up recursively by the sorts of techniques that are familiar from the construction of truth definitions. In what follows, I will in fact assume that the problem of naturalizing representation reduces to the problem of naturalizing it for atomic symbols (mutatis mutandis, atomic *mental states* if it is mental representation that is being naturalized).[10]

F1 and F2 are more closely related than may appear since we can assume that '*P*s cause *S*s' is counterfactual supporting only if it's a law. The connection between information and nomologicity that is explicit in F2 is therefore implicit in F1. Because the notions of law and counterfactual support are so close to the heart of both Skinner's and Dretske's views of semantics, the theories share a feature that will be important to us much later in the discussion: both imply that what your words (thoughts) mean is dependent entirely on your *dispositions* to token them, the *actual history* of their tokenings being semantically irrelevant.

This principle—that actual histories are semantically irrelevant—follows from the basic idea of informational semantics, which is that the content of a symbol is determined solely by its nomic relations. To put it roughly but intuitively, what laws subsume a thing is a matter of its *subjunctive* career; of *what it would do* (or would have done) *if* the circumstances were (or had been) thus and so. By contrast, a thing's actual history depends not just on the laws it falls under, but also on the circumstances that it happens to encounter. Whether Skinner and Dretske are right to suppose that a naturalized semantics can ignore actual histories in favor of purely subjunctive contingencies is a question we'll return to late in chapter 4. Till then, we will cleave rigorously to the principle that only nomic connections and the subjunctives they license count for meaning.

For the present, then, I propose to take F2 as my stalking horse. It formulates a doctrine that is within hailing distance of both Skinner's version of naturalized semantics and Dretske's, and it makes clear the intimate connection between the information that's generated by a causal transaction and the existence of a causal law that "covers" the transaction.[11] And as far as I can tell, the problems we're about to raise for F2 will have to be faced by any version of information-based semantics that can claim to be remotely plausible.

2.   Error and the Disjunction Problem

You have to get error in somewhere, and so far we've made no room
for it. In fact, there looks to be a dilemma about this. Suppose, to
put it crudely, that "dog" means *dog* (and thus has dogs and only
dogs in its extension) because it's a law that dogs cause "dogs." Then
there are two possibilities:

First Possibility
Only dogs cause "dog"s. If this is so, then only things in the extension of "dog" cause it to be tokened; so it looks as though all the
tokens of "dog" must be true.

Second Possibility
Some non-dogs cause "dog"s. Suppose, for example, that either
being a dog or being (the right sort of) cat-on-a-dark-night is sufficient to cause a "dog" token. F2 says, in effect, that symbols express
the properties whose instantiations are nomically sufficient for their
tokening. So "dog" expresses the property of being *either a dog or a
cat-on-a-dark-night*. So the extension of "dog" is the union of the dogs
and the cats-on-dark-nights. So tokens of "dog" that are caused by
cats on dark nights are *true*, and we still don't have a story about
falsehood and error.
  If F2 is the best that a causal theory of content can do, it looks as
though such theories can't distinguish between a true token of a
symbol that means something that's disjunctive and a false token of
a symbol that means something that's not. The literature on informational semantics has come to call this the "disjunction problem."
  What, exactly, is going on here? Well, it seems plausible that the
least you'd want of a false token of a symbol is that it be caused by
something that is not in the symbol's extension. But this is a condition
that F2 has trouble meeting. Because:

> (*i*)   it's a truism that *every* token of a symbol (including the false
> ones) is caused by something that has some property that is
> sufficient to cause a tokening of the symbol

and

> (*ii*)   according to F2, any property whose instantiation is suffi-
> cient to cause the tokening of a symbol is thereby expressed by
> that symbol.

Since the extension of a symbol is just the set of things that have the
property that the symbol expresses, it appears to follow from (*i*) and

(*ii*) that *every* token of a symbol is caused by something that belongs to its extension; hence that no token of a symbol can be false. This is, to put the case mildly, not satisfactory.

Indeed, it is *so* not satisfactory that the question whether a naturalistic semantics is possible has recently come to be viewed as identical in practice to the question whether the disjunction problem can be solved within a naturalistic framework. Accordingly, most of the rest of this paper will be about the vicissitudes of recent attempts to find such a solution.

With an exception that I will retail later, all the standard attempts to solve the disjunction problem exhibit a certain family resemblance. The basic idea is to distinguish between two types of situations, such that lawful covariation determines meaning in one type of situation but not in the other. The revised theory says, in effect, that a symbol expresses a property if instantiations of the property are nomically sufficient for instantiations of the symbol *in situations of type one*. Since the tokens of a symbol that occur in type one situations are ipso facto caused by things that are in its extension, it follows that all such tokens are true. However, properties whose instantiations cause tokens of a symbol (only) *in situations of the second type* are *not* thereby expressed by the symbol; so tokens of a symbol that occur in type two situations are *not* ipso facto caused by things in its extension; so it is left open that such tokens may be false.

The strategy of the revised theory is thus to solve the disjunction problem by localizing it. It's accepted that symbol tokens in type one situations are ipso facto true;[12] and it's thereby conceded that if tokenings of a symbol are caused by more than one sort of thing *in type one situations* then it follows that the meaning of the symbol is disjunctive. But, according to the new story, not *all* sorts of situations enjoy this privilege of conveying infallibility; for example, type two situations don't. So the new story does make room for the possibility of error, which, as we've seen, the old story failed to do.

Here's a slightly different, though convergent, way to think about this distinction between type one and type two situations. It might reasonably occur to a philosopher to wonder, "Why is it that our canonical specifications of thoughts, beliefs and the like operate by employing phrases—embedded 'that' clauses—that (apparently) express actual or possible states of affairs? Why, for example, do we pick out the thought that it's raining by using the expression 'it's raining'? What is it about thoughts, and about states of affairs, that makes this practice possible?" (Papineau, 1988, wonders this sort of thing, circa p. 88, as does Loar, 1981). This is closely related to a revealing question that I believe was first raised by Donald Davison:

how are we to understand the fact that the expressions that can appear as freestanding declarative sentences can also appear as the complements of verbs of propositional attitude?

All informational accounts tell essentially the same story about this; what's going on, they say, is a species of *etiological* identification. When we use "it's raining" to specify the intentional object of the thought that it's raining, we are picking the thought out by reference to the state of affairs that would, in certain circumstances, cause it to be entertained. It's rather like an alcoholic stupor; you specify the state by reference to the sort of thing that brings it on.

All right so far; but since, in general, the tokening of an intentional state can have any of a variety of different kinds of causes (unlike, by the way, tokenings of alcoholic stupors) the problem arises, under *which* circumstances the cause of a thought is ipso facto identical to its intentional object. Answer: By definition, this coincidence obtains in situations of type one. The moral is that the disjunction problem is a, but not the only, consideration that might motivate an informational semanticist to try to draw a type one/type two distinction. Other philosophical interests point to the same desideratum.

So everything is fine; all we need is a convincing—and, of course, naturalistic—explication of the type one/type two distinction and we will understand, within the framework of an informational account of content, both how error is possible and how it is possible to individuate intentional states in the ways that we do. As it turns out, however, convincing naturalistic explications of this distinction have proved to be a little thin on the ground.

3.   Dretske's Story about Error

The first attempt was owing to Dretske (1981). In a nutshell, Dretske's idea was to identify the type one (i.e., meaning-bestowing) situations with the ones *in which a symbol is learned*:

> In the learning situation special care is taken to see that incoming signals have an intensity, a strength, sufficient unto delivering the required piece of information *to* the learning subject. . . . Such precautions are taken in the learning situation . . . in order to ensure that an internal structure is developed with the information that s is F. . . . But once we have meaning, once the subject has articulated a structure that is selectively sensitive to information about the F-ness of things, instances of this structure, tokens of this type, can be triggered by signals that *lack* the appropriate piece of information. . . . We (thus) have a case of

misrepresentation—a token of a structure with a false content. We have, in a word, meaning without truth. (emphasis Dretske's).

See chapter 2 for an extended discussion of this proposal; the heart of the matter is as follows.

F2 implies that S expresses the property that, as a consequence of the training, came to be nomically sufficient for causing S-tokens. It therefore matters a lot which property this is, and the crucial point is that its identity is *not* determined by the actual S-tokenings that the trainee produces during the learning period. For example, even a learner all of whose "dog" tokens are caused by dogs throughout the course of his training may nevertheless be using "dog" to mean not *dog* but *dog or cat-on-a-dark-night*. Whether he is doing so won't show in his overt behavior (in his tokenings of "dog") unless he happened to run into a cat-on-a-dark-night; which, by assumption, he didn't. But remember, in informational semantics, it's the subjunctives, *counterfactuals included*, that count. That is, it's the actual *and counterfactual S*-tokenings in training situations that fix the identity of the property that S expresses. Since it goes without saying that there must always be indefinitely many properties whose instantiations are *not* encountered in any finite linguistic apprenticeship, there are always indefinitely many disjunctive properties that the trainee's use of "dog" could express, *consonant with all of his actual tokenings of "dog" being dog-occasioned*. This creates a dilemma for Dretske's proposal that is itself just a version of the disjunction problem.

Case one. If a cat-on-a-dark-night had been encountered during the learning period, it would have caused a "dog" token. But then the consequence of training has been that "dog" means *dog or cat-on-a-dark-night*, and tokens of "dog" caused by cats on dark nights outside the training situation are true. So there is still no room for false tokens.

Case two. If a cat-on-a-dark-night had been encountered during the learning period, it would *not* have caused a "dog" token. Then, the consequence of the training has been that cats-on-dark-nights don't cause "dog" tokens after all; presumably, only dogs do. (If a cat-on-a-dark-night encountered *during* the training period wouldn't have caused a "dog" token, why on Earth should a cat-on-a-dark-night encountered *after* the training period cause one?) But if only dogs cause "dog" tokens, all such tokens are true and again there's no room for errors.

The moral seems to be that when you take the counterfactuals into the reckoning, the story about the training doesn't help with the disjunction problem.

I once heard Dretske make what I took to be the following suggestion: What determines the identity of the concept the student has learned is *not* the actual and counterfactual distribution of his tokenings (as per the preceding), but rather the distribution of actual and counterfactual *punishments and rewards* that prevails in the training situation. So, for example, imagine a student who has been reinforced for positive responses to *apples*, and suppose that no *wax apples* have been encountered. Then what determines that the student has learned the concept APPLE rather than the disjunctive concept APPLE OR WAX APPLE is that, *were he* to respond positive to a wax apple, the teacher (or some other environmental mechanism) *would contrive to punish the response*.

But I don't think Dretske really wants to hold this (and it's entirely possible that I have misconstrued him in thinking that he thinks that he does). For, on this account, *it would be impossible to mistakenly learn a disjunctive concept when a nondisjunctive one is being taught.* Suppose you are trying to teach me APPLE; i.e., suppose that you would punish me for positive responses to wax apples. And suppose that it somehow nevertheless gets into my head that the concept you are trying to teach me is the disjunctive APPLE OR WAX APPLE. On the current view, however explicitly I think that that *is* the concept that you are trying to teach me, and however much it is the case that I *would* respond positive to instances of WAX APPLE were any such to be presented, still the concept that I have in fact acquired is not APPLE OR WAX APPLE but APPLE. Because: the proposal is that it's the objective distribution of (actual and counterfactual) punishments and rewards in the training situation that determines the identity of the concept that I learn; and, by hypothesis, in this training situation it's APPLEs and not APPLE OR WAX APPLEs, to which the actual and counterfactual rewards accrue. This, surely, is a reductio of the proposal. If the objective reinforcement contingencies determine which concepts we acquire we'd all be practically infallible and induction would be a snap. Alas, what constitutes my concepts is not *the objective reinforcement contingencies,* but rather *the reinforcement contingencies that I take to obtain.* Cf. a point that Chomsky made against Skinner: what's reinforced is one thing, what's learned is often quite another.

None of this shows, of course, that you can't get out of the disjunction problem by restricting the circumstances under which causation makes content. But it does suggest that the identification of type one situations with *learning* situations won't do the trick.

4.   *Teleological/Functional Solutions*

The basic idea for dealing with the disjunction problem was to define a *type one situation* such that:

> (*i*)   If it's a law that *P*s cause *S*-tokens in type one situations, then *S* means *P* (and if *P* is disjunctive, then so be it);

and

> (*ii*)   not all situations in which *S* gets tokened qualify as type one, so that tokens of *S* that happen in *other* sorts of situations are ipso facto free to be false.

Well, it looks as though type one situations can't be learning situations; but here's an alternative proposal. *Normal* situations are just the sort of situations we require. We are now about to spend some time looking at this proposal.

Prima facie, this kind of idea is sort of attractive; it's sensitive to the plausible intuition that errors are cases where *something has gone wrong*: "Where beliefs are false . . . we also expect some explanation for the deviation from the norm: either an abnormality in the environment, as in optical illusions or other kinds of misleading evidence, or an abnormality in the internal belief-forming mechanisms, as in wishful thinking or misremembering" (Stalnaker, 1984, p. 19). Conversely, normal situations are maybe just the one's where *everything has gone right*. In which case—since it's plausible (perhaps it's tautological) that when everything has gone right what you believe is true—it's maybe OK if S-tokens are all true in normal situations.

So maybe it's OK if, in normal situations, the conditions for meaning and truth come out to be the same. *Normal*—at least when it's used this way—is a normative notion,[13] and *true* is a normative notion, so maybe it's not surprising if the former notion reconstructs the latter. So, at least, one might be inclined to argue at first blush.

Of course, if the intentional circle is to be broken by appeal to *Normal* situations for symbol tokenings, we had better have some naturalistic story to tell about what it is for a situation to be *Normal* in the relevant respect. What might such a story look like? Roughly, the suggestion is that *Normality* should somehow be cashed by appeal to (natural) teleology; e.g., to some more-or-less Darwinian/historical notion of biological mechanisms *doing what they were selected for*.

So, then, here's a sketch of the story: an organism's mental-state tokens get caused by, for example, events that transpire in the organism's local environment. There are, of course, mechanisms—typically neuronal ones—that mediate these causal transactions. And these mechanisms have presumably got an evolutionary history. They are presumably the products of processes of selection, and it's not implausible that what they were selected *for* is precisely their role in mediating the tokening of mental states. So there are these cognitive mechanisms, and there are these cognitive states; and the function of the former is to produce instances of the latter upon environmentally appropriate occasions.

Strictly speaking, it doesn't, of course, follow, that *the cognitive states themselves*—states like believing that *P* or desiring that *Q* or doubting that the Dodgers will ever move back to Brooklyn—have a Normal function; in fact, it doesn't follow that they have any function at all. (You could perfectly well have a machine whose function is to produce things that are themselves functionless. In a consumer society you might have quite a lot of these.) Since the assumption that there is a teleological story to be told about the mechanisms of belief *fixation* does not imply that there is a teleological story to be told about *beliefs*, it a fortiori does not imply that beliefs (or, mutatis mutandis, other intentional states) can be *individuated by reference to their functions*. This is important because it's more intuitive that belief-fixing mechanisms (nervous systems, for example) have functions than that beliefs do; and the implausibility of the latter idea ought not to prejudice the plausibility of the former.

Nor would a teleological solution of the disjunction problem require that intentional states can be functionally individuated. All solving the disjunction problem requires is a distinction between Normal and abNormal circumstances for *having* a belief (hence between type one circumstances for having a belief and others). There would be such a distinction even if there were no such things as Normally functioning beliefs, so long as there are such things as Normally functioning mechanisms of belief fixation. Per se, teleological solutions to the disjunction problem do not therefore require that there be Darwinian (or, indeed, any) answers to questions like, "What is the belief that seven is prime for?"

There seems to be a certain amount of confusion about this point in papers like Millikan (1986). Millikan thinks that beliefs, desires and the like must have "proper functions," and she thinks this because she thinks that "there must, after all, be a finite number of general principles that govern the activities of our various cognitive-state-making and cognitive-state-using mechanisms and there must be explanations of why these principles have historically worked to aid our survival" (p. 55).

But the assumption that the mechanisms that make/use cognitive states have functions does not entail that cognitive states themselves do. And the assumption that it's useful to have cognitive states does not entail that you can distinguish among cognitive states by reference to their uses. It's a sort of distributive fallacy to argue that, if having beliefs is functional, then there must be something that is the distinguishing function of each belief. The function of the human sperm cell is to fertilize the human ovum; what, then, is the distinguishing function of *this* sperm cell? The hair on your head functions to prevent the radiation of your body heat; what, then, is the distinguishing function of *this* hair (or, for that matter, of *red* hair)?

Conversely—and contrary to Millikan—if there is nothing that the belief that seven is prime is *for* (and that the belief that four is even is not for), it wouldn't follow that "our cognitive life is an accidental epiphenomenal cloud hovering over mechanisms that evolution devised with other things in mind." Having toes is a good idea; I suppose there's even a selectional story about why we have them. It does not follow that each toe has its distinguishing function, or that this toe has any function that one hasn't. Nor, for all that, are my toes at all like epiphenomenal clouds hovering over something.

Millikan's idea is that, on the one hand, cognitive states are distinguished by their functions and, on the other, it's the function of a cognitive state that determines its intentional object. ". . . the descriptions we give of desires [and the like] are descriptions of their most obvious proper functions [so that the fact that] desire(s) are . . . individuated . . . in accordance with content is as ordinary a fact as . . . that the categories 'heart', 'kidney', and 'eye' are carved out by reference to *their* most obvious proper functions" (pp. 63–64). The idea that content reduces to Normal function is one of the two main threads in the story we're examining (the other being the idea that function reduces to selectional history, of which a lot more presently).

Now there is, right at the beginning, something fishy about the idea that the content of a mental state is to be understood by reference to its function since this sort of account leaves it mysterious why the identification of content with function works *only* for intentional states; why beliefs have intentional content in virtue of their functions but hearts, eyes, and kidneys don't. In any event, the disanalogy between the functional individuation of propositional attitudes and the functional individuation of hearts, eyes, and kidneys would seem to be glaring. Functions are, I suppose, species of Normal effects. We find out that the function of the heart is to pump the blood when we find out that, among the Normal effects of heart beat, blood circulation (and not, say, heart noise) is the effect that hearts are designed to produce. But how would the corresponding analysis go in the case of intentional states like desires? What is it that the desire to be rich and famous can Normally be relied upon to effect in the way that hearts can Normally be relied upon to effect the circulation of blood? *Trying to become rich and famous* is perhaps a candidate since, I suppose, people who want to become that do Normally try to become it. But trying is no good for the job at hand since it is itself an intentional state. *Actually becoming rich and famous* would do, except that it's so wildly implausible that it is, in any nonquestion-begging sense, a Normal effect of *wanting* to become it.

Contrary to what Millikan claims, it's just not on the cards that "the proper function of every desire . . . is to help cause its own fulfillment." (p. 63) For, on the one hand, nothing is the proper function of Xs except what Xs Normally help to cause; and, on the other, if Xs Normally help to cause Ys, then presumably *when the situation is Normal Ys can be relied upon to happen when(ever) it's the case that X*. Thus the activity of the heart helps to cause a state of affairs— viz., that the blood circulates—that can Normally be relied upon to happen when the heart beats (i.e., that can be relied upon to happen when the heart beats and the situation is Normal). But does Millikan really believe that wanting to become rich and famous helps to cause a state of affairs—viz., that one becomes rich and famous—which can Normally be relied upon to happen if one wants that it should? And, if she really does believe this, isn't that because she's sort of sneaked a look at the intentional object of the want?[14]

Millikan remarks—in one breath, as it were—that "a proper function of the desire to eat is to bring it about that one eats; [and] a proper function of the desire to win the local Democratic nomination for first selectman is to bring it about that one wins the local Democratic nomination for first selectman" (p. 63). But while there is arguably a *law* that connects desires to eat with eatings (ceteris paribus) and a law that connects functioning hearts with blood pumpings (ceteris paribus), what's the chance that there is any Normally reliable, nonintentional connection between desires to win elections and election winnings? Stevenson wanted to win just as much as Eisenhower did, and the circumstances were equally Normal for both. But Eisenhower won and Stevenson didn't. In Normal circumstances, not more than one of them could have, what with elections being zero-sum games. So how could it be that, in virtue of a law or other reliable mechanism, in Normal circumstances everybody wins whatever elections he wants to? When the situation is Normal, the lion wants to eat and the lamb wants not to be eaten. But. . . .

The proposal is that the proper function of a desire is to bring about the state of affairs that it Normally helps to cause, and that the state of affairs that a desire would bring about were it performing its proper function is its intentional object. Thus far I've been running the discussion of this proposal on the reading of 'Normally helps to cause' that examples like hearts, eyes, kidneys, and the like most obviously suggest: 'if X Normally helps to cause Y, then "if X then Y" is true if the situation is Normal.' But, as Tim Maudlin has pointed out to me, it's entirely possible that Millikan has a less robust notion of 'Normally helping to cause' in mind; perhaps it's enough for X Normally helping to cause Y that the probability of Y given X is Normally greater than the probability of Y given not-X.[15] This would cope with the kinds of counterexamples I've been offering since it wouldn't require that when the situation is Normal you actually get Ys whenever you get Xs.

This revised proposal is, however, clearly too weak. For example: the recording that I want to buy is the Callas *Tosca*, but I'm prepared to "suboptimize": I'll settle for the Milanov if Milanov is all they've got. So my wanting to buy the one recording increases the probability that I'll actually buy the other; "all ships float on a rising tide," as Granny is always saying. Nor is there the slightest reason to doubt that this sort of suboptimizing has survival value; probably if we didn't do it, we'd all go mad. (Perhaps if we didn't do it we'd already *be* mad since our willingness to suboptimize is arguably a constituent of our practical rationality.) In short, *helping me to get the Milanov Tosca* satisfies the revised condition for being the proper function of my wanting the Callas *Tosca*. (As does, of course, help me get the Callas *Tosca*. One consequence of this construal of 'proper function' being too weak is that it fails to yield unique proper functions.) But it is, for all that, the Callas *Tosca* and not the Milanov *Tosca* that is the intentional object of my want.

Other sorts of cases point the same moral. Normally, my desiring to win the lottery increases at most very slightly the likelihood that I will do so. It increases considerably more the likelihood that I shall presently be five dollars poorer, five dollars being the price of a ticket. For all that, what I want is to win the lottery, not to get poorer; getting poorer comes in not as the intentional object of my want but merely as a calculated risk.

So, for one reason and another, the revised construal of 'Normally helping to cause' is too weak; but like the original construal it is also too strong, and this is the more serious fault. It is simply intrinsic to the logic of wants that they can be causally isolated from the states of affairs whose occurrence would satisfy them, even when things are perfectly Normal. So, I can want like stink that it will rain tomorrow and spoil Ivan's picnic. Not only is it not the case that my wanting this is Normally sufficient to bring it about; my wanting it doesn't alter in the slightest scintilla the likelihood that it will happen. That it is possible to have wants that are arbitrarily causally inert with respect to their own satisfaction is, indeed, one of the respects in which wants are intentional; it's what makes wanting so frightfully nonfactive. "If wishes weren't causally isolated from horses, beggars would ride ceteris paribus," as Granny is also always saying.

As we've seen, however, the teleological solution to the disjunction problem doesn't have to go Millikan's way; in particular, it doesn't require either that intentional states (as opposed to cognitive mechanisms) should have proper functions, or that the putative proper functions of intentional states should determine their contents. Let us therefore leave Millikan and return to the main line of argument.

There are—let's assume—these cognitive mechanisms whose function is to mediate the causal relations between environmental states on the one hand and mental states on the other. Of course, they don't mediate those relations in just *any old* circumstances. Organisms don't hear well when they have carrots in their ears, and they don't see well when they have dust in their eyes . . . etc. But if there is an evolutionary story about a cognitive mechanism, then presumably there must be naturalistically specifiable circumstances C such that

> (*i*)   ceteris paribus, the mechanism in question mediates the relations in question whenever circumstances C obtain;

and

> (*ii*)   ceteris paribus, possession of the mechanism bestows selectional advantage because it does mediate the relation whenever circumstances C obtain.

Let's suppose that all of this is so. Then we identify 'Normal' (hence, type one) situations as the ones in which it's the case that C; and we say that if mental state tokens of type S are caused by P-instantiations in such situations, then tokens of mental state S mean (express the property) P. Since situations where it isn't the case that C are ipso facto not Normal for the tokening of S, and since it's only in Normal circumstances that causation is supposed to be constitutive of content, S-tokens that transpire when it isn't the case that C are free to be caused by anything they like. In particular, they are free to be false.

So, then, Darwinian teleology underwrites the appeal to Normal functioning and the appeal to Normal functioning solves the disjunction problem and naturalizes content. In consequence, if you say to an informational semantical "Please, how does meaning work?" you are likely to get a song and dance about what happens when frogs stick their tongues out at flies. "There is," so the song goes, "a state S of the frog's nervous system such that:

> (*i*)   S is reliably caused by flies in Normal circumstances;
> (*ii*)   S is the Normal cause of an ecologically appropriate, fly-directed response;
> (*iii*)   Evolution bestowed S on frogs because (*i*) and (*ii*) are true of it."

S, one might say, Normally resonates to flies. And it is only because it Normally does so that Mother Nature has bestowed it on the frog. And it is only because Mother Nature bestowed it on the frog only because it Normally resonates to flies that tokens of this state *mean fly even in those (abNormal) circumstances in which it is not flies but something else to which the S-tokens are resonating.*[16]

So that, at last, is the full-blown causal/teleological/historical-Darwinian story about how to solve the disjunction problem and naturalize content.[17]

Now, anybody who takes the picture of evolutionary selection that this teleological story about Normal circumstances presupposes to be other than pretty credulous should look at Gould and Lewontin's splendid paper, "The Spandrels of San Marco" (1979). It is, I think, most unlikely, even on empirical grounds, that Darwin is going to pull Brentano's chestnuts out of the fire. For present purposes, however, I'm going to bypass the empirical issues since there are internal reasons for doubting that the evolutionary version of the teleological account of intentionality can do the work for which it has been promoted.

In the first place—contrary to advertisements that you may have seen—the teleological story about intentionality does *not* solve the disjunction problem. The reason it doesn't is that teleological notions, insofar as they are themselves naturalistic, always have a problem about indeterminacy just where intentionality has its problem about disjunction. To put it slightly more precisely, there's a kind of dilemma that arises when you appeal to the function of a psychological mechanism to settle questions about the intentional content of a psychological state. If you specify the function of the mechanism *by reference to* the content of the state (for example, you describe the mechanism as mediating the initiation of actions under certain maxims or the fixation of beliefs *de dicto*) then you find, unsurprisingly, that you get indeterminacy about the function of the mechanism wherever there is ambiguity about the content of the state. And if, on the other hand, you describe the function in some way that is intentionally neutral (e.g., as mediating the integration of movements or the fixation of beliefs *de re*) you may get univocal functional ascriptions but you find, still unsurprisingly, that they don't choose between competing ascriptions of content. Either way then, the appeal to teleology doesn't help you with your disjunction problem.

We can see this dilemma play itself out in the case of the frog and the flies. Here is David Israel (1987) expounding a teleological solution to the frog's disjunction problem:

> We've talked of [a certain neural state of the frog's as] . . . *meaning* that there's a fly in the vicinity. Others have said that what 'fly' means to the frog is just [a] characteristic pattern of occular irradiation—i.e., as of a small black moving dot. This is just backwards. The facts are that, in a wide range of environments, flies are what actually cause that pattern on the frog's eyes and that *flies on the fly are what the frog is after*. This convergence of the 'backward looking' (environment-caused) and 'forward looking' (behavior-causing) aspects of the state is a good thing (from the frog's parochial point of view of course) (pp. 6–7). . . . Talk of belief is essentially functional talk: the crucial function . . . of belief states is that they represent the world as being a certain way and, together with desire states, cause bodily movements. What movements? . . . . If things go well, they cause those movements which, if the world is as it is represented, will constitute the performance of an action that satisfies the agent's desires. If the world is not the way it is represented as being, the bodily movement is considerably less likely to succeed. (p. 15)

The trouble is, however, that this doesn't *solve* the disjunction problem; it just begs it. For, though you *can* describe the teleology of the frog's snap-guidance mechanism the way that Israel wants you to—in Normal circumstances, it resonates to flies; so its function is to resonate to flies; so its intentional content is *about* flies—there is precisely nothing to stop you from telling the story in quite a different way. On the alternative account, what the neural mechanism in question is designed to respond to is little ambient black things. It's little ambient black things which, "in a wide range of environments

. . . are what actually cause that pattern on the frog's eyes" and little ambient black things are "what the frog is after." Hence, a frog is responding *Normally* when, for example, it snaps at a little ambient black thing that is in fact *not* a fly but a bee-bee that happens to be passing through.

Notice that, just as there is a teleological explanation of why frogs should have fly detectors—assuming that that is the right intentional description of what they have—so too there is a teleological explanation of why frogs should have little-ambient-black-thing detectors—assuming that *that* is the right intentional description of what they have. The explanation is that *in the environment in which the mechanism Normally operates* all (or most, or anyhow enough) of the little ambient black dots are flies. So, in this environment, what ambient-black-dot detectors Normally detect (de re, as it were) is just what fly detectors Normally detect (de dicto, as it were); viz., flies.

It bears emphasis that *Darwin doesn't care which of these ways you tell the teleological story.* You can have it that the neural mechanism Normally mediates fly snaps, in which case snaps at bee-bees are ipso facto errors. Or you can have it that the mechanism Normally mediates black dot snaps that are, as one says at Stanford, "situated" in an environment in which the black dots are Normally flies. (On the latter reading, it's not the frog but the world that has gone wrong when a frog snaps at a bee-bee; what you've got is a Normal snap in an abNormal situation.) It is, in particular, true *on either description* of the intentional object of the frog's snaps that, if the situation is Normal, then "if the world is as it is represented [snapping] will constitute the performance of an action that satisfies the agent's desires."

Correspondingly, both ways of describing the intentional objects of the snaps satisfy what Millikan (1986) apparently takes to be the crucial condition on content ascription: Both make the success of the frog's feeding behavior not ". . . an accident [but] . . . the result of the elegant self-programming of his well designed nervous system. More explicitly [they both make it a] result of his nervous system's operating in accordance with general principles that also explained how his ancestors' nervous systems programmed themselves and used these programs so as to help them to proliferate" (p. 68). Huffing and puffing and piling on the teleology just doesn't help with the disjunction problem; it doesn't lead to univocal assignments of intentional content.[18]

The Moral, to repeat, is that (within certain broad limits, presently to be defined) Darwin doesn't care how you describe the intentional objects of frog snaps. All that matters for selection is how many flies the frog manages to ingest in consequence of its snapping, and this number comes out exactly the same whether one describes the function of the snap-guidance mechanisms with respect to a world that is populated by flies that are, de facto, ambient black dots, or with respect to a world that is populated by ambient black dots that are, de facto, flies.[19] "Erst kommt das Fressen, denn kommt die Morale." *Darwin cares how many flies you eat, but not what description you eat them under.* (Similarly, by the way, flies may be assumed to be indifferent to the descriptions under which frogs eat them.) So it's no use looking to Darwin to get you out of the disjunction problem.

I've been arguing that a teleologically based theory of content will have to put up with a lot of intentional indeterminacy. In defiance, probably, of prudence, I propose to push this line of argument further. Let's ask *how much* intentional indeterminacy one would have to put up with on the teleological story.

I think that the right answer is that appeals to mechanism of selection won't decide between *reliably equivalent* content ascriptions; i.e., they won't decide between any pair of equivalent content ascriptions where the equivalence is counterfactual supporting. To put this in the formal mode, the context: *was selected for representing things as F* is transparent to the substitution of predicates reliably coextensive with *F*. A fortiori, it is transparent to the substitution of predicates *necessarily* (including *nomologically* necessarily) coextensive with *F*. In consequence, evolutionary theory offers us no contexts that are as intensional as 'believes that. . . .' If this is right, then it's a conclusive reason to doubt that appeals to evolutionary teleology can reconstruct the intentionality of mental states. Let's look at the frog case again with this in mind.

It might be argued that there is a real indeterminacy about whether frogs snap at flies or at little black dots. But, surely, if there are any matters of fact about content, it's one of them that frogs don't snap at flies under the description *fly or bee-bee*. Yet, as far as I can see, it's equally OK with Darwin which way you describe the intentional objects of fly snaps, so long as it's reliable (say, nomologically necessary; anyhow, counterfactual supporting) that all the local flies-or-bee-bees are flies. The point is, of course, that if all the local flies-or-bee-bees are flies, then it is reliable that the frog that snaps at one does neither better nor worse selection-wise than the frog that snaps at the other. So evolutionary teleology *cannot tell these frogs apart.*

Here one has to be a little careful to avoid red herrings. It might be argued that you can't have a fly-or-bee-bee concept unless you have a bee-bee concept, and, since having a bee-bee concept would do the frog no good, we do, after all, have Darwinian reason to suppose that it's flies, and not flies-or-bee-bees that frogs snap at. This argument is in jeopardy of proving that *we* don't have the concept UNICORN. And, anyhow, its major premise is false. In principle, the frog could perfectly well have a *primitive* concept whose *extension* is disjunctive (from our point of view, as it were). In particular, it could perfectly well have the concept *fleebee*, whose extension embraces the flies and the bee-bees but which has neither the concept *bee-bee* nor the concept *fly* as constituents. The present question, then, is whether considerations of evolutionary (or other) utility can distinguish the hypothesis that the intentional object of the frog's snap is a fleebee from the hypothesis that it's a fly. And I claim that the line of argument I've been running strongly suggest that they cannot. Selectional advantage cares how many flies you get to eat in Normal circumstances; and, in Normal circumstances you get to eat the same number of flies whether it's flies or fleebees that you snap at.

Notice, by the way, how exactly analogous considerations show that, if "F iff G" is reliable, then just as *evolutionary theory* cannot appeal to a difference in probable utility to distinguish organisms that respond to Fness from organisms that respond to Gness, so too *reinforcement theory* cannot distinguish between such organisms by appealing to a difference in probable reward. This is what generated the traditional problem about "what is learned" over which Skinnerians used to agonize; it's precisely what one should expect given the very close similarity between Darwinian accounts of how environments select genotypes and Skinnerian accounts of how environments select behavioral phenotypes.

Suppose, in an operant conditioning paradigm, I train an organism to prefer green triangles to some negative stimulus. Is it then the greenness or the triangularity or both that the animal is responding to? I can tell only if I can "split" the greenness from the triangularity (e.g., by providing a red triangle or a green nontriangle as a stimulus) and see which way the animal generalizes. Similarly, I can teach a preference for greenness *as opposed to* a preference for triangularity only if *greens are triangles and vice versa* is not counterfactual supporting in the training situation, since that's the only circumstance in which responses to greenness and responses to triangularity can be differentially reinforced.[20] Since, however, *responding to Fness* and *responding to Gness* can be distinct intentional states even when 'F iff G' is reliable, I take this to be a sort of proof that there could not be a conditioning-theoretic solution of the disjunction problem. Contexts like "whether the stimulus is . . . determines the probability of reinforcement" slice specifications of the stimulus thicker than typical intentional contexts do; if 'F' makes this context true, so too does

'G,' so long as 'Fs are Gs' is reliable. So, the same reasoning that shows that Darwin is no use to Brentano shows that Skinner is no use to him either.[21]

Perhaps you are now yourself prepared to bite the bee-bee; perhaps you are now prepared to say that it's OK after all if there's no fact of the matter about whether the intentional objects of the frog's snaps are fleebees rather than flies. But notice that that isn't *solving* the disjunction problem; it's just deciding to live with it. Specifically, it's deciding to live with the massive intentional indeterminacy that the disjunction problem implies. But, if all you want to do is *not* solve the disjunction problem, then unvarnished, *non*teleological/*non*evolutionary versions of causal theories of content will do that quite adequately *without* appealing to the Darwin stuff. So, either way, it wouldn't appear that the Darwin stuff is buying you anything.

Let me pause a bit to rub this in. Dennett (1987) argues that Dretske and I have this disjunction problem *because* we don't take account of "utility." ". . . when we adopt the intentional stance . . . the dictated attributions are those that come out veridical *and useful* (sic). Without the latter condition . . . [one is] stuck with Fodor's and Dretske's problem of disjunctive dissipation of content . . . " (p. 311). But as far as I can see, usefulness is useless for the purposes at hand. After all, it *is* useful, in fact it's simply *super* (for a frog) to eat *flies or bee-bees* in any world in which the *flies or bee-bees* are reliably flies. It's eating flies-or-bee-bees in worlds like that that keeps frogs going.

I suppose it might be a way out of this fix to appeal to counterfactuals about what *would* happen if the locally reliable coextension between flies and flies-or-bee-bees were broken. The thought would be that snapping at flies-or-bee-bees would be bad for the frog in a world where many of the flies or bee-bees are bee-bees. But:

First, Dennett is explicit in rejecting the sort of theory that makes content rest on the causal relations that *would* hold in (merely) counterfactual circumstances (see p. 309). For Dennett (as for Millikan) it's selectional *history* that determines content.

Second (to revert to a point I made in discussing Papineau; see note 19), it's not clear how to decide which counterfactuals are the ones that count; fleebee snaps aren't advantageous in abNormal worlds where the fleebees mostly aren't flies *unless* it happens that the bee-bees in those worlds are edible.

Third (and this is the crucial point), going counterfactual to define function (and hence content) would be to give up on a Darwinian solution to the disjunction problem since utility that accrues only in *counterfactual* environments *doesn't produce actual selectional advantages*. This means that you can't reconcile appeals to counterfactual advantages with an analysis that construes content and function in terms of selection history.

That ought to be just obvious. Consider, for example, the brightly colored fish that, according to popular legend, are found in sunless ocean deeps. I don't know what the evolutionary explanation is supposed to be, but one thing is for certain: it can't be that the fish are colored because for them to be so *would be* advantageous if their environment *were* lit up. How could the selectional advantages that would accrue if you lived in an illuminated world (which, we're assuming, you don't) explain your being colored in *this* world (which, we're assuming, you are). Merely counterfactual advantages don't affect actual histories of selection. So appeals to merely counterfactual advantages can play no role in Darwinian explanations.

Well, similarly, in the present case, if it's reliable that all the flies-or-bee-bees are flies, then that's true not just of all the flies-or-bee-bees that *this* frog has encountered, but also of all the flies-or-bee-bees that its Granny encountered, and that its Granny's Granny encountered . . . and so on back to the primordial protoplasmic slime. But then, by what mechanism could selection have preferred frogs that snap at flies to frogs that snap at flies-or-bee-bees? What selection wants is that some actual frogs should actually go hungry in consequence of actually snapping at the wrong sort of things. But that won't ever happen if, in point of nomological necessity, all the frog-or-bee-bee-snaps that are prompted by bee-bees are ipso facto counterfactual.

It can't be overemphasized, in this context, that Darwinian explanations are species of *historical* explanations: they account for the geneotypical properties of organisms (or, if you prefer, for the statistical properties of gene pools) by reference to the actual—not the counterfactual—histories of predecessors. (See, for example, Millikan, 1984, p. 3: "The 'functions' of these natural devices are, roughly, the functions upon which their continued reproduction or survival has depended." Note the tense and mood.)

So far, I've followed Dennett, Millikan, et al. and assumed that it's essential to teleological semantics to be Darwinian. But, of course, one might just give up on the reduction of content to selectional history and try for a *nonhistorical* theory of content; one in which content is determined not by the selectional pressures that *actually* governed the evolution of a psychological state but by the selectional pressures that would apply if certain counterfactuals were true. E.g.: Either fly-snaps and fly-or-bee-bee snaps are equally advantageous in *this* world. But the intentional objects of frog snaps are flies and not flies-or-bee-bees because fly-snaps would be selected in nearby worlds where there are flies *whether or not there are bee-bees there* but fly-or-bee-snaps would not be selected in nearby worlds where there are bee-bees *unless there are also flies there*. In effect, there's a question about which of two locally confounded properties selection is contingent on; so one applies the method of differences across counterfactual worlds to deconfound them. Appealing to the counterfactuals licenses an intensional (with an 's') notion of selection; it distinguishes the effects that selection *really* cares about (getting flies in) from those that are merely adventitious (getting fleebees in).

But the question arises why these counterfactuals should matter for determining *content* even if, as seems quite plausible, they are exactly what matters for determining *function*. Consider the following case: I suppose that the function of the preference for sweets is to get sugars (hence calories) aboard, and I suppose that the ingestion of saccharine is nonfunctional. This works out fine on the counterfactual approach to function: A preference for sweets would be a good thing to have in a world where all the sweet things are sugar but it would lack survival value in a world where all the sweets are saccharine. But the trouble is that, in this sort of case, function and content come apart. The function of a sweet tooth is to get you to ingest sugar; but its intentional object is—not sugar but—sweets; that's why saccharine satisfies the craving. N.b., saccharine *satisfies* the craving for sweets; it doesn't just cause the craving to go away.[22]

It looks to me as though the evolutionary line on content makes two mistakes, either of which would be adequately fatal: On the one hand, it supposes that you can get a historical/selectional analysis of function (that the function of a state is what it was actually selected for) whereas what you need for function is pretty clearly some kind of counterfactual analysis (the function of a state is what it would have been selected for even if. . .). And, on the other hand, it supposes that if you're given the function of a state you are thereby given its intentional object, and the sweet tooth case strongly suggests that this isn't so.

In my view, what you've got here is a dead theory.

One last point before I stop jumping up and down on this dead theory. One way that you can really confuse yourself about the value of appeals to Darwin in grounding intentionality is to allow yourself to speak, sort-of-semi-seriously as you might say, of evolutionary teleology in terms of "what Mother Nature has in mind." The reason that this can be so confusing involves a point I called attention to above: The expressions that are deployed where we seriously and nonmetaphorically explain things by appealing to people's purposes, intentions, and the like, are far less transparent to the substitution of coextensive predicates than those that evolutionary explanations use.

As far as I can see, so long as we're dealing strictly in Darwinian (viz., historical) explanations, there's no sense to the claim that a state is selected for being F but not for being G in cases where it's necessary that F and G are coextensive.[23] In effect, Darwinian explanations treat reliably coextensive representations as synonymous; whereas, of course, psychological explanations don't. So if you're in the habit of thinking of evolutionary explanations on the model of appeals to an invisible engineer, you are likely to think that they're doing you a lot more good than they really can do when it comes to the individuation of contents.

Look, if Granny builds a mechanical frog, she may have it in mind that her frog should snap at flies, and not have it in mind that her frog should snap at things that are flies-or-bee-bees. So her mechanical frog is a fly-snapper and not a fly-or-bee-bee snapper, however reliably all the local fly-or-bee-bees are flies. (This is just like Dennett's "two-bitser," though apparently our intuitions don't agree about such cases. On my view, but not on his, if I build a machine that I intend to go into state S whenever I put a quarter in, then the machine is a quarter-accepter even if there are, in some other part of the forest, Mexican rupees which are physically very like quarters and hence *would* make the machine go into state S if it *were* to encounter any.) Attributions of (so-called) "derived intentionality," unlike specifications of "what Mother Nature has in mind" are typically opaque to the substitution of reliably coextensive expressions. In particular, they can distinguish between fly-snaps and fly-or-bee-bee snaps.

So there is no disjunction problem for derived intentionality. Where we have things whose states have derived intentionality (the intentionality of all the artifacts that Granny's made so far, by the way) we can construe very fine distinctions among the contents of their states. That's because we can construe very fine distinctions among the contents of *our* states, and derived intentionality is intentionality that's derived *from us*. Ascriptions of derived intentional objects to *Granny's frog* can distinguish between reliably coextensive contents because attributions of mental states to *Granny* can distinguish between reliably coextensive contents. There really is a difference between mechanical fly-snappers and mechanical fly-or-bee-bee snappers *because* there really is a difference between Grannies who intend their frogs to snap at the one and Grannies who intend their frogs to snap at the other.

The logic of teleological explanations that appeal to selectional advantage would appear, however, to be *very* different. As we've seen, it's quite unclear that appeals to "what Mother Nature has in mind" can rationalize distinctions between reliably equivalent content attributions. Indeed you might put Brentano's thesis like this: The difference between Mother Nature and Granny is precisely that Granny does, and Mother Nature doesn't, honor merely intentional distinctions. I don't say that Granny is *smarter* than Mother Nature; but I do say she's much more *refined*.

It is, in consequence, *very*, *very* misleading to say that since ". . . in the case of an organism . . . [content] . . . is not independent of the intentions and purposes of Mother Nature, [it is] just as derived as . . . the meaning in [states of an artifact]" (Dennett, p. 305).[24] The putative analogy gets it wrong about attributions of derived intentionality since it underestimates the distinctions among contents that such attributions can sustain relative to those that attributions of content to "Mother Nature" can. And—what is maybe worse—it deeply misinterprets the Darwinian program, which was precisely to *purge* biology of anything that has the logic of the kinds of explanation that are intentional with a 't.' Really (as opposed to metaphorically), Darwinian explanation isn't *anything like* ascribing goals to Mother Nature. Contrary to what Dennett says, Darwin's idea is not that " . . . we are artifacts designed by natural selection . . . " (p. 300). Darwin's idea is much deeper, much more beautiful, and appreciably scarier: We are artifacts designed by selection in exactly the sense in which the Rockies are artifacts designed by erosion; which is to say that we aren't artifacts and nothing designed us. We are, and always have been, entirely on our own.

Of course Darwin has nothing to say to Brentano; the whole point of Darwin's enterprise was to get biology out of Brentano's line of work.

And that's not all that's wrong with the evolutionary/teleological treatment of the disjunction problem. Many paragraphs back, I remarked on the naturalness of the intuition that grounds the teleological story, the intuition that error is what happens when something goes wrong. But you need more than this to license a teleological solution to the disjunction problem; you also need it that when things go right—more particularly, when things are Normal—whatever causes a symbol to be tokened is ipso facto in the extension of the symbol. It's this that ties the *teleological* story about Normalcy to the *causal* story about content. Teleology defines the class of situations in which everything is Normal; but it's the assumption that Normally

caused symbols ipso facto *apply* to their causes that brings the semantics in. In particular, it's this assumption that licenses the identification of the Normal situations with the ones in which causation
makes content.

As it turns out, however, this key assumption—that when the
situation is teleologically Normal, symbol tokens ipso facto apply to
what they are caused by—is simply no good. What's true at best is
that when symbol tokens are caused by what they apply to the
situation is de facto teleologically Normal. Maybe it's plausible that
when everything goes right what you believe must be true. But it's
certainly *not* plausible that when everything goes right what causes
your belief must be the satisfaction of its truth conditions. To put it
still another way, if all that the appeal to Normal functioning allows
you to do is abstract from *sources of error*, then the Normal situations
are *not* going to be identical with the type one situations.

The glaring counterexample is the occurrence of representation *in
thought*. Suppose, having nothing better to do, I while away my time
thinking about frogs. And suppose that, in the course of this medi-
tation, by a natural process of association as it might be, my thoughts
about frogs lead me to thoughts about flies. The result is a token of
the mental state type *entertaining the concept FLY*, which is, surely,
caused in a perfectly Normal way (the teleology of mental functioning
may abstract from *error*, but surely it doesn't abstract from *thinking*).
But it is *not* an instance of an intentional state that was caused by
what it means. What caused me to think about flies was thinking
about frogs; but the effect of this cause was a thought about flies for
all that. It may be that there are causal connections to flies *somewhere*
in the historical background of thoughts about flies that are prompted
by thoughts about frogs. But such thoughts haven't got the sort of
causal histories that Skinnerian/Dretskian accounts contemplate the
reduction of content to: they aren't *occasioned* by flies, and they don't
carry information about flies in any sense in which what symbols
carry information about is their causes. Specifically, the "covering"
law that connected my fly-thought tokening with its cause projects
the relation between fly-thoughts and frog-thoughts, *not* the relation
between fly-thoughts and flies.

Compare Papineau: " . . . sometimes [a belief] will be triggered by
'abnormal' circumstances, circumstances other than the one that in
the learning process ensured the belief had advantageous effects and
which therefore led to the selection of the disposition behind it. My
suggestion is that the belief should be counted as false in these
'abnormal' circumstances—. . . the truth condition of the belief is the
'normal' circumstance in which, given the learning process, it is

biologically supposed to be present" (pp. 65–66). The basic idea is that all of the following pick out the same state of affairs:

- P's truth condition,
- the 'normal' (viz., the Normal) circumstance for entertaining P,
- the situation in which P is biologically supposed to be present.

But this can't be right. Thinking is a circumstance in which beliefs are, often enough, Normally entertained; and, I suppose, it's a circumstance in which biology intended that they should occur. But the matrix of mental states in which a belief is tokened in the course of mental processing is patently not to be identified with its truth condition. (Here as elsewhere, coming down heavily on "the learning process" doesn't help much. Lots of words/concepts aren't learned ostensively.)

This is, I think, a real problem. In fact, it's the disjunction problem in still another guise. What we want is that fly-occasioned "fly"s, and bee-bee occasioned "fly"s, *and representations of flies in thought* all mean FLY. At best, teleological solutions promise to allow us to say this for the first two cases—bee-bee-occasioned tokens are somehow 'abNormal'; hence not type one; hence their causation is not relevant to the content of "fly"—though we've seen that it's a promise that they welsh on. But teleological theories don't even pretend to deal with the third case; they offer no reason not to suppose that fly-thoughts mean *fly or thought of a frog* given that both flies and thoughts of frogs normally cause fly-thought tokens.

God, by definition, doesn't make mistakes; His situation is always Normal. But even God has the disjunction problem on the assumption that the content of His thoughts is determined by their causes and that some of His thoughts are caused by some of His others. The sad moral is, we still have the disjunction problem even after we idealize to infallibility.

I think a lot of philosophers (and a lot of psychologists in the Dewey/Gibson/American Naturalist tradition) believe deep down that content starts with perceptual states that are closely implicated in the control of action. It's perception—and, specifically, such perceptions as eventuate in characteristic corresponding behaviors, as in orient and capture reflexes—that provides the aboriginal instance of intentionality. Thought and the like come later, *not just phylogenetically but also in the order of explanation*. Thus, Israel remarks that, in theorizing about naturalized semantics, "it makes sense to look first at perceptual states of living organisms before moving on to anything more sophisticated" (p. 6). Since, as we've seen, Israel holds that the content of a state is determined by its function, he must be assuming that the function of perception is, at least in principle, dissociable from its role in the fixation of belief;[25] if the connection between perception and belief fixation is internal, the advice to look at perception first doesn't noticeably simplify the theorist's problems.

But even on this dubious assumption, this is dubious advice. Presumably, perception and thought are intentional *in the same sense*, so it's likely that a semantics that works only for the former works for the wrong reason. In perception there is generally a coincidence between what a cognitive state carries information about and what it represents (viz., between its Normal cause and its intentional object). But the intentionality of thought shows that this coincidence is an artifact; it's not essential to content.

In light of all this, I'm inclined to think that the teleological story about content is just hopeless. On the one hand, the appeal to teleologically normal conditions doesn't provide for a univocal notion of intentional content; specifically it doesn't solve the disjunction problem. And, on the other hand, type one situations can't be identified with teleological Normal conditions; it's just not true that Normally caused intentional states ipso facto mean whatever caused them. So we need a nonteleological solution of the disjunction problem. So be it.

Notes

1. This would be true even if, as functionalists suppose, physicalistic formulations of *necessary and sufficient* conditions for being in psychological states are typically not lawlike.

2. Some intentional laws constrain the relations among the states of a given organism at a given time (e.g., ceteris paribus, if you believe P & Q then you believe P). These laws could generalize even over organisms that had *none* of their mental states in common; in the present case, there's no P or Q that two organisms both have to believe in order that both should fall under the law.

   But laws that quantify into opaque contexts, e.g.: *(x) (y) (if x believes that y is dangerous then ceteris paribus x tries to avoid y)*, look to be in deep trouble if holism is true, since such laws purport to generalize over organisms *in virtue of the shared intentional contents of their mental states*. Similarly for laws that constrain the mental states of a given organism across time, including, notably, the laws that govern belief fixation in reasoning, learning, and perception (about 96.4% of serious psychology, at a rough estimate). Suppose, for example, that it's a law that, ceteris paribus, the more of the xs an organism comes to believe are F, the more the organism comes to believe $(x) Fx$. Such a law would presuppose that an organism can hold the same (quantified) belief for different reasons at different times. But it's hard to square this with an intentional holism that implies that changing any one of one's beliefs changes the content of all the rest.

3. To avoid repetition, I shall use this as a technical term for a theory of content that is both physicalistic and atomistic; i.e., a theory according to which (i) and (ii) are both false.

4. Maybe it starts earlier—with the breakdown of image theories of Ideas. The theory that Ideas refer to what they resemble is, after all, both physicalistic (on the assumption that resemblance is some sort of geometrical relation and that physics contains geometry) and atomistic (since, presumably, what one of one's Ideas resembles does not depend on what other Ideas one has). Alas, the image theory, though naturalistic, is, by general consensus, untenable.

5. Quine isn't, of course, the only one. See the first two chapters of Putnam's *Representation and Reality* (1988) where it's assumed without *any* argument that if you're holist about confirmation you've got to be holist about meaning too.

6. On this view, there's an interesting analogy between the semantical role of the theories that one espouses and the semantical role of the instruments of observation that one deploys: They both just function to sustain the head/world coordinations that constitute meaning. As I remarked in *Psychosemantics* (1987), the Operationalists were right in thinking that "star" means *star* because we have procedures that have stars on one end and "star"s on the other; they went wrong— they stumbled into holism—by supposing that such procedures are *constitutive* of meaning, so that "star" meant something different with the invention of telescopes.

   By the way, not just one's own skills, theories, and instruments, but also those of experts one relies on, may effect coordinations between, as it might be, "elms" in the head and elms in the field. That would be quite compatible with the meaning relation being both atomistic *and individualistic*, assuming, once again, the Skinnerian view that the conditions for meaning are purely functional and that they quantify over the mechanisms that sustain the semantically significant functional relations. Putnam (1988) argues that since appeals to experts mediate the coordination of one's tokens of "elm" with instances of *elm*, it follows that "reference is a social phenomenon." Prima facie, this seems about as sensible as arguing that since one uses telescopes to coordinate one's tokens of "star" with instances of *star*, it follows that reference is an optical phenomenon.

   That Putnam, of all people, should make this mistake is heavy with irony. For, it is Putnam who is always—and rightly—reminding us that ". . . 'meanings' are preserved under the usual procedures of belief fixation . . . " (1988, chapter 1, p. 14). I take this to be a formulation of anti-instrumentalist doctrine: the ways we have of telling when our concepts apply are *not*, in general, germane to their semantics. Why, I wonder, does Putnam make an exception in the case where our way of telling involves exploiting experts?

7. The nicety at issue is that my revised Skinnerian story isn't, strictly speaking, naturalistic as I've been telling it: it requires a counterfactual supporting correlation between dogs and *dog-thoughts* (token states of entertaining the concept DOG); and, 'is a dog-thought' is a nonnaturalistic predicate; it picks out a thought by reference to its intentional object. Skinner gets around the corresponding problem in the original version of his theory by (tacitly) assuming that he can specify the content-bearing expressions of natural languages "formally": e.g., phonologically or orthographically. (Thus, the regularity in virtue of which the English word "dog" expresses the property *dog* connects instances of *dog* with tokens of the expression #"d"^"o"^"g"#.) A Skinnerian semantics for mental states would have to assume analogously formal specifications for the tokens of mental states.

8. This may not strike you as sounding a lot like Dretske. That's because—at least as late as the BBS Precise (1983)—Dretske actually has two stories about content running together. There's the one I've sketched in the text, which takes the notion of nomic connectedness as basic; and there's one that's elaborated in terms of

conditional probabilities (roughly, whether an event e1 carries information about an event e2 is a function of the conditional probability of e2 given e1). It's not clear just how these two theories fit together, or what the second one buys you that the first one doesn't. To give just one example, on the nomic-connectedness story, the transitivity of 'carries information about' (what Dretske calls the "Xerox Principle") follows from the transitivity of 'is lawfully connected to'; on the conditional probability story, by contrast, it requires special stipulation. (Specifically, it requires the stipulation that e1 carries information about e2 only if the conditional probability of e2 given e1 is one.)

I think that the conditional probability story is a dead end and that connecting content to nomic relatedness is the really interesting idea in *Knowledge and The Flow of Information*. Anyhow, I propose to read Dretske that way for purposes of this discussion.

9. A subsidiary argument is that it's required to guarantee the Xerox principle. See preceding footnote.

10. According to this view, a semantic theory provides a naturalized condition for content in terms of nomic relations among properties; roughly, the symbol S expresses the property P if it's a law that Ps cause S-tokens. This condition is perfectly general in the sense that it can be satisfied both by atomic symbols and complex ones. Correspondingly, the appeal to recursive ("Tarskian") apparatus in a semantic theory functions *not* as part of the definition of content, but rather to show how the conditions for content could be satisfied by infinitely many formulas belonging to a productive system of representations. The idea is that content emerges from lawful relation between tokenings (in the world) of the property that a symbol expresses and tokenings (in the organism) of the symbol; and the internal representation of the Tarskian apparatus is part of the computational mechanism that mediates this lawful relation.

These remarks are intended to soothe philosophers who hold that ". . . a Tarskian truth characterization . . . makes no contribution at all to a solution of the problem of intentionality for semantic notions . . . [because] even if the in-quirer has a materialistically acceptable explanation of what it is about the simpler sentence A and its relation to the world that makes it true, he gets no help at all from the truth definition in his search for an explanation of the physical basis of the semantic status of the complex sentence" (Stalnaker, 1984, p. 31). Still there's something to what Stalnaker says. As we'll see in chapter 4, no nomic connection theory could account for the content of complex predicates that can't be instantiated (e.g., "is a square circle" and the like). And, for just the reason that Stalnaker points out, adding Tarskian apparatus doesn't help with the naturalization problem in these areas.

11. As F2 understands 'information carried', there is a metaphysical assumption that if x causes y, then there are properties of x and y in virtue of which it does so, and there is a law that subsumes ("covers") the causal interaction and relates the properties. See also chapter 5.

12. This approach to the disjunction problem thus exhibits a certain spiritual affinity with 'paradigm case' arguments in epistemology. Both assume that there are situations such that the fact that a sort of symbol is applied to a sort of thing in those situations is *constitutive* of the symbol meaning what it does. '"Dog" can't but be true of Rover because it's constitutive of the meaning of "dog" that Rover is a paradigm of the kind of thing that one says "dog" about. So pooh to people who think that there's a skeptical doubt about whether there are dogs!' But if this is not to beg the argument against skeptics, 'Rover is a paradigm of the kind of

thing that one says "dog" about' can't mean 'Rover is the kind of thing that "dog" is true of'; rather, it's got to mean something like 'Rover is the kind of thing that "dog" is said of'. And now there needs to be a caveat: viz., Rover has to be the kind of thing that "dog" is said of *when the conditions for dog-spotting are pretty good*. (There are *other* conditions—dark nights and such—when cats are paradigmatic of the kind of thing that "dog" is said of; a consideration that's grist for the skeptic mill.) In effect, paradigm case arguments presuppose that there is a distinction between type one situations and others; and that dark nights don't count as type one situations for saying "dog." It was not, however, in the tradition of paradigm case arguments to be explicit about much of this.

13. Cf. examples like *normal pulse rate* rather than examples like *snafu*. I shall follow the convention initiated by Ruth Millikan and write "Normal" with a cap N when I want to stress that a normative rather than a statistical notion of normalcy is intended.

14. I should emphasize that what's being denied here isn't just the statistical claim that all or most or much of the time if you want to become rich and famous you do become it. I'm claiming that a situation in which somebody wants very much to become rich and famous can be perfectly Normal in *any* reasonable sense of the term, and yet what's wanted very much may nevertheless fail to come off. This seems to me to be a truism.

15. Notice that Normalcy isn't a statistical notion even on this account. It's assumed that if X Normally causes Y, then *if the situation is Normal* then if X then it's relatively likely that Y. This is, of course, perfectly compatible with Xs never causing what they Normally cause because the situation is never Normal. Dennett (in a 1988 manuscript called "Fear of Darwin's Optimizing Rationales") succumbs to ill temper because he thinks I have misread Millikan as proposing a statistical account of normal functioning. But she doesn't and I haven't and none—I mean *none*—of the arguments I've proposed depends upon assuming that she does. I am a little miffed about this.

16. So, to keep the record straight: whereas Millikan apparently wants to define the content of a belief state in terms of its selectional history, the alternative proposal defines belief content by reference to the teleology of the belief fixing mechanisms (roughly, a belief is about what would cause it to be tokened in the sort of circumstances in which the mechanisms of belief fixation were designed to operate). The present proposal includes both nations so as not to prejudice the case against either.

17. Though other sorts of teleological accounts are not precluded in principle, I assume in what follows that any naturalistic story about teleology is going to rest on some sort of appeal to evolutionary history. But actually, as far as I can tell, the main line of argument goes through just as well if it's assumed only that the account of teleology is consequentialist and not subjunctive; i.e., that the purpose of a biological mechanism is somehow determined by the good results it (actually) produces, whether or not *good result* is itself construed in terms of selectional advantage.

18. Millikan has this to say about the frog/fly/bee-bee example: "We say that the toad thinks the pellets are bugs merely because we take it that the toad's behavior would fulfill its proper functions (its 'purpose') Normally only if these (viz., the pellets) were bugs *and* that this behavior occurs Normally (not necessarily normally) only upon encounter with bugs" (pp. 71–72). But assume that the toad thinks that the bee-bees (and the bugs) are black spots (so the bee-bee elicited snaps are "true"). If the Normal environment for snapping at black spots is one

where black spots are predominantly bugs, it still goes through that frog snaps at bee-bees would fulfill their proper functions Normally only if the bee-bees were bugs. This is because, in the cases where the black dots that the frog snaps at *aren't* bugs, the environment, ipso facto, isn't Normal. And, for the same reason, it still goes through that frog snaps occur Normally "only upon encounter with bugs." So we still haven't got a solution to the disjunction problem even after we've satisfied the conditions that Millikan imposes; i.e., satisfying her conditions on the Normal function of frog snaps is compatible with taking the intentional objects of the snaps to be (not flies but) little black dots.

19. Millikan and Israel are by no means the only philosophers who are hoist on this petard (whatever, precisely, a petard may be). David Papineau, who runs a teleological line on content in *Reality and Representation* (1988), suggests that ". . . the biological function of any given desire type is to give rise to a certain result: the result is then the desire's satisfaction condition" (p. 64). But this assumes that a naturalistic account of the teleology of desires will specify a *unique* biological function for each desire type; in particular, it supposes that the teleology will be univocal in cases where the disjunction problem would otherwise make intentional content indeterminate. Papineau provides no argument that natural teleology is univocal in this respect, and we've just seen why, if it's grounded by appeals to selection, it pretty clearly won't be.

Correspondingly, Papineau suggests that "the truth conditions for beliefs are . . . the circumstances in which they will have effects that will satisfy the desires they are working in concert with." Well, suppose that what the frog desires is food; suppose, even, that what it desires is that it should ingest flies. It's still true that (given Normal circumstances), *either* the belief that there are flies *or* the belief that there are black dots will have effects that will satisfy the frog's desire.

It's also true, of course, that snapping at black dots won't satisfy the frog's desire for flies in the *abNormal* circumstance where the black dots are bee-bees; and some of the things that Papineau says (p. 72) suggest that he wants to rest on this. But that won't do since there are other, also abNormal, circumstances in which *snapping at flies* won't satisfy the desire to ingest flies either (the frog's tongue is covered with silicon, and the flies slip off; the flies are of a new high-tech variety and can fly faster than frogs can snap, etc.). The moral is that you can rely on the frog's fly-beliefs leading to fly-ingestions (and thus bestowing selectional advantage when entertained in the presence of flies) only if you are taking it for granted that the frog's ecology is Normal. But then we've just seen that if you *are* taking it for granted that the frog's ecology is Normal, the requirement that its beliefs should operate in conjunction with its desires to produce successes isn't strong enough to motivate unique assignments of intentional content to the beliefs. Dilemma.

20. Strictly speaking, given the possibility of higher-order conditioning, it may be that getting an organism to respond to the triangularity rather than the greenness of green triangles doesn't depend on *green* and *triangle* being dissociated in the course of training, so long as *some* colors are dissociated from *some* shapes. A general habit of responding to shape rather than color could perhaps be established by differential reinforcement in those cases. I have no idea whether this would actually work, and, anyhow, it's just a curiosity; it suggests, contrary to fact, that if "green iff triangular" is reliable, it can't be that an organism is responding to triangularity rather than greenness unless it has a disposition to respond to shape rather than color *in general*.

21. It should now be clear that the argument against Darwinian theories of content was, in effect, that "Mother Nature" can select for organisms that snap at flies—as opposed to organisms that snap at fleebees—only if she can perform a "split stimulus" experiment; i.e., only if she can contrive to present the frog with fleebees that aren't flies; i.e., only if she can contrive to present the frog with fleebees that are bee-bees; a fortiori, only if "all the fleebees are flies" isn't reliable in the frog's ecology.

22. I'm very grateful to David Rosenthal for a conversation that helped to get this sorted out. The saccharine case isn't exceptional, by the way; any example of what ethnologists call a "supernormal" stimulus serves to point the same moral.

23. Till now I've been arguing that appeals to selectional history can't distinguish an organism that *represents things* from F from an organism that represents them as G in a world where it's counterfactual supporting that all and only the Fs are Gs. A parallel line of argument secures the present claim that appeals to evolutionary history can't distinguish selection for *being F* from selection for *being G* when F and G are necessarily coextensive: If you always get Fs and Gs together, then a mechanism that selects one *thereby* selects the other, so the utility of being F and being G always comes out the same.

   This has philosophically interesting consequences. For example, even assuming that it's a law that hearts and only hearts make the noises they do, still it's intuitively plausible that the function of the heart is pumping the blood, not making the noises. If the line of argument I've been selling is right, then appeals to selectional history do not, in and of themselves, underwrite this intuition. This does not, of course, imply that it's false that the function of the heart is blood pumping; it only implies that facts about function don't reduce to facts about selectional history. Dennett (1987) says that "if you want to maintain that it is perfectly respectable to say that eyes are for seeing . . . you take on a commitment to the principle that natural *selection* is well named . . . there is not just selection *of* features but selection *for* features . . . without this 'discriminating' prowess of natural selection, we would not be able to sustain functional interpretations at all" (p. 316; his italics). But no argument is given for this, and, as we saw above, it could turn out that function gets an analysis in terms (not of selectional history but) of *counterfactuals*. The governing intuition is, perhaps, that it would be OK if the heart stopped making noise as long as it kept pumping, but not so good the other way 'round.

24. Similarly, mutatis mutandis: Teddy bears are artificial, but *real bears are artificial too*. We stuff the one and Mother Nature stuffs the other. Philosophy is *full* of surprises.

25. The idea that "the" function of perception is to guide movement rather than to fix belief is also a main theme in the American Naturalist tradition; and in what is sometimes described as the evolutionary approach to the mind (see Patricia Churchland, 1987). For discussion, see chapter 9.

Chapter 4

A Theory of Content, II:

The Theory

". . . the appeal to teleologically Normal conditions doesn't provide for a univocal notion of intentional content . . . it's just not true that Normally caused intentional states ipso facto mean whatever causes them. So we need a nonteleological solution of the disjunction problem. So be it." So the first part of this discussion concluded. But that did rather beg the question against the guy who holds that *there isn't going to be a solution of the disjunction problem* because there are no intentional states, and hence no matters of fact about the disjunctiveness, or otherwise, of their intentional contents. What you need, to put the matter brutally, is one thing; what you are likely to get is quite another. What on earth would a naturalistic and nonteleological theory of content be like?

This rest of this paper explores and extends an approach to the disjunction problem that I first sketched in *Psychosemantics* (1987) and in "Information and Representation" (forthcoming). This solution is broadly within the tradition of informational approaches to content[1] but it does not equate what a symbol means with the information that its tokens carry; and it does not try to solve the disjunction problem by distinguishing type one situations (those in which whatever causes a symbol to be tokened is ipso facto in its extension) from type two situations (those in which symbols are allowed to be caused by things that they don't apply to.)[2] In the second respect, at least, it differs from all the other treatments of the disjunction problem that I've seen in the literature.

I must acknowledge at the outset the existence of what seems to be quite an impressive consensus—among the maybe six or eight people who care about these matters—that my way of doing the disjunction problem won't work. But Granny says I'm not to be disconsolate; Rome wasn't deconstructed in a day, she says. Accordingly, I now propose to run through more or less all of the objections to my treatment of the disjunction problem that I've heard of, and a few that I've dreamed up. Partly this is to show you that I am not disconsolate; partly it is to try to convince you that my story actually copes pretty well with the putative counterexamples; and partly it's to provide an opportunity to refine and deepen the theory.

Asymmetric Dependence (and Teleology for Almost the Last Time)

Errors raise the disjunction problem, but the disjunction problem isn't really, deep down, a problem about error. What the disjunction problem is really about deep down is the difference between *meaning* and *information*. Let's start with this.

Information is tied to etiology in a way that meaning isn't. If the tokens of a symbol have two kinds of etiologies, it follows that there are two kinds of information that tokens of that symbol carry. (If some "cow" tokens are caused by cows and some "cow" tokens aren't, then it follows that some "cow" tokens carry information about cows and some "cow" tokens don't). By contrast, *the meaning of a symbol is one of the things that all of its tokens have in common, however they may happen to be caused. All "cow" tokens mean cow;* if they didn't, they wouldn't be "cow" tokens.

So, information follows etiology and meaning doesn't, and that's why you get a disjunction problem if you identify the meaning of a symbol with the information that its tokens carry. Error is merely illustrative; it comes into the disjunction problem only because it's so plausible that the false tokens of a symbol have a different kind of causal history (and hence carry different information) than the true ones. But, as we saw in chapter 3, there are other sorts of examples of etiological heterogeneity (including representation in thought) and they produce disjunction problems too.

To put the same point another way, solving the disjunction problem requires not a theory of *error* but a theory of *meaning*; if a theory of meaning is any good, the conditions for disjunctive meaning should fall out as a special case (see the discussion in Fodor, forthcoming. If one is sympathetic to the Skinner-Dretske tradition, the trick in constructing such a theory is to explain how the meaning of a symbol can be insensitive to the heterogeneity of the (actual and possible) causes of its tokens even though, on the one hand, meaning is supposed somehow to reduce to information and, on the other hand, information varies with etiology.

You can now see what's *really* wrong with teleological theories of content. The heart of a teleological theory is the idea that "in Normal circumstances" the tokens of a symbol can have only *one kind* of cause—viz., the kind of cause that fixes meaning. (Normally, only cows cause "cows," so the teleological story goes.) But surely this underestimates what one might call the *robustness* of meaning: In actual fact, "cow" tokens get caused in *all sorts* of ways, and they all mean *cow* for all of that. Solving the disjunction problem and making clear how a symbol's meaning could be so insensitive to variability in the causes of its tokenings are really two ways of describing the same undertaking. If there's going to be a causal theory of content, there has to be some way of picking out *semantically relevant* causal relations from all the other kinds of causal relations that the tokens of a symbol can enter into. And we'd better not do this by implicitly denying robustness—e.g., by idealizing to contexts of etiological homogeneity.

Well, then, how *are* we to do it? Here's a first approximation to the proposal that I favor: Cows cause "cow" tokens, and (let's suppose) cats cause "cow" tokens. But "cow" means *cow* and not *cat* or *cow or cat* because *there being cat-caused "cow" tokens depends on there being cow-caused "cow" tokens, but not the other way around.* "Cow" means *cow* because, as I shall henceforth put it, noncow-caused "cow" tokens are *asymmetrically dependent upon* cow-caused "cow" tokens. "Cow" means *cow* because *but that "cow" tokens carry information about cows, they wouldn't carry information about anything.*

Notice that this sort of story has the desirable property of not assuming that there are such things as Type one situations; in particular, it doesn't assume that there are circumstances—nomologically possible and naturalistically and otherwise nonquestion beggingly specifiable—in which it's semantically necessary that only cows cause "cows". Nor does it assume that there are nonquestion-beggingly specifiable circumstances in which it's semantically necessary that *all* cows would cause "cows."[3] All that's required for "cow" to mean *cow*, according to the present account, is that some "cow" tokens should be caused by (more precisely, that they should carry information about) cows, and that noncow-caused "cow" tokens should depend asymmetrically on these.

Teleological theories say that what's special about false tokens is that they can't happen when circumstances are Normal; if it's supposed that things actually are Normal some of the time (as, indeed, it must be if the theory is historical/Darwinian) it follows that some of the time what's said (or thought) can't but be true. By contrast, the theory I'm selling says that false tokens can happen whenever they like; only if *they* happen, so too must tokenings of other kinds: No noncow-caused "cow"s without cow-caused "cow"s; false tokens are metaphysically dependent on true ones.[4] Since the satisfaction of the asymmetric dependence condition is compatible with any amount of heterogeneity in the causal history of "cow" tokens, this way of solving the disjunction problem is compatible with meaning being arbitrarily robust.[5]

This story also has the desirable property of being naturalistic in the sense discussed in chapter 3. It's atomistic ("cow"s could be asymmetrically dependent on cows in a world in which no other asymmetric dependencies obtain) and it's physicalistic (you can say what asymmetric dependence is without resort to intentional or semantic idiom).[6] But despite its having these desirable properties, the proposal I've just sketched is *only* a first approximation. As it stands there's lots to be said against it. Before we commence to look at the problems, however, I have three prefecatory remarks I want to make: a shortish one about a doctrine that you might call "pansemanticism," a longish one about ontology, and then a very short one about who has the burden of argument.

Pansemanticism
Here's a clash of intuitions for you.
  On the one hand:

> . . . symbols and mental states both have representational *content*. And nothing else does that belongs to the causal order: not rocks, or worms or trees or spiral nebulae. . . . the main joint business of the philosophy of language and the philosophy of mind is the problem of representation. . . . How can anything manage to be *about* anything; and why is it that only thoughts and symbols succeed? (Me, in *Psychosemantics*, 1987, p. xi)

And on the other hand:

> Clouds *mean* rain. Spots of a certain kind *mean* measles. . . . In all such cases there is a lawlike or nomological regularity connecting one type of situation with another. Instances of these regularities are cases in which one situation means something or carries information about another: and, of course, in such cases there need be neither minds nor symbols used by minds. (Israel, 1987, p. 3; emphasis his)

In fact, the idea that meaning is just *everywhere* is a natural conclusion to draw from informational analyses of content. If, after all, meaning reduces (more or less)[7] to reliable causal covariance, then since there is patently a lot of reliable causal covariance around, it looks to follow that there must be a lot of meaning around too. And the intuition that "means" is univocal—and means *carries information about*—in '"smoke" means *smoke*' and 'smoke means fire' is close to the heart of information-based semantics.

But this can't be right. If it were, then (since "carries information about" is transitive) it would follow that "smoke" means *fire*; which it doesn't. On the asymmetric dependence account, by contrast, this sort of case comes out all right. "Smoke" tokens carry information about fire (when they're caused by smoke that's caused by fire). But they don't *mean* fire because their dependence on fire is asymmetrically dependent on their dependence on smoke. Break the *fire* → *smoke* connection, and the *smoke* → *"smoke"* connection remains intact; our using "smoke" in situations where there's fire doesn't depend on smoke's carrying information about fire. But break the *smoke* → *"smoke"* connection and the *fire* → *"smoke"* connection goes too; our using "smoke" in situations where there's fire does depend on "smoke"'s carrying information about smoke.

There is, in short, a lot less meaning around than there is information. That's because all you need for information is reliable causal covariance, whereas for meaning you need (at least) asymmetric dependence too. Information is ubiquitous but not robust; meaning is robust but not ubiquitous. So much for pansemanticism.

Ontology

As I remarked in chapter 3, I assume that if the generalization that Xs cause Ys is counterfactual supporting, then there is a "covering" law that relates the property of being X to the property of being a cause of Ys: counterfactual supporting causal generalizations are (either identical to or) backed by causal laws, and laws are relations among properties. So, what the story about asymmetric dependence comes down to is that "cow" means *cow* if (*i*) there is a nomic relation between the property of being a cow and the property of being a cause of "cow" tokens; and (*ii*) if there are nomic relations between other properties and the property of being a cause of "cow" tokens, then the latter nomic relations depend asymmetrically upon the former.

Ontologically speaking, I'm inclined to believe that it's bedrock that the world contains properties and their nomic relations; i.e., that truths about nomic relations among properties are deeper than—and hence are not to be analyzed in terms of—counterfactual truths about individuals. In any event, *epistemologically* speaking, I'm quite certain that it's possible to know that there is a nomic relation among properties but not have much idea which counterfactuals are true in virtue of the fact that the relation holds. It is therefore, *methodologically* speaking, probably a bad idea to require of philosophical analyses that are articulated in terms of nomic relations among properties that they be, as one says in the trade, "cashed" by analyses that are articulated in terms of counterfactual relations among individuals.

This methodological point is one about which I feel strongly. So much so that I am prepared to succumb to a digression. Here come several paragraphs about how a philosopher can get into trouble by taking it for granted that truths about laws need to be analyzed by, or into, counterfactual truths.

The context is Kripke's critical discussion (1982) of dispositional accounts of rule following. According to such accounts, meaning *plus* by "+" is analyzed in terms of a disposition to "respond with the sum of [the] two numbers" when asked things like "What's m + n?" Kripke says this sort of analysis won't do because we have no such dispositions: our computational powers are finite; we make mistakes; and so forth. To which he imagines his interlocutor replying that: ". . . the trouble arises solely from too crude a notion of disposition: *ceteris paribus* notions of dispositions, not crude and literal notions, are the ones standardly used in philosophy and in science." So what's imagined is, in effect, a dispositional story about rule following that is backed by an appeal to the performance/competence distinction.

But, according to Kripke, that won't do either. For ". . . how should we flesh out the *ceteris paribus* clause? Perhaps [by invoking counterfactuals] as something like: If my brain had been stuffed with sufficient extra matter to grasp large enough numbers, and if it were given enough capacity to perform such a large addition . . . [etc.] . . . , then given an addition problem involving two large numbers *m* and *n*, I would respond with their sum. . . . But how can we have any confidence of this? How in the world can I tell what would happen if my brain were stuffed with extra brain matter. . . . Surely such speculation should be left to science fiction writers and futurologists. We have no idea what the results of such experiments would be. They might lead me to go insane. . . . [and so forth]"

Apparently Kripke assumes that we can't have reason to accept that a generalization defined for idealized conditions is lawful unless we can specify the counterfactuals which would be true if the idealized conditions were to obtain. It is, however, hard to see why one should take this methodology seriously. For example: God only knows what would happen if molecules and containers actually met the conditions specified by the ideal gas laws (molecules are perfectly elastic; containers are infinitely impermeable; etc.); for all *I* know, if any of these things were true, the world would come to an end. After all, the satisfaction of these conditions is, presumably, *physically impossible* and who knows what would happen in physically impossible worlds?

But it's not required, in order that the ideal gas laws should be in scientific good repute, that we know anything like all of what would happen if there really were ideal gasses. All that's required is that we know (e.g.) that if there were ideal gasses, then, ceteris paribus, their volume would vary inversely with the pressure upon them. And *that* counterfactual *the theory itself tells us is true.*[8]

Similarly, if there are psychological laws that idealize to unbounded working memory, it is not required in order for *them* to be in scientific good repute that we know all of what would happen if working memory really were unbounded. All we need to know is that, if we did have unbounded memory, then, ceteris paribus, we would be able to compute the value of $m+n$ for arbitrary m and n.[9] And that counterfactual the theory itself tells us is true.

Similarly again, we can know that there are asymmetric dependences among nomic relations between properties without knowing much about which counterfactuals these asymmetric dependences make true. All we need to know is that if the nomic relation between $P1$ and $P2$ is asymmetrically dependent on the nomic relation between $P3$ and $P4$, then, ceteris paribus, breaking the relation between $P3$ and $P4$ would break the relation between $P1$ and $P2$. And that counterfactual the theory itself tells us is true. As per above.

Having gotten all that off my chest, I shall join the crowd and talk counterfactuals from time to time, faut de mieux. And, since it's widely supposed that talk about counterfactuals itself translates into talk about possibilia, I shall sometimes equate "there is a nomic dependence between the property of being a Y and the property of being a cause of Xs" with "Ys cause Xs in all (nearby? see below) nomologically possible world". But I am not happy about any of this; it seems to me to be just the sort of reductive move that is always blowing up in philosophers' faces. I suspect, in particular, that some of the troubles we're about to survey stem not from there being anything wrong with the proposal that content rests on asymmetrical dependences among nomological relations, but rather from there being everything wrong with the assumption that claims about nomological relations need counterfactual/possible world translations.[10]

Who Has the Burden of Argument
The theory of meaning that I'm going to propose is elaborated largely in terms of subjunctive conditionals. It has this in common with all informational theories of meaning; it's in the nature of such theories to claim that a symbol means such-and-such because *if there were* instances of such-and-such they *would cause* tokenings of the symbol. So it may occur to you, in the course of these proceedings, to object

as follows: "Why should I believe that the counterfactuals that are being invoked are true? Why should I believe that if there actually were such-and-suches they actually would cause symbol tokenings in the ways that your theory requires?"

The answer is: Don't forget, this stuff is supposed to be philosophy. In particular, it's an attempt to solve Brentano's problem by showing that there are naturalistically specifiable, and atomistic, sufficient conditions for a physical state to have an intentional content. In *that* context, I get to *stipulate* the counterfactuals. It's enough if I can make good the claim that *"X" would mean* such and such if so and so *were to be* the case. It's not also incumbent upon me to argue that since *"X" does* mean such and such, so and so *is* the case. That is, solving Brentano's problem requires giving sufficient conditions for intentionality, not *necessary* and sufficient conditions. So, if you want to argue with the metaphysical conclusions of this paper, you've got to construct a world where my counterfactuals are all in place but where *"X"* doesn't mean what I say it does. Fair enough; let's see one.

OK, now to business.

To begin with, not an objection, but something more like a vague discomfort: *Even if you can get the theory to cope with the examples, I don't see why the theory should be true; I don't see why asymmetric dependence should, as it were, make the difference between information and content.*

Let's start by forgetting about the naturalization problem (we'll return to it in a couple of paragraphs). I want to make it seem plausible that asymmetric dependence might have deep roots in the analysis of semantical phenomena when the phenomena are viewed commonsensically, outside the context of metaphysical issues about reduction. And let's, for the moment, talk about linguistic rather than mental representation in order to keep the facts as much as possible out in the open. So, then:

We have, I suppose, a variety of practices with respect of the linguistic expressions we use. And I suppose it's plausible that these practices aren't all on a level; some of them presuppose others in the sense that some work only because others are in place. For a banal example, there's the business of having people paged. How it works is: Someone calls out "John" and, if everything goes right, John comes. Why John? I mean, why is it *John* that you get when you call out "John"? Well, because the practice is that the guy who is to come is the guy whose name is the vocable that is called. This much, surely, is untendentious.

Notice that you have to invoke the practice of naming to specify the practice of paging. So the practice of paging is parasitic on the practice on naming; you couldn't have the former but that you have the latter. But not, I suppose, vice versa? Couldn't you have the practices that are constitutive of naming (so that, for example, the convention is that "John is pink" is true if it's the person whose name is "John" that is pink) even if there were no practice of paging people by calling out their names? I take it to be plausible that you could, so I take it to be plausible that paging is *asymmetrically* dependent on naming.

Oh, no doubt, I could have an arrangement with my dog according to which my dog comes when I whistle; and this though the sound that I make when I whistle for my dog isn't, of course, my dog's name. But here learning the language game really *is* just training. The whistling works because there's a *pre*arrangement between me and my dog; I've taught the dog what to do when I make that noise. By contrast, I can page John by calling his name without this sort of prearrangement. When a convention of naming is in place, there's room for a practice of paging that is perfectly abstract: Anyone who has a name can be paged just by calling his name.

So, the *productivity* of the paging arrangement depends on there being a convention of naming. Similarly, mutatis mutandis, for the productivity of the practice in virtue of which I bring you a slab when you say "bring me a slab." That it's one of *those* things that you get when you say this has essentially to do with those being the kinds of things that are *called* "slabs" (with its being the case, for example, that those are the kinds of things that have to be pink if "slabs are pink" is true.) But not, surely, vice versa; surely the practices in virtue of our pursuit of which "is a slab" means *is a slab* could be in place even if there were no convention of bringing slabs when they're called for. So then it's plausible that the cluster of practices that center around bringing things when they're called for is asymmetrically dependent on the cluster of practices that fix the extensions of our predicates.

These kinds of considerations show one of the ways that asymmetric dependence gets a foothold in semantic analysis: Some of our linguistic practices presuppose some of our others, and it's plausible that practices of *applying* terms (names to their bearers, predicates to things in their extensions) are at the bottom of the pile.[11] But what, precisely, has all this got to do with robustness and with the relation between information and content? The idea is that, although tokens of "slab" that request slabs carry no information about slabs (if anything, they carry information about wants; viz., the information that a slab is wanted), still, *some* tokens of "slab" presumably carry information about slabs (in particular, the tokens that are used to predicate slabhood of slabs do); and, but for there being tokens of "slab" that carry information about slabs, I couldn't get a slab by using "slab" to call for one. My "slab" requests are thus, in a certain sense, *causally dependent on slabs even though there are no slabs in their causal histories.* But they're not, of course, causally dependent on slabs in the way that (according to informational semantics) my "slab" predications are. So then there are *two* semantically relevant ways that "slab" tokens can be causally dependent on slabs consonant with their meaning *slab*: by being "slab" tokens that are caused by slabs, and by being "slab" tokens that are asymmetrically dependent upon "slab" tokens that are caused by slabs. Equivalently: By being "slab" tokens that carry information about slabs, and by being "slab" tokens that asymmetrically depend upon "slab" tokens that carry information about slabs.

So far so good; we can see how asymmetric dependences among our linguistic practices might explain how a token of "slab" could mean *slab* even when, as in the case of slab requests, it's a want rather than a slab that causes the tokening; and how a token of "John" could mean *John* even though, if it's used to page John, it's caused not by John but by his absence. Which is to say that we can see something of the connection between asymmetric dependence and robustness.

But, of course, as it stands none of this is of any use to a reductionist. For, in these examples, we've been construing robustness by appeal to asymmetric dependences among *linguistic practices.* And linguistic *practices* depend on linguistic *policies*; the asymmetric dependence of my pagings on my namings comes down to my undertaking that, ceteris paribus, I will call out "John" only when the man I want to come is the one whom I undertake that I will use "John" to name; and so forth. Since, however, being in pursuit of a policy is being in an intentional state, how could asymmetric dependence among linguistic practices help with the naturalization problem?

The first point is that words can't have their meanings *just* because their users undertake to pursue some or other linguistic policies; or, indeed, just because of any purely *mental* phenomenon, anything that happens purely 'in your head'. Your undertaking to call John "John" doesn't, all by itself, make "John" a name of John. How could it? For "John" to be John's name, there must be some sort of *real relation* between the name and its bearer; and intentions don't, per se, establish real relations. This is because, of course, intentions are (merely) intentional; you can intend that there be a certain relation between "John" and John and yet there may be no such relation. *A fortiori*, you can intend that there be a certain *semantical* relation between "John" and John—that the one should name the other, for example—and yet there may be no such relation. Mere undertakings connect nothing with nothing; "intentional relation" is an oxymoron. For there to be a relation between "John" and John, something has to happen *in the world*. That's part of what makes the idea of a *causal* construal of semantic relations so attractive. (And it's also, I think, what's right about Wittgenstein's "private language" argument. Though, as I read the text, he has it muddled up with irrelevant epistemology. For "John" to mean *John*, something has to happen in the world. It doesn't follow that for "John" to mean John someone has to be in a position to *tell* that that thing has happened.)

Linguistic policies don't make semantic relations; but maybe they make *causal* relations, and maybe causal relations make semantic relations. This, anyhow, is a hope by which informational semantics lives. I pursue a policy according to which I use "is a slab" to predicate slabhood, and a policy according to which I use "bring a slab" to request slabs, and a policy according to which the second of these practices is asymmetrically dependent on the first. My pursuing these policies is my being in a certain complex mental state, and my being in that mental state has causal consequences: in particular it has the consequence that there is a certain pattern of causal relations between slabs and my tokenings of "is a slab;" and that there is a certain (very different) pattern of causal relations between slabs and my tokenings of "bring a slab;" and that the second pattern of causal relations is asymmetrically dependent on the first.

Now maybe we can kick away the ladder. Perhaps the policies per se aren't what matters for semantics; maybe all that matters is the patterns of causal dependencies that the pursuit of the policies give rise to. That one kind of causal relation between "slab"s and slabs should depend asymmetrically upon another kind of causal relation between "slab"s and slabs might be enough to explain the robustness of "slab" tokenings, *however* the relations are sustained. (Cf. a doctrine of Skinner's cited with approval in Chapter 3: semantics depends on a "functional relation"—a relation of nomic dependence—between symbols and their denotata. How this relation is mediated—e.g., that it is neurologically mediated, or for that matter, psychologically mediated—isn't part of the *semantical* story.)

The point is, if the asymmetric dependence story about robustness can be told just in terms of symbol-world causal relations, then we can tell it *even in a context where the project is naturalization*. No doubt, it's the linguistic policies of speakers that give rise to the asymmetric causal dependences in terms of which the conditions for robustness are defined; but the conditions for robustness *quantify over* the mediating mechanisms, and so can be stated without referring to the policies; hence their compatibility with naturalism.

At a minimum, nobody who is independently committed to the reduction of semantic relations to causal ones should boggle at this way of accommodating the facts about robustness. Informational theories, for example, define "information" in just this sort of way: i.e., they appeal to reliable covariances while quantifying over the causal mechanisms by which these covariances are sustained. By doing so, they explain why information (indeed, why the very *same* information) can be transmitted over so many different kinds of channels.

Well, similarly, if it's the causal patterns themselves that count, rather than the mechanisms whose operations give rise to them, then perhaps our *mental* representations can be robust just in virtue of asymmetric dependences among the causal patterns that our concepts enter into.[12] That is, perhaps there could be mechanisms which sustain asymmetric dependences among the relations between mental representations and the world, even though, patently, we have no policies with respect to the tokenings of our mental representations. If that were so, then the conditions for the robustness of linguistic expressions and the conditions for the robustness of mental representations might be *identical* even though, of course, the mechanisms in virtue of whose operations the two sorts of symbols satisfy the conditions for robustness would be very, very different. Some races are won by sailboats and some are won by steamboats, and the mechanisms whose operation eventuates in winning the two sorts of races are very, very different. But the conditions for winning quantify over the mechanisms and are the same for both sorts of races; however you are driven, all you have to do to win is come in first (on corrected time, to be sure).

So much for some of the intuitions that are running the show. Now let's see to the counterexamples.

1. *First Objection*: "What about 'unicorn'? It seems implausible that nonunicorn-caused 'unicorn' tokens should depend on unicorn-caused 'unicorn' tokens since, as you may have noticed, there are many of the former but none of the latter."

First reply: That's one of the reasons why I want to do the thing in terms of nomic relations among properties rather than causal relations among individuals. I take it that there can be nomic relations among properties that aren't instantiated; so it can be true that the property of being a unicorn is nomologically linked with the property of being a cause of "unicorn"s *even if there aren't any unicorns.* Maybe this cashes out into something like *"there wouldn't be nonunicorn-caused "unicorn" tokens but that unicorns would cause "unicorn" tokens if there were any unicorns.* And maybe *that* cashes out into something like: *there are nonunicorn-caused "unicorn" tokens in worlds that are close to us only if there are unicorn-caused "unicorn" tokens in worlds that are close to them.* But this is very approximate. For example, I suppose that "unicorn" is an (uninstantiated) kind term. It will become clear later, when we worry about doppelgängers of things that are in the extensions of kind terms, that this entails that, ceteris paribus, no world in which only nonunicorns cause "unicorns" can be as close to ours as some world in which only unicorns do. And anyhow, for reasons previously set out, I am not an enthusiast for such translations.

Two subsidiary points should be noticed. First, this way of compensating for the lack of unicorns won't work if the lack of unicorns is *necessary* (e.g., nomologically or metaphysically necessary). For, in that case, it's not a law that if there were unicorns they would cause "unicorn" tokens; laws aren't made true by vacuous satisfactions of their antecedents. Similar lines of argument suggest what appears to be quite a strong consequence of the asymmetric dependence story: *no* primitive symbol can express a property that is necessarily uninstantiated. (There can't, for example, be a primitive symbol that expresses the property of being a round square).

One would think that a theory that makes so strong a claim should be pretty easy to test. Not so, however, in the present case. For one thing, the notion of primitiveness that's at issue here isn't entirely clear. You could, presumably, have a *syntactically* primitive symbol[13] that means *is a round square* so long as it is 'introduced by' a definition. Whatever, precisely, *that* may mean. In short, although the claim that all necessarily uninstantiated properties may be expressed by complex symbols looks to rule out a lot of possibilities, I, for one, can't think of any way to decide whether it's true. Suggestions are gratefully solicited.

2. *Second Objection*: Why doesn't "horse" mean *small horse*, seeing that, after all, if horses cause "horses" it follows that small horses cause "horses".

Second Reply: That's another reason why I want to do the thing in terms of nomic relations among properties rather than causal relations among individuals. Being struck by lightning caused the death of the cow. The bolt that killed the cow was the fourth that Tuesday, so being struck by the fourth bolt on that Tuesday caused the death of the cow; "cause" is transparent to that sort of substitution. But though it's true (given the assumptions) that being struck by the fourth bolt on Tuesday killed the cow, the law that "covered" that causal transaction applies to cows and lightning bolts qua cow and lightning bolts (or, perhaps, qua organisms and electrical discharges?); it was because it was a lightning bolt—and not because it was the fourth such bolt that Tuesday—that its hitting the cow caused the cow to die.

Well, similarly in the semantic case. Small horses cause "horse"s if horses do; but nothing follows as to the identity of the properties involved in the law that covers these causal transactions (except that small horses must be in the extension of the one and token "horse"s in the extension of the other). As it turns out, routine application of the method of differences suggests that it must be the property of *being a horse* and not the property of *being a small horse* that is connected with the property of *being a cause of "horse" tokens* since many things that have the first property have the third despite their lack of the second: large horses and medium horses simply spring to mind. (Similar considerations explain why "horse" means *horse* rather than, as it might be, *animal*; consider this a take-home assignment.)

3. *Third Objection* (suggested independently by Steven Wagner, Tim Maudlin, and Scott Weinstein, in reverse chronological order.)

Aha! But how about this: Consider, on the one hand, Old Paint (hereinafter OP) and, on the other hand, all the horses except Old Paint (hereinafter HEOPs). It's plausible that OP wouldn't cause "horse"s except that HEOPs do; and it's also plausible that HEOPs would cause "horse"s even if OP didn't. So OP's causing "horse"s is asymmetrically dependent on HEOPs causing "horse"s; so "horse" means *all the horses except Old Paint*.

Third Reply: This is a third reason why I want to do it in terms of nomic relations among properties rather than causal relations among individuals. In what follows, I will often have claims to make about what happens when you break the connection between Xs and "X"s. In thinking about these claims *it is essential* to bear in mind that 'break the connection between Xs and "X"s' is always shorthand for 'break the connection between the property in virtue of which Xs cause "X"s and the property of being a cause of "X"s'. In the present case, *by stipulation* the property in virtue of which OP causes "horse"s is the property of *being a horse*. But if you break the connection between *that* property and the property of being a cause of "horse"s, then the connection between HEOPs and "horse"s fails too (since, of course,

HEOPs are causes of "horse"s not in virtue of being HEOPs, but in virtue of being horses).

So OP's causing "horse"s is not, after all, asymmetrically dependent on HEOPs causing "horse"s, and the counterexample fails.

Next Worry: Does asymmetric dependence really solve the disjunction problem?

Asymmetric dependence finds *a* difference between, on the one hand, false tokens, representation in thought, and the like and, on the other hand, symbol tokens that are caused by things that they apply to. But is it the *right* difference? Does it, for example, explain why it's only in the case of the latter sort of tokenings that etiology determines meaning? I now propose to look rather closely at some worries about how the asymmetric dependence story copes with the disjunction problem.

4. *Baker's Objection:* Here is a passage from a critical discussion of asymmetric dependence in a recent paper by Lynne Rudder Baker (in press).

> Let us consider this account in light of a particular case. Suppose that, although there are many ordinary cats around, a certain person, *S*, learns a particular Mentalese symbol solely from artifacts (say, Putnam's robot-cats) that impinge on sensory surfaces in exactly the same way as cats. Now (for the first time) *S* sees a real cat. . . . How should Fodor interpret the cat-caused token? . . . There seem to be three possibilities . . .

none of which, Baker thinks, is tolerable. These are:

(a) the token means *cat* and is thus true of the cat. But this can't be right because ". . . if there is any asymmetric dependence, it goes the other way. *S*'s present disposition to apply 'cat' to a real cat depends upon her corresponding current disposition to apply it to robot-cats."

(b) the token means *robot-cat* and is thus false of the cat. But this can't be right since it ignores relevant counterfactuals. Specifically, it ignores the fact that—although only robots did cause *S*'s "cats"—cats *would* have caused them if *S* had happened to encounter any. ". . . the [counterfactual supporting] correlation is between tokens of a certain type and (cats or robot-cats). It is simply an accident that the actual causes of *S*'s early representations were all robot cats. . ."

This is a form of argument I accept; see the discussion of Dretske's "learning period" account of the disjunction problem in Chapter 3.

(c) the token means *robot-cat or cat* and is thus true of the cat. But this can't be right because it ". . . just rekindles the disjunction problem. . . . [Moreover, on this account] both the cat-caused and the robot-caused tokens are veridical after all—even when S, on subsequently discovering the difference between cats and robot-cats, exclaims, 'I mistook that robot for a cat!' [Option C] seems to preclude saying that S made an error. We would have to say that her mistake was to think that she had made a mistake, and try . . . to find some way to make sense of her 'second-order' mistake."(All quotes from ms. pp. 6–8, passim).

So none of the three options is any good. So there must be something wrong with the way the asymmetric dependence story treats the disjunction problem. What to do then, what to do?

For reasons that will become clear when we discuss the *echt* Twin Earth problem (the one about H_2O and XYZ), Baker's case is in certain important respects underdescribed. However, given just the information that she provides and the choices that she offers, I opt for (c); that first "cat"[14] token means *cat or robot* and is thus true of the cat that it's applied to.[15] I am pleased to be able to tell you that at least one other philosopher shares this intuition. Fred Dretske somewhere considers the following variant of a Twin Earth example: There are both H_2O and XYZ on Twin Earth, but, just fortuitously, some speaker of the local dialect learns "water" only from ostensions of samples of H_2O. Dretske's intuition (and mine) is that this speaker's tokens of "water" mean H_2O *or XYZ*; in this case, though not in the standard Twin cases, the fact that the speaker would have called XYZ samples "water" counts for determining the extension that term has in his mouth. Since Baker's cat/robot case seems to be much the same sort of example, I take it that Dretske would share my view that "cat" means *cat or robot-cat* in the circumstances that Baker imagines.[16]

How good are the objections Baker raises against this analysis? Baker says that to opt for (c) "rekindles the disjunction problem," but I don't see that that is so: It is OK for *some* predicates to be disjunctive as long as not all of them are. One can perfectly consistently hold, on the one hand, that "cat" means *robot or cat* when it's *accidental* that you learned it just from robot-cats; while denying, on the other hand, that it would mean *cat or robot* if you had learned it in a world where all you *could* have learned it from were robot-cats (e.g., because there aren't any cats around.) Similarly, Dretske can consistently hold that "water" is true of H_2O or XYZ in the case he describes while agreeing that it is true of H_2O and false of XYZ in the case that Putnam describes.

But what of S's sense, on subsequently discovering the difference between robots and cats, that she used to be mistaken when she applied "cats" to robots? If her "cat" tokens meant *cat or robot*, then they were true of *both* the cats and the robots that she applied them to. Is she, then, mistaken to suppose that she used to be mistaken? There is, I think, an easy answer and an interesting answer.

Easy Answer: S used not to distinguish between cats and robots; her indiscriminate application of the same term to both was a symptom of her failure to distinguish between them. Not distinguishing between cats and robots was a serious mistake (by S's current lights. And, of course, by ours).

Interesting Answer: This depends on formulating the disjunction problem a little more carefully than one usually needs to. A typical instance of the disjunction problem is: "Why does the extension of 'cat' not contain both cats and rats, assuming that both cats and rats cause 'cat's?" This isn't quite the same as: "Why doesn't 'cat' *mean cat or rat* given that both cats and rats cause 'cats'?" The difference makes a difference in Baker's case.

Suppose that option (c) is right. Then, if S used to use "cat" in the way that Baker imagines, cats and robots were both in its extension. But this doesn't, of course, imply that S used "cat" to express the disjunctive concept CAT OR ROBOT (i.e., to mean *cat or robot*). Quite the contrary, S *couldn't* have used "cat" to express that concept because, by assumption, she didn't *have* that concept. Nobody can have the concept CAT OR ROBOT unless he has the constituent concepts CAT and ROBOT; which by assumption, S didn't.

So, then, what concept *did* S use "cat" to express according to option (c)? There just isn't any way to say; English provides only a disjunctive formula (viz., the expression "cat or robot") to pick out the extension {cats U robots}, and this disjunctive formula expresses a disjunctive concept (viz., the concept CAT OR ROBOT), hence not the concept that S had in mind. (Rather similar arguments show that English won't let you say what "water" means in the mouth of my Twin Earth twin; and, mutatis mutandis, that English$_2$ won't let my twin say what "water" means in my mouth.)

Now we can see what mistake S used to make when she applied "cat" to robots. No doubt what she said when she did so was something true. But she said it because she took it that the robots that she called "cats" had a certain nondisjunctive property which they shared with everything else in the set {cats U robots}. By her present lights, by contrast, *there is no such property*. By her present lights, the only property that cats and robots share qua cats and robots is the disjunctive property of BEING A CAT OR A ROBOT. So, by her present lights, when she used to say "cat" of robots (or of cats for that matter) she was saying something true, but she was saying it *for the wrong reason*. Hence her present (well-founded) intuition that there was some sort of mistake underlying her usage.

Given all this, I take it that Baker's case doesn't refute the asymmetric dependence account of content.

5. *Indeterminacy.* We saw in Chapter 3 that teleological solutions to the disjunction problem have the following nasty habit: Teleology goes soft just when you need it most; you get indeterminacies of function in just the cases where you would like to appeal to function to resolve indeterminacies of content.

In the notorious frog and bug case, for example, one would think that a good theory of content should decide—and should give some reasons for deciding—whether the intentional objects of the frog's snaps are flies or little-black-things (in effect, whether the content of the frog's mental state is 'there's a fly' or 'there's a fly-or-bee-bee').[17] But, on inspection, the teleological story about content fails to do so. To recapitulate the argument I gave in Chapter 3: You can say why snapping is a good thing for frogs to do given their situation, whichever way you describe what they snap *at*. All that's required for frog snaps to be functional is that they normally succeed in getting the flies into the frogs; and, so long as the little black dots in the frog's Normal environment *are* flies, the snaps do this equally well on either account of their intentional objects. The mathematics of survival come out precisely the same either way. (This is the sort of thing that makes philosophers feel—incorrectly but understandably—that, deep down, *content makes no difference*. First Darwinism, then nihilism when Darwinism fails; a career familiar enough from nineteenth century moral theory.)

The asymmetric dependence story, by contrast, decides the case. The frog's snaps at flies are asymmetrically dependent on its snaps at little black dots. So it is black dots, not flies, that frogs snap at. (De dicto, of course; de re it's true both that frogs snap at little black dots *and* that they snap at flies since Normally flies are the only little black dots that frogs come across.)

Three subsidiary objections now need to be considered. To wit:

(i) "What makes you so sure that the counterfactuals are the way that you're assuming? Who says that the fly snaps are asymmetrically dependent on the black-dot snaps and not vice versa?"

Strictly speaking, this is a sort of question I do not feel obliged to answer; it suffices, for the present metaphysical purposes, that there are naturalistically specifiable conditions, not known to be false, such that *if* they obtain there is a matter of fact about what the frog is snapping at. (See above, the discussion of who has the burden of argument.) However, just this once:

The crucial observation is that frogs continue to snap at (and ingest) bee-bees even when they have plenty of evidence that the bee-bees that they're snapping at aren't flies. That is: frogs continue to snap at dots in worlds where there are dots but no flies; but they don't snap at flies in worlds where there are flies but no dots.[18] (In fact, frogs won't even snap at *dead* flies; it's *moving* black dots they care about.) I take it that this strongly suggests that either there is no nomic relation between the property of being-a-fly and the property of being-a-cause-of-frog-snaps, or that, if there is such a relation, it depends asymmetrically upon the nomic relation between the property of being-a-black-dot and the property of being-a-cause-of-fly-snaps.

So far as I can tell, there's nothing special here; just a routine employment of the method of differences.

> (ii) "Doesn't asymmetric dependence capitulate to the argument from illusion? If the intentional object of the frog's fly-snaps is little black dots when (de re) the frog snaps at flies, then maybe the intentional object of my fly-swats is little black dots when (de re) I swat at flies. If the fact that frogs sometimes snap at little black dots that aren't flies means that they haven't got a FLY-concept, doesn't the fact that I sometimes swat at little black dots that aren't flies mean that I haven't got a FLY-concept either?"

The relevant consideration isn't however, *just* that frogs sometimes go for bee-bees; it's that they are prepared to go on going for bee-bees *forever.* Sometimes I swat at mere fly-appearances; but usually I only swat if there's a fly. Sometimes Macbeth starts at mere dagger appearances; but most of the time he startles only if there's a dagger. What Macbeth and I have in common—and what distinguishes our case from the frog's—is that *though he and I both make mistakes, we are both in a position to recover.*[19] By contrast, frogs *have no way at all* of telling flies from bee-bees. If you think of frog snaps at black dots as *mistaken* when the black dots are bee-bees, then such mistakes are *nomologically necessary* for the frog; and this not just in the weakish sense that it's a law that black dots elicit snaps if flies do in *this* world, but also in the stronger sense that black dots elicit snaps if flies do in *all* relevant worlds where the frog's psychological constitution is the same as here.

There is no world compatible with the perceptual mechanisms of frogs in which they can avoid mistaking black dots for flies. Whereas even if, freakishly, I mistake all the dagger appearances I actually come across for daggers; and even if, still more freakishly, I never do recover from any of these mistakes, still, that would be an *accident* since it is nomologically consonant with the way that I'm constructed that I should distinguish daggers from dagger appearances some of the time. But it is *not* nomologically consonant with the way that frogs are constructed that they should ever distinguish black dots from flies.

So Macbeth and I have dagger detectors and not dagger-or-dagger-appearance detectors but frogs have black-dot detectors and not fly detectors.

Here, then, is an interesting consequence of the present story about content: An organism can't have a kind of symbol which it *necessarily* misapplies, i.e., which it misapplies in every world compatible with its psychology. Suppose that Xs look a lot like Ys; suppose they look enough like Ys that S-tokens are quite often applied to them. Still, if S means Y and not X, then (according to the theory) there *must* be worlds, consonant with the organism's psychology in *this* world, in which S-tokens are applied to Ys but withheld from Xs. (And, of course, the asymmetric dependence condition requires that, ceteris paribus, some such worlds are nearer to ours then any worlds in which S-tokens are applied to Xs but withheld from Ys; see sections 8 and 10 below). The bottom line is that it's impossible for frogs to have FLY concepts but not impossible for *us* to have FLY concepts. This is because it's consonant with our psychology, but not with theirs, to sometimes distinguish flies from bee-bees.

This consequence constrains robustness. There are, after all, some mistakes that can't be made; viz., mistakes from which it is nomologically impossible to recover, consonant with the character of one's psychology. To this extent, the asymmetric dependence story is an attenuated sort of verificationism. I think that perhaps it captures what's *true* about verificationism; but, of course, I would think that.[20]

> (iii)   "How do you avoid saying that frogs are really snapping at their retinas?"

The point about black dots was that (we're assuming) in the frog's ecology, 'is a black dot' is a description Normally true of flies. So our problem was to choose—from among the descriptions that flies Normally satisfy when frogs snap at them—the descriptions that frogs snap at them under. There may, however, be Xs other than flies, and Fs other than being a black dot, such that flies getting snapped at by frogs is asymmetrically dependent on Xs being F. If there are such, the question would arise: Why aren't Xs that are Fs the intentional objects of fly snaps?

For example: it's presumably a law that no fly gets snapped at except as some proximal projection of the fly produces some state of excitation of the retina of the frog; a retinal excitation that is, in turn, causally implicated in producing the snap. Moreover, it's plausible that such states of retinal excitation would be sufficient for causing frog snaps even if they (the excitations) weren't produced by proximal projections of flies. If all this is true, then the frog's fly-elicited fly snaps are asymmetrically dependent on these states of retinal excitation. So why aren't the excitation states the intentional objects of the frog's snaps?

I don't know what the story is with frogs, but in the general case there is no reason at all to suppose that the causal dependence of perceptual states on distal objects is asymmetrically dependent on the causal dependence of *specific arrays of proximal stimuli* on the distal objects; e.g., that there are specifiable sorts of proximal traces that a cow has to leave on pain of the cow → COW connection failing. On the contrary, in the usual case there are a heterogeneity of proximal arrays that will eventuate in cow perception, and there's a good reason for this: Since,—due to the laws of optics, inter alia—cows are mapped one-many onto their proximal projections, the mechanisms of perception—constancy, bias, sharpening, and the like— must map the proximal projections many-one onto tokenings of COW. Given the vast number of ways that cows may impinge upon sensory mechanisms, a perceptual system which made COW tokenings intimately dependent upon specific proximal projections wouldn't work as a cow-spotter.

It might still be said, however, that the dependence of cow thoughts on distal cows is asymmetrically dependent on their dependence on *disjunctions* of proximal cow projections; distal cows wouldn't evoke COW tokens but that they project proximal whiffs or glimpses or snaps or crackles or . . . well, or what? Since, after all, cow spotting can be mediated by theory to any extent you like, the barest whiff or glimpse of cow can do the job for an observer who is suitably attuned. Less, indeed, than a whiff or glimpse; a mere ripple in cow-infested waters may suffice to turn the trick. On the present view, cow thoughts do *not*, of course, owe their intentional content to the belief systems in which they are embedded; what determines their content is simply their asymmetric causal dependence on cows. But it is quite compatible with this that belief systems should *mediate* these semantically salient causal dependencies. They can form links in the causal chain that runs from cows to COW tokens, just as instruments of observation form links in the causal chain that runs from galaxies to GALAXY tokens.[21] To the extent that this is so, just about *any* proximal display might mediate the relation between cows and cow-thoughts for some cow-thinker or other on some or other cow-spotting occasion.

So barring appeals to *open* disjunctions, it seems likely that there is just no way to specify an array of proximal stimulations upon which the dependence of cow-thoughts upon cows is asymmetrically dependent. And here's where I quit.[22] I mean, it does seem to me that the price of intentional univocality is holding that primitive intentional states can't express open disjunctions. The idea might be that, on the one hand, content depends on *nomic* relations among properties and, on the other, nothing falls under a law by satisfying an *open* disjunction (open disjunctions aren't projectible). Like the prohibition against primitive symbols that express impossible properties, this strikes me as a very strong consequence of the present semantical theory; but not an embarrassment because not obviously false.[23]

6. *What about the Logical Vocabulary?* I don't know what about the logical vocabulary. Since I think that Kripke's objection fails (see above), I'm inclined to think that maybe there is *no* objection to the idea that "+", "and", "all" and the like have the meanings they do because they play a certain causal role in the mental lives of their users. This would, of course, be to accept a distinction in kind between the logical and the nonlogical vocabularies. (The semantics for the former would be a kind of 'use' theory, whereas the semantics for the latter would depend on nomic, specifically mind-world, relations.) Gilbert Harman somewhere suggests that to be a logical word *just is* to be the sort of word of which a use-theory of meaning is true. That proposal strikes me as plausible.

You may wonder how anybody who claims to be implacably opposed to inferential role semantics can have the gall to identify the meaning of a logical word with its use. Answer: the trouble with use theories is that they invite holism by well-known paths of argument (see chapter 3 above and, more extensively, *Psychosemantics*, chapter 3). But these holistic arguments depend on the acknowledged impossibility of *defining* most terms (specifically, on the impossibility of distinguishing defining from merely nomic biconditionals). It is therefore unclear that they apply to the logical vocabulary since terms in the logical vocabulary generally *are* definable: Anything counts as meaning *plus* that expresses a function from the numbers m,n to $m+n$; anything counts as meaning *and* that expresses a function from propositions to truth values and assigns *true* to P,Q iff it assigns *true* to $P\&Q$.

Correspondingly, it is arguably a sufficient condition for a speaker's meaning *plus* by "+" that, ceteris paribus, he takes "$m+n$" to designate the sum of m and n; a sufficient condition for a speaker's meaning *and* by "and" that, ceteris paribus, he takes "P and Q" to be true iff he takes "P" to be true and "Q" to be true; and so forth. (Relations like "taking to express," "taking to be true"—which, on this construal, hold between symbol users and symbols they use—would have to receive a causal/dispositional reconstruction if circularity is to be avoided. But there are familiar proposals for wedding functionalist construals of these relations to functional role theories of content: Thus, a speaker means *and* by "and" iff, ceteris paribus, he has "P and Q" in his belief box iff he has "P" in his belief box and he has "Q" in his belief box. In the case of logical vocabulary, I know of no principled reason why some such proposal shouldn't be endorsed.)

7. *What about Predicates that Express Abstractions (like "Virtuous")?* All predicates express properties, and all properties are abstract. The semantics of the word "virtuous," for example, is determined by the nomic relation between the property of being a cause of tokens of that word and the property of being virtuous. It isn't interestingly different from the semantics of "horse."

8. *Block's Problem.* The following characteristically insightful objection was pointed out to me by Ned Block in the following conversation; I suppose I'm grateful to him.

> Look, your theory comes down to: "cow" means *cow* and not *cat* because, though there are nomologically possible worlds in which cows cause "cow"s but cats don't, there are no nomologically possible worlds in which cats cause "cow"s but cows don't. But such face plausibility as this idea may have depends on equivocating between two readings of "cow". In fact, there's a dilemma: If you mean by "cow" something like *the phonological/ orthographic sequence #c^o^w#*, then there's just no reason at all to believe the claim you're making. For example, there is surely a possible world in which cows don't cause #c^o^w#s but trees do, viz., *the world in which #c^o^w# means tree*. So, if when you write "cow" what you mean is #c^o^w#, then it clearly can't be

nomologically necessary in order for "cow" to mean *cow* that nothing causes "cows" in worlds where cows don't.

Notice that it does no good to protest that the asymmetric dependence condition is supposed to be sufficient but not necessary for content. There is *no* orthographic/phonetic sequence 'X' which mightn't mean *tree* in some nomologically possible world or other, whatever 'X' happens to mean here. Given the conventionality of meaning, there couldn't be. It follows that there is no orthographic/phonetic sequence 'X' the nomologically possibility of tokenings of which is dependent on 'X's being caused by Xs. So there is no such sequence that satisfies your sufficient condition for meaning X. A sufficient condition for content that *nothing* satisfies needn't much concern Brentano. Or us.

It wouldn't, of course, be a way out of this to amend the proposal to read '#cˆoˆw# means *cow* only if, in every world in which you break the cow → #cˆoˆw# connection, *either* nothing causes #cˆoˆw#s, *or* #cˆoˆw# doesn't mean *cow*'. For, though that would indeed exclude the unwanted cases, it would do so by appealing to a semantical condition and would therefore be circular. Well, for the same sort of reason it's also no good arguing that, in the world imagined, tokens of #cˆoˆw# don't count as tokens of the (viz., *our*) word "cow"; i.e., to read "cow" in "cows's are asymmetrically dependent on cows" as naming the *word* "cow" rather than the orthographic/phonological sequence #cˆoˆw#. For, that would be to appeal implicitly to a semantical construal of the conditions for type identifying words. Barring circularity, the orthographic/phonological construal of 'same word' is accessible to a naturalistic semantics, but the semantical construal of 'same word' is not.

So, to put it in a nutshell, if you read "cow" orthographically/phonologically the claim that "cow" means *cow* because "cow"s are asymmetrically dependent on cows is false; and if you read "cow" morphemically the claim that "cow" means *cow* because "cow"s are asymmetrically dependent on cows is circular. Either way, it's a claim that seems to be in trouble.

This is a pretty nifty line of argument. Just the same, I think the problem it raises is actually only technical.

Block is, of course, perfectly right that for the purposes of a naturalistic semantics the only nonquestion-begging reading of "cow" is #cˆoˆw#. Henceforth be it so read. However, the asymmetric dependence proposal is that *all else being equal*, breaking cow → "cow" breaks X → "cow" for all X.[24] Correspondingly—to put the point intuitively—what's wrong with Block's argument is that all else *isn't* equal in the worlds that he imagines. To get those worlds, you need to suppose *not only* that cow → "cow" is broken, *but also and independently* that tree → "cow" is in force. It's this independent supposition that violates the 'all else equal' clause.

Here's a way to make the same point in terms of possibilia. If you put in 'all else equal', then what the theory requires is *not* that cows cause "cow"s in *every* nomologically possible world where Xs cause cows. Rather, what's required is just that there be worlds where cows cause "cows" and noncows don't; and that they be nearer to our world than any world in which some noncows cause "cows" and no cows do. Notice that, on this formulation of the asymmetric dependence condition, the nomological possibility of Block's world where #cˆoˆw# means *tree* is compatible with "cow" meaning (and hence being asymmetrically dependent upon) cows in our world. At least, it is on the intuitively plausible assumption that worlds that are just like ours except that it's the case that cows don't cause "cow"s are ipso facto nearer to us than worlds that are just like ours except that it's both the case that cows don't cause "cows" *and* that trees do.

Let's do this one more time: To get the nearest semantically relevant world to here, you break cow → "cow". All the X → "cow" relations that nomically depend on cow → "cow" will, of course, go too, since to say that X → "cow" is nomically dependent on cow → "cow" is to say that [not (X → "cow") unless (cow → "cow")] is nomologically necessary. What the present theory claims is that, in the world that's just like ours except that cow → "cow" and everything nomologically dependent on it are gone, X → "cow" is false for all X (where, to repeat, "cow" is read as #cˆoˆw#.) Well, if this is what you mean by 'the nearest possible world in which cow → "cow" is gone', then, clearly, Block's world doesn't qualify. To get to Block's world, you have to both break cow → "cow" and stipulate tree → "cow". So the nomological possibility of Block's world is compatible with "cow" meaning *cow* according to the present version of the asymmetric dependence criterion. So everything would seem to be OK.

Corollary: Suppose that, in *this* world, there happens to be a language L in which "cow" (viz #cˆoˆw#) means *tree*. Presumably *our* (English-speakering) use of "cow" for cows is causally independent of L's use of "cow" for trees. So, then, the nearest world to ours in which cow → "cow" goes (taking with it everything that's nomically dependent on it) still has tree →"cow" intact; and the nearest world to ours in which tree → "cow" goes (taking with it everything that's nomically dependent on it) still has cow → "cow" intact. But by assumption (specifically, by the assumption that only L and English use #cˆoˆw#), in the nearest world in which *both* cow → "cow" *and* tree → "cow" goes for every X. So, for every X, either X → "cow" depends on cow → "cow" or X → "cow" depends on tree → "cow", neither of which depends upon the other. So, if there is a language in which "cow" means *cow* and a language in which "cow" means *tree*, then there are two different ways in which tokens of "cow" satisfy the asymmetric dependence condition. So "cow" (viz., #cˆoˆw#) is ambiguous. This is, I take it, the intuitively correct solution.

Next objection?

9. *Why Doesn't "WATER" Mean the Same as "H₂O"?* After all, it's plausible that they express the same property; in which case, it presumably follows that neither concept is asymmetrically dependent on the other.

Actually, I'm inclined to think that "WATER" *does* mean the same as "H₂O." What doesn't follow—and isn't true—is that having the concept WATER is the same mental state as having the concept H₂O. (I.e., it's not the case that concepts are individuated by their contents. For a discussion of this sort of distinction, see chapter 6). Would you, therefore, kindly rephrase your objection?

OK. Why, given that they express the same property, is having the concept WATER not the same mental state as having the concept H₂O?

Reply: Because you can't have the concept H₂O without having the concept HYDROGEN and you can have the concept WATER without having the concept HYDROGEN; as, indeed, is evident from the fact that the (Mentalese) expression "H₂O" has internal lexico-syntactic structure.

10. *Do the Twin Cases.* Tell me why "water" doesn't mean XYZ. And don't tell me that "water" does mean XYZ; XYZ isn't even in its extension.

I suppose the worry is that an English speaker exposed to XYZ would call it "water," and the truth of this counterfactual suggests that there's a nomic dependence between the property of being a cause of "water" tokens and the disjunctive property of being H₂O or XYZ. Since, according to the present proposal, content arises from such nomic dependencies, the problem is to explain why H₂O is, but XYZ is not, in the extension of "water." (Less precisely, it's to explain why "water" doesn't mean something disjunctive.)

The thing to keep your eye on is this: It's built into the way that one tells the Twin Earth story that it's about kind-terms (mutatis mutandis, kind-concepts). In particular, it's part of the story about "water" being a kind-term that English speakers intended it to apply to all and only stuff of the same (natural) kind as paradigmatic local samples (and similarly for "water2" as it's used by speakers of English2.) A fortiori, it's part of "water" and "water2" being kind-terms that speakers intend *not* to apply them to anything that is distinguishably *not* of the same kind as their local samples. (There are, of course, sorts of expressions with perfectly kosher semantics whose uses are not controlled by these sorts of intentions, that are therefore not used to pick out natural kinds, and whose extensions are therefore disjunctive in the sense that things of more than one natural kind belong to them. The expression "stuff sort of like water" is, I suppose, one such.)

My point is that the intention to use "water" only of stuff of the same kind as the local samples has the effect of making its applications to XYZ asymmetrically dependent on its applications to H_2O ceteris paribus. Given that people are disposed to treat "water" as a kind term (and, of course, given that the local samples are all in fact H_2O) it follows that—all else equal—they would apply it to XYZ only when they would apply it to H_2O; specifically, they would apply it to XYZ only when they *mistake* XYZ for H_2O; only when (and only because) they can't tell XYZ and H_2O apart. Whereas, given a world in which they *can* tell XYZ and H_2O apart (and in which their intentions with respect to "water" are the same as they are in *this* world), they will continue to apply "water" to H_2O and refrain from applying it to XYZ.

Notice that worlds in which speakers intend to use "water" as a kind-term and XYZ is distinguishable from H_2O are 'nearby' relative to worlds in which speakers do not intend to use "water" as a kind-term and XYZ is distinguishable from H_2O. So the possibilities play out like this:

- In nearby worlds where XYZ *can't* be distinguished from H_2O, if you break the H_2O/"water" connection you lose the XYZ/ "water" connection and vice versa.
- In nearby worlds where XYZ *can* be distinguished from XYZ, if you break the H_2O/"water" connection you lose the XYZ/ "water" connection, but *not* vice versa.

So, ceteris paribus, there are nearby worlds where you get the H_2O/ "water" connection without the XYZ/"water" connection, but no nearby worlds where you get the XYZ/"water" connection without the H_2O/"water" connection. I.e., it's nomologically possible for the XYZ/water connection to fail without the H_2O/water connection failing, but not vice versa. So applications of "water" to XYZ are asymmetrically dependent on applications of "water" to H_2O. So "water" means H_2O and not XYZ in the conditions that the Twin Earth story imagines; just as the standard intuitions require.[25]

So much for H_2O and XYZ. It may be useful, by way of summary, to bring together what I've said about the unicorn worry, the Baker worry and the H_2O/XYZ worry, since all three involve cases where a semantic theory is required to make intuitively correct determinations of the extension of a term with respect to merely possible entities.

To begin with, you can now see why I said that the Baker example (about cats and robot-cats) was underdescribed. In the *echt* Twin cases, it's always assumed that the speaker intends the word in question to be a natural kind-term, and the speaker's having this intention has the effect of making the semantically relevant asymmetric dependencies true of his use of the word. In Baker's case, by contrast, we know that the speaker eventually comes to apply "cat" to cats and not to robots, but we *don't* know whether this is in virtue of a previous standing disposition to use "cat" as a kind-term. Baker doesn't say, so I've assumed that the speaker had no such standing disposition. So Baker's "cat" means *cat or robot* because, on the one hand, *S* would (indeed, does) use "cat" for either; and, on the other, there's nothing in Baker's description of the case that suggests a mechanism (such as an intention to use "cat" as a kind-term) that would make the use for the robots asymmetrically dependent upon the use for the cats (or vice versa).

"Unicorn" means unicorn because you can have lawful relations among uninstantiated properties (and people would apply 'unicorn' to unicorns if there were any). By contrast, "water" means water (and not XYZ) because, although people would use "water" of XYZ if there were any (XYZ is supposed to be indistinguishable from H_2O) nevertheless, they have a settled policy of using "water" as a kind-term (of using it only for substances actually of the same kind as water), and their adherence to this policy makes their use of "water" for XYZ asymmetrically dependent on their use of "water" for H_2O: there's a break in the XYZ/"water" connection *without* a break in the H_2O/"water" connection in nearby world where H_2O is distinguishable from XYZ. (If, however, you don't like this story about why "water" doesn't mean XYZ, I'll tell you a different one presently.)

11. *Absolutely Last Objection*: But *how could* asymmetric dependence be sufficient for content? Surely you can have cases where one nomic relation is asymmetrically dependent on another but where there is no *semantical* relation at issue?

Well, maybe, but I've only been able to think of two candidates: asymmetric dependences that arise from causal chains and asymmetric dependences that involve nomic relations at different levels of analysis. And what's striking about both these cases is that the asymmetric dependences they generate aren't the right kind to produce robustness. Since mere stipulation can ensure that only asymmetric dependencies that do produce robustness count for semantic purposes, neither of these kinds of cases poses a real threat to my story. Let's have a look at this.

Interlevel Relations: Suppose you have a case where a microlevel law $(B \to C)$ provides the mechanism for a macrolevel law $(A \to D)$ (in the way that, for example, Bernoulli's law provides the mechanism for laws about airfoils). Then it might be that the $A \to D$ law is asymmetrically dependent on the $B \to C$ law. You might get this if, for example, $B \to C$ is necessary but not sufficient to sustain $A \to D$; in that case, breaking the $B \to C$ connection would break the $A \to D$ connection in all nomologically possible worlds, but there might be nomologically possible worlds in which the $A \to D$ connection goes even though the $B \to C$ connection is intact. Since it is, to put it mildly, not obvious that C has to mean B in such cases, it seems that asymmetric dependence isn't sufficient for content after all.

Reply: The point of appeals to asymmetric dependence in theories of content is to show how tokens of the same type could have heterogeneous causes compatible with their all meaning the same thing; i.e., it's to show how robustness is possible. Correspondingly, if a sufficient condition for content is going to be fashioned in terms of asymmetric dependence, it must advert to the dependence of one causal law *about "X" tokens* upon another causal law *about "X" tokens*. But the sort of asymmetric dependences that interlevel cases generate don't meet this condition. What we have in these cases is a law that governs the tokening of one thing (Ds in the example) that's dependent on a law that governs the tokening of some other thing (Cs in the example). This sort of asymmetric dependence doesn't produce robustness, so it's not semantically relevant.

Causal Chains: We discussed these in a slightly different context when we asked why the frog's retinal irradiations are not the intentional objects of its fly-snaps: The causal link between distal stimuli and mental representations is mediated by (and thus depends asymmetrically upon) causal links between proximal stimuli and mental representations. In that example, we were given a state whose intentional object was assumed to be one of its causes, and the question was *which* one. The present issue is slightly different: Since causal chains give rise to a species of asymmetrical dependence, and since every event belongs to some causal chain or other, how are we to avoid concluding that everything means something? Pansemanticism gone mad.

Short Form: Suppose As (qua As) cause Bs (qua Bs), and Bs (qua Bs) cause Cs (qua Cs), and assume that As are sufficient but not necessary for the Bs. Then the law $A \rightarrow C$ is asymmetrically dependent on the law $B \rightarrow C$. Why doesn't it follow that Cs mean B?

Answer: Because, although the causal chain makes the $A \rightarrow C$ connection asymmetrically depend on the $B \rightarrow C$ connection, the dependence of Cs on Bs that it engenders is not ipso facto robust, and content requires not just causal dependence but robustness too. The dependence of Cs on Bs *is robust only if there are non-B*-caused Cs. But the causal chain $A \rightarrow B \rightarrow C$, engenders an asymmetric dependence in which *all the A-caused Cs are also B-caused.* So the asymmetric dependence of $A \rightarrow C$ on $B \rightarrow C$ doesn't satisfy the conditions on robustness; so it's not semantically relevant.

But suppose we have both $A \rightarrow B \rightarrow C$ and $D \rightarrow B \rightarrow C$.

> (*i*)   C still doesn't mean B because every C is B-caused and robustness fails.
>
> (*ii*)   C doesn't mean A because Cs being caused by non-As doesn't depend on Cs being caused by As, (i.e., you don't get $X \rightarrow C$ relations that are asymmetrically dependent on $A \rightarrow C$ relations). An analogous argument shows that C doesn't mean D either.
>
> (*iii*)   C *doesn't mean (A or D)* because X-caused Cs that are asymmetrically dependent on A- or D-caused Cs are ipso facto asymmetrically dependent on B-caused Cs. Intuitively, what's wanted is that 'X' means X only if Xs are the *only* sorts of things on which Xs are robustly dependent. Take-home problem: Formulate the asymmetric dependence condition to make this the case.

All that this technical fooling around shows is that if we stipulate that asymmetric dependence engenders content only if it produces robustness, then perhaps we can avoid Crazy Pansemanticism: the doctrine that everything means something. But, of course, some causal chains—viz., the ones that do meet conditions for information and robustness—*will*, ipso facto, meet the present conditions for content. So, the really interesting question is whether meeting the conditions for information and robustness really *is* meeting the conditions for content. We'll return to this at the end.

So much for all the objections I've been able to think of.

Unverificationist Interlude

We arrive at a major watershed. If we accept the theory as it has been developed so far, we're committed to a form of verificationism. For, according to the theory, it's a semantical truth (it follows from the nature of semantical relations as such) that:

> P: You cannot have a symbol (/concept) which expresses property X unless it is nomologically possible for you to distinguish X-instantiations from instantiations of any other property.

Or, to put it slightly differently:

> P': If "X" expresses at least X, and if there is a Y which it is not nomologically possible for you to distinguish from X, then "X" expresses Y as well as X (e.g., it expresses the disjunctive property X *or* Y.)[26]

Now, I don't know of any perfectly clear counterexamples to P (Paul Boghossian has struggled manfully to produce one, but I'm not convinced that he's succeeded).[27] But, on the other hand, I don't see why P or P' have to be true. *Why* should having a word that means X but not Y depend on being able, even in principle, to tell Xs and Ys apart? After all (by assumption) being X is a different state of affairs from being Y even if (by assumption) the worlds in which differences between Xs and Ys show up are too far away for us to get to. But if the difference between being X and being Y is real, then so too, surely, is the difference between being X and being (X or Y). And if the difference between being X and being (X or Y) is real, why shouldn't we be able to talk (/think), in ways that respect that difference?

I don't know how convincing you will find that line of thought; I'm not at all sure, for that matter, how convincing *I* find it. Put it, at a minimum, that the successes of verificationist philosophizing have not, over the years, been exactly staggering. Perhaps it would be well, if only as an exercise, to see what we would have to change about the story we've been telling if we want it not to entail P or P'.

I think the answer is pretty clear. The story up to now has had two parts: there's an "information" condition (roughly, "X" expresses

X only if Xs qua Xs cause "X"s); and there's an "asymmetric dependence" condition which is supposed to take care of the 'robustness' cases; the cases where "X"s are caused by things *other* than Xs.[28] It is the first of these—the information condition—that entrains the verificationism. Correspondingly, the cost of getting rid of the verificationism is a semantical theory that is, in a sense that should presently become clear, not purely informational. I propose to lay out the relevant geography, leaving it to you to decide whether or not being a verificationist is worth it at the price.

You may recall that in chapter 3, when we discussed the Skinner-to-Dretske tradition in semantics, I suggested that the following claim is close to its heart: What your words (/thoughts) mean is dependent entirely on your *dispositions* to token them (on what I called the "subjunctive history" of their tokenings), *the actual history* of their tokenings being semantically irrelevant.

The discussion up till now has stuck with Skinner and Dretske in assuming that this doctrine is correct—that semantic relations are, as I shall now say, purely informational[29]—and it's pretty clear how the verificationism follows. Consider the Twin cases. Perhaps the first thing one is inclined to point to as relevant to distinguishing the WATER concept from the WATER2 concept is that the former, but not the latter, is formed in an environment of H_2O. But (purely) informational theories don't acknowledge this appeal. Such theories distinguish between concepts only if their tokenings are controlled by different laws. Hence only if different counterfactuals are true of their tokenings. Hence only if there are (possible) circumstances in which one concept would be caused to be tokened and the other concept would not. So if you want to have the WATER concept distinct from the WATER2 concept, and you want to play by the rules of a purely informational semantics, you have to assume a world where WATER is under the control of H_2O but *not* under the control of XYZ,[30] i.e., a world where H_2O and XYZ are distinguished (a fortiori, a world in which H_2O and XYZ are distinguishable). That is how you get from informational semantics to verificationism.

Correspondingly, the way you avoid the verificationism is: You relax the demand that semantic relations be construed solely by reference to subjunctive conditionals; you let the actual histories of tokenings count too. What follows is a sketch of a mixed theory of this sort. I propose three conditions on the relation between (a symbol) "X" and (a property) X, such that, when they are simultaneously satisfied, "X" expresses X. Or so I claim. I'll then comment, briefly, on the sorts of considerations that motivate each of these conditions. And then I'll say something about what sorts of facts are hard for this kind of theory to accommodate. And then I'll do a little tidying up and a little moralizing. And then—you'll be glad to hear—I propose to stop.

I claim that "X" means X if:

1. 'Xs cause "X"s' is a law.
2. Some "X"s are actually caused by Xs.
3. For all Y not=X, if Ys qua Ys actually cause "X"s, then Ys *causing "X"s* is asymmetrically dependent on Xs *causing "X"s.*

Comments:

Condition 1: 'X $\rightarrow$ "X"' is a law.

- This just follows Dretske. It ensures that "X"s *at least* carry information about Xs (but not, N.B., that they carry information *only* about Xs.)
- It also explains why "horse" means HORSE and not SMALL HORSE (even though small horses cause "horses" if horses do. The idea is that when small horses cause "horses" the covering law is *horse* $\rightarrow$ *"horse"* and not *small horse* $\rightarrow$ "horse" (see above).
- Notice, however, that condition 1 doesn't rule out "horse" means HORSE OR (COW ON A DARK NIGHT) since the connection between the property of being a "horse" token and the property of being an instance of *cow on a dark night* (unlike the connection between the property of being a "horse" token and the property of being an instance of *small horse*) presumably *is* nomic on the operative assumption that cows on dark nights qua cows on dark nights are sometimes mistaken for horses. That is, the information requirement doesn't, in and of itself, solve the disjunction problem. By now this should come as not news.

Condition 2: Some "X"s are actually caused by Xs.

- This invokes the actual history of "X" tokens as constitutive of the meaning of "X" and thereby violates the assumptions of pure informational theories.
- It rules out '"horse" means Twin-horse', '"water" means XYZ', and the like.
- It also allows the intuition that the first nonrobot-caused "cat" (in Baker's example) was *false,* in case that's the intuition that you feel inclined to have. (It doesn't *require* this intuition, however. If you don't have it, you're free to argue that, for semantical purposes, a causal history that includes only Xs counts as including Xs and Ys when the exclusion of the Ys was accidental;

in which case, the intuition should be that the first cat-occasioned "cat" means CAT OR ROBOT and is therefore true.)

Condition 3: Asymmetric dependence.

- This is the heart of the solution of the disjunction problem for the mixed theory as it was for the pure one: It rules out "horse" means HORSE OR COW ON A DARK NIGHT, given (a) the assumption that some cows on dark nights actually do cause "horses," and (b) the usual assumption about counterfactuals (viz., that cows on dark nights wouldn't cause "horses" but that horses do).

- Notice that we can't rely on condition 2 to do this job. It's one thing to assume that the actual history of "*X*" must contain Xs so that "horse" can't mean TWIN HORSE. It's quite another thing to suppose that it must contain *only* Xs (so that, if some cows on dark nights have caused "horses" then "horse" means HORSE OR COW ON A DARK NIGHT.) Having condition 2 in the theory allows actual histories of tokening to be constitutive of the semantic properties of symbols; condition 3 allows symbols to be robust with respect to their actual histories of tokening as well as with respect to their counterfactual histories. That is, it allows tokens of a symbol actually to be caused by things that are not its extension.

- Condition 3 is also required to rule out '"horse" means HORSE PICTURE', to account for the dependence of the metaphorical uses of "horse" upon its literal uses, and the like. Remember that not all non horse-occasioned "horse"s are ipso facto false.

General comment: The mixed theory is itself just a *soupçon* verificationist, but only in a way that might surely be considered untendentious. We used to have to say that "*X*"s meaning X requires the nomological possibility of distinguishing X from any property that *would* cause "*X*"s *if it were instantiated.* (Hence we had to say that "water" means something disjunctive unless there is a nomologically possible world in which H_2O is distinguished from XYZ, etc.) Now all we require is that it be nomologically possible to distinguish X from any property that is *actually* instantiated in the causal history of "*X*"s. (Any property that *doesn't* actually cause "*X*"s ipso facto fails to meet condition 2; that's why "water" doesn't mean XYZ according to the present account.) The theory is residually verificationist only in assuming that if cows-on-dark-nights actually do cause "horses," either "horse" means something disjunctive or it is nomologically possible to distinguish horses from cows-on-a-dark-night. (I.e., the residual verificationism is required so that tokens of "horse" that are caused by cows on dark nights can fall under condition 3.)

I think, in fact, that this much verificationism is probably built into causal theories of content per se. Thus, you get actual causal histories to bear on the semantics of kind-concepts by taking terms like "water" to mean something like *whatever bears the same-kind relation to the local samples*. This will make XYZ be not in the extension of "water" *on the assumption that there's no XYZ in the local samples*. If, by contrast, water tokens actually *are* caused indifferently by H_2O and XYZ, you can't appeal to actual histories to exclude XYZ from the extension of "water." And if they *would be* caused by H_2O and XYZ indifferently in any nomologically accessible world (if, that is to say, it's not nomologically possible to tell them apart) then you can't appeal to subjunctive causal conditionals to exclude XYZ from the extension of "water." So there seems to be *nothing left* to keep XYZ out of the extension of "water" consonant with assuming that what "water" means must have *something* to do with the causation of its tokens. My advice is, if this be verificationism, swallow it.

Notice, by the way, that it's still true, on the mixed view, that frogs snap at black dots rather than flies. For: some frog snap are caused by black dots (black dots satisfy condition 2); and there is no world compatible with the frog's psychology in which frogs snap at flies but not at black dots (flies fail to satisfy condition 3). Conversely, it's daggers—rather than dagger appearances—that Macbeth's DAGGER concept expresses because, although daggers and dagger appearances both cause DAGGER tokens in this world, still there are possible worlds in which Macbeth can tell them apart. Even if you don't want a *lot* of verificationism, you probably want a *little* verificationism to deal with semantical versions of the argument from illusion.

Here's what's happened: Where we used to have a *causal law* account of semantic properties, we now have an account that invokes both causal laws and actual causal histories. The resultant story is only minimally verificationist, which is arguably a good thing. But, of course, there is the usual nothing free for lunch. Pure informational theories aren't gratuitous; there are things they do better than mixed theories can. In particular, they're very good at unicorns.

Pure informational theories can treat "unicorn"s just the same way they treat "table"s and "chair"s. Since, according to such theories, all that semantic relations require is the right nomic connections among properties, and since you can have nomic connections among *uninstantiated* properties, all that's required for "unicorn"s to mean *unicorns* is a nomologically possible world in which the former are elicited by the latter, together with the satisfaction of the usual asymmetric dependence constraints. Uninstantiation is not, according to pure informational theories, a semantically *interesting* property of properties.

Mixed informational theories, by contrast, take quite a serious view of uninstantiation; in particular, "unicorn" can't mean UNICORN in virtue of satisfying conditions 1 to 3 since it fails egregiously to satisfy 2. The upshot is that, whereas pure theories can treat UNICORN as a *primitive* concept, mixed theories have to treat it as, in effect, an abbreviated description. Mixed theories have to say, in effect, that concepts that express uninstantiated properties are ipso facto constructions out of concepts that express instantiated properties; there is, no doubt, something quaintly Russellean in this. Perhaps, however, it's not a tragedy. Even pure theories have to say that "square circle" can't be primitive since, of course, there isn't a nomologically possible world in which "square circles" are caused by instantiations of *square circle*hood. So, if the mixed theory that embraces 1 to 3 can't be *necessary* for content, neither can the corresponding pure theory that omits condition 2.

Pure and mixed theories both have to acknowledge primitive/derived as a distinction of kind. Still, pure theories can tolerate a rather closer connection between being *semantically* primitive and being *syntactically* simple than mixed theories can. I used to think (see "The Current Status of the Innateness Controversy" in Fodor, 1981c) that "primitive concept" just about meant "lexical concept" (viz., concept expressed by a syntactically simple predicate of, as it might be, English). I'm now inclined to think it just about means "lexical and instantiated concept." Extensionally, this probably makes vanishingly close to no difference because *uninstantiated lexical properties are very, very rare*. So rare that one might risk the speculation that their rarity isn't an accident. Maybe the *instantiated lexical concepts* constitute a semantical natural kind.

Summary: How God Knows What You're Thinking.

"Even God couldn't tell, just by looking in your head, the intentional content of your neural states."[31] That's a way of summarizing the "externalist" view of content. It's also a way of rejecting "functional role" semantics since, according to functional role theories, when you know the facts about the intramental causal relations of a mental state, you know the facts on which its content supervenes.

Robustness ups the ante. If, as I've been supposing, the etiology of the tokens of an intentional state can be practically arbitrarily heterogeneous consonant with all the tokens having the same content, then it presumably follows that even God couldn't tell what the content of a mental state is just by looking at its *actual* causal relations. And this may seem unsatisfactory, because really *causal*—as opposed to informational—theories would have it that the actual causal relations of a mental state token are what *determines* its content. At the heart of such theories is the intuition that it must be something like *being caused by a cat* that makes a certain thought a *cat*-thought. The tug of war between this sort of intuition and the facts about robustness has been a main theme in our discussion; indeed, the 'mixed' story about content is an attempt to give both the causal and the nomic theories their due.

What's in your head doesn't determine content and actual causal relations don't determine content, but: If God has a look at both the actual causal relations of your mental state *and* the surrounding space of counterfactual causal relations, *then* He can tell the content of your state. The content of a state supervenes on its actual causal relations together with certain counterfactuals. Or so I claim.

If this is true then (barring some caveats we'll look at presently) it solves Brentano's problem about the possibility of providing a naturalistic account of content. So if it's true, it's important. Just by way of making the claim graphic, I propose to run through an example that shows how, assuming the theory, Omniscience might consult the actual causal relations of a mental state, together with relevant counterfactuals, to resolve a simple case of the disjunction problem. This may do as a summary of the body of doctrine that I've been developing.

For simplicity, I assume that what God sees when He looks in your head is a lot of light bulbs, each with a letter on it. (High-tech heads have LCDs.) A mental-state type is specified by saying which bulbs are on in your head when you are in the state. A token of a mental-state type is a region of space time in which the corresponding array of bulbs is lit. This is, I imagine, as close to neurological plausibility as it is ever necessary to come for serious philosophical purposes.

What God sees when he looks at the relations between what's in your head and what's in the world is that there are many cases in which the bulbs turn on and off in lawful correlation with features of, say, the local distal environment. He can tell that these relations *are* lawful because He can tell that they are counterfactual supporting. And He can tell that they are counterfactual supporting because, by assumption, He can see not just actual causal relations but the space of counterfactuals that surround them.

Let's suppose that here is how it looks to Him in a particular case; say, in *your* particular case. There is a light bulb marked *c* that regularly goes on when there are cats around; and there is light bulb marked s that regularly goes on when there are shoes around. We can assume that the right story is that c's being on means *cat* (i.e., it constitutes your entertaining as a token of the concept CAT) and s's being on means *shoe*.

But God can't assume this; at least, not yet. The reason He can't is that He's got problems about robustness. It turns out that though some of the c tokenings in your head are caused by cats, it's also true that some of your c tokenings are caused by shoes. Moreover, like the cat $\to c$ causal pattern, the shoe $\to c$ causal pattern supports counterfactuals; there are circumstances in which shoes cause cs *reliably*. (I assume that the statistics don't matter; that is, it doesn't matter to the intentional content of c-states what the relative frequency of shoe-caused cs to cat-caused cs turns out to be. God doesn't play dice with intentional ascriptions.)

Also, God has trouble with Twin-cats. Twin-cats are robots, hence neither cats nor shoes. But they would turn on the c bulb in virtue of the similarity between Twin-cats and real cats, and they would turn on the s-bulb in virtue of the similarity between Twin-cats and real shoes. Since God can see counterfactuals, He is able to see that all of this is true.

Because God has these troubles with robustness and Twins, He has a disjunction problem. The way it's *supposed* to come out is that the cs Twin-cats would cause, like the cs that shoes do or would cause, are semantically just like the cs that cats do cause, viz., they all mean *cat*. Cases where shoes cause cs are cases where shoes are *mistaken* for cats; cases where Twin-cats cause cs are cases where Twins would be mistaken for cats if there were any.

God, cannot, however, take the way it's supposed to turn out for granted. Charity requires that He consider an alternative hypothesis, viz., that c is ambiguous, with some c tokens meaning *shoe* and some meaning *Twin-cat*.[32] Here's how God resolves the dilemma. He asks Himself, "What was the actual causal pattern like?" and "What would the causal patterns have been like in a world that's relevantly like the real one except that, in the counterfactual world, cs aren't caused by cats?"

The answer to the first question rules out the Twins; there are no Twin-cats in the actual causal history of c tokenings, so c tokenings don't mean Twin-cats.[33] The answer to the second question is supposed to rule out the shoes. There are two relevant possibilities here:

One is that you would have gotten the shoe-caused c tokens even if the cat $\to c$ connection hadn't been in place. But then, these shoe-caused c tokens can't mean *cat*. For: No symbol means *cat* unless it carries information about cats. But no symbol carries information about cats unless its tokenings are somehow nomically dependent upon cats. But, on the present assumptions, shoe-caused c-tokenings *aren't* nomically dependent on cats; you'd get them even in worlds where the cat $\rightarrow$ c connection is broken. The point is that if shoes causing cs isn't *somehow* nomically dependent on cats causing cs, then God can only take shoe-caused cs to mean *cat* if He is prepared to give up the basic principle of information-based semantics; viz., that the content of a symbol is *somehow* dependent on the lawful causal relations that its tokens enter into. I assume that God is not about to give this up.

The other relevant possibility is that shoes wouldn't cause cs if cats didn't cause cs. If this counterfactual is true, then God can square the assumption that c means *cat* with—on the one hand—there being cs that aren't caused by cats (robustness) and,—on the other hand— the foundational intuition that a symbol means *cat* in virtue of some sort of reliable causal connection that its tokens bear to cats. If even shoe-caused cs are causally dependent on cats—in the sense that if cats didn't cause cs then shoes wouldn't either—then it's OK for God to read a c-token as meaning *cat* even when it's caused by a shoe.

So God can tell the intentional content of your neural state by looking at its actual causal relations and at relevant counterfactuals; in effect, He can apply the method of differences, just like any other rational agent. So there's a fact of the matter about what the intentional content of your neural state *is*. So God doesn't have to worry about Brentano's problem. And neither do we.

Or so it seems.

Conclusion: Have We Solved Brentano's Problem?

Suppose that everything in this paper is true. Then what we have is an explication of a semantical relation (viz., the semantical relation between a syntactically primitive predicate and the property it expresses) couched in a vocabulary that involves only naturalistic (specifically causal) expressions and expressions that denote intensional with-an-s objects (specifically expressions that denote laws and properties.) It comes out of this treatment that symbols can be both robust and informative, consonant with the basic symbol-making relation being nomic dependence. Since, moreover, the account is entirely atomistic, it follows that the connection between intentionality and holism isn't *intrinsic*, ever so many fashionable philosophers recently to the contrary notwithstanding.

So, does this solve Brentano's problem? Or, to put it another way, *does information plus robustness equal content*? Are information and robustness all you need for intentionality?

I don't know the answer to this question. The standard objection to the identification of content with information is the disjunction problem. Correspondingly, I've tacitly assumed throughout this paper that if you can get a theory of content that squares the intuition that "*X*" means *X* only if "*X*" tokens carry information about *X*-instantiation with the intuition that "*X*" means *X* only if you can have *X*-tokens that aren't caused by *X*s, then you've done all that a solution to Brentano's problem is required to do. Maybe, however, there are reasons for wanting more than information and robustness for content. What might these reasons be?

Well, there are people who think that you have to throw in some consciousness, for example. However, to insist on an internal connection between content and consciousness in the face of a successful research program, from Freud to Chomsky, that depends on denying that there is one, seems to me vaguely Luddite.)[34] I don't, therefore, propose to take this idea seriously; but I do agree that if I'm wrong, and it is a serious idea, then the problem of intentionality is probably hopeless because the problem of consciousness is probably hopeless.

Another possibility is that you have to throw in some normativity. I am sort of in sympathy with this. Robustness captures the point that some ways of using symbols are ontologically parasitic on others. But we surely want more; we want it to turn out that some ways of using symbols are *wrong*.[35] Where, in the picture of representation that we've been constructing, does the idea get a foothold that there are *mis*representations; and that they are things to be avoided?

One might consider trying to derive the normative relations from the ontological ones, but at second thought, this seems not plausible. There's no obvious reason why the fact that one way of using a symbol is asymmetrically dependent on another implies that we should prefer the second way of using it to the first. It seems, not just here but also in the general case, that ontological priority is normatively neutral, Plato to the contrary notwithstanding. What to do?

The reader who has followed the argument the whole weary way to here may now be feeling a twinge of nostalgia for the teleological account of content deprecated in chapter 3. As I remarked at the time, talk of function brings (a kind of, anyhow) normative talk in its train; wherever you have functions, you have the logical space for misfunctions and malfunctions too. It's therefore arguable that teleological theories go some way toward reconciling the demands of naturalism with the normativity of intentional ascription, with semantic evaluations being really evaluative. Too bad teleological theories are so rotten at resolving intentional indeterminacy.

It's not, however, out of the question that we might have it both ways. The arguments in chapter 3 seem to me to show pretty conclusively that you cannot derive the intentional content of a mental state from its biological function (not, at least, if your account of its biological function is grounded in its selectional history). But it might be well-advised to try going the other way 'round: given an independent, nonteleological, naturalistic account of content (like, for example, the one that we've been working on), you might try construing the function of a mental state by reference to what it represents. For example, the function of the belief that P is to represent the world as being such that P on (certain) occasions when it's the case that P. Talking this way does nothing to offend naturalistic scruples given that the notion of representation is independently defined.

It is, moreover, an argument for this order of analysis that the account of the function of intentional states that it provides is plausibly *true*. I assume that (anyhow, higher) organisms are species of decision theoretic machines; plus or minus a bit, they act in ways that will maximize their utilities if (and, except by luck, only if) their beliefs are true. What is therefore required of a belief in order that it should perform its function in such a machine is that it should *be* true. So, to that extent, false beliefs ipso facto fail to perform their functions. It might turn out, on this sort of view, that there are no normative implications of representation per se. Representation is just a certain kind of causal relation—it's just information plus asymmetric dependence—and as such it's neither a good thing nor a bad. Evaluation gets a grip when representational states have functions that are defined by reference to their contents (when a state that represents the world as such and such has the function of representing the world as such and such). In these cases, misrepresentations are failures of function and are, as such, to be deplored.

This is, however, all very complicated; there's a lot more to be done if this sort of story is to be made convincing. For example, if Freud was right some false beliefs perform *a* function by screening unbearable truths. Do they thereby perform *their* function? If so, it looks like false beliefs can be functional, so semantic evaluation and functional evaluation come apart. This throws doubt on the current project, which proposes, in effect, that misrepresentation is a bad thing *because* it's a species of malfunction. I don't know how seriously one should take such examples, and I don't propose to explore the issue any further here. Perhaps we could leave it at this: *if* you're moved by the idea of a teleological account of the normativity of intentional ascription, that option is still open even if you think (as I think you ought to) that teleological accounts of *content* are hopeless.

Well, then, suppose we can finesse the normativity issue in something like the way I've just discussed. Would it *then* be reasonable to claim to have solved Brentano's problem? Here's a thought intended to placate philosophers who hold it a matter of principle that no philosophical problem should ever be solved: Even if it's true that intentionality equals information plus robustness, it wouldn't have to follow that information plus robustness is sufficient for *mentality*. Sufficient conditions for being in a state with intentional content needn't also be sufficient conditions for having a belief or a desire or, indeed, for being in any other *psychological* condition.

It's arguable, for example, that beliefs aren't just states that have content; they're states that have content *and* whose causal relations obey the axioms of some reasonable decision theory; and the axioms of some reasonable theory of inference, etc. No argument I've heard of shows that you can't satisfy the intentionality condition for being a belief without satisfying these others. (Functional-role theories of content might well entail this since they generally connect content with 'minimal rationality'; so much the worse for them.) If content is just information plus robustness, a good theory of content might license the literal ascription of (underived) intentionality to thermometers, thermostats, and the like; that is, it might turn out on a good theory of content that some of the states of such devices are semantically evaluable. I don't think that should count as a reductio, though (in my view) the ascription of beliefs and desires to thermometers or thermostats certainly would.

In short, it might turn out that the intentional is a big superset of the psychological, and that might be acceptable so long as it isn't a *crazy* superset of the psychological (so long as it doesn't include everything, for ex. mple). It's good to remember this when you're working over your intuitions, looking for counterexamples to putative solutions of Brentano's problem; one does not refute a theory that entails that state S has content such-and-such just by showing that S is not a propositional attitude. It's also good to remember that the intentional might be a big superset of the psychological if you're inclined to weep over the possibility of Brentano's problem being solved. Solving Brentano's problem might, after all, leave most of the philosophy of mind still in the old familiar mess; so no technological unemployment need result.

Last Word. Suppose we had naturalistically sufficient conditions for content. It wouldn't, of course, follow that any of our neural states, or any of our public symbols have the content that they do because they satisfy the conditions on offer. Indeed, it wouldn't follow from the mere existence of sufficient conditions for content that anything in the universe has actually got any. '*P* implies *Q*' is neutral about *Q*. God can accept the consequents of any true hypotheticals whose antecedents He doesn't know to be false; but we can't.

On the other hand, if there are naturalistic sufficient conditions for content, and if we don't know these conditions not to be satisfied, then we would at least be in a position to claim, for example, that "cat" *could* mean *cat* for all we know to the contrary. This would be a satisfactory situation for the philosophy of mind (or the philosophy of language, or whatever this stuff is) to have finally arrived at. For, the prima facie plausibility that "cat" *does* mean *cat* is, after all, pretty substantial. I don't know about you guys, but when friends in other lines of work ask me what philosophers are into these days, and I tell them that these days philosophers are into claiming that really, deep down—in a first-class conceptual system, you know?—*it's not true* that "cat" means *cat* . . . they laugh at me. I do find that embarrassing.

Acknowledgments

I want to express a special indebtedness to Paul Boghossian for very helpful conversations on these topics and for having caught a bad mistake in an earlier draft of this paper. Literally dozens of other people have made suggestions I've found illuminating. They include all, but not only, the following (and I hereby apologize to anyone I have left out): Louise Antony, Lynne Baker, Ned Block, Dan Dennett, Michael Devitt, Joe Levine, Barry Loewer, Tim Maudlin, Brian McLaughlin, Georges Rey, Steve Wagner, and many graduate students at Rutgers and CUNY.

Notes

1. A variant of the theory that I'll discuss near the end departs significantly from the letter of informational semantics, though perhaps less significantly from its spirit.
2. For the type one/type two distinction, see chapter 3.
3. Compare *Psychosemantics* (1987), in which I took it for granted—wrongly, as I now think—that an information-based semantics would have to specify such circumstances. As far as I can tell, I assumed this because I thought that any informational theory of content would have to amount to a more or less hedged version of 'all and only cows cause "cow"s'. This, too, was a failure to take semantic robustness sufficiently seriously. It's no more plausible that there are nonquestion-beggingly

specifiable situations in which it's semantically necessary that all cows cause "cows" than that there are such situations in which, necessarily, only cows do. How *could* there be circumstances in which the content of a thought guarantees that someone will think it?

4. As are all other "nonlabeling" uses of a symbol. See Fodor [in press].

5. Well, *almost* arbitrarily robust; see below.

6. Though not, of course, without resort to intentional (with-an-"s") idiom. The asymmetric dependence story is up to its ears in Realism about properties, relations, laws, and other abstracta. Whether this sort of Realism prejudices a semantic theory's claim to be physicalistic—and whether, if it does, it *matters* whether a semantic theory is physicalistic—are questions of some interest; but not ones that I propose to take on here. Suffice it that *naturalism*, as I understand the term, needn't imply *materialism* if the latter is understood as denying independent ontological status to abstract entities.

7. The caveat is because informational semanticists rarely straight out identify "meaning that. . . ." with "carrying the information that . . . ." (though Isreal seems to be right on the edge of doing so in the passage cited in the text). Dretske, for example, adds constraints intended to ensure that the information carried should be *perfectly* reliable, and that it should be "digitally" encoded (this is Dretske's way of ensuring that "dog" means *dog* rather than *animal*.) Also, the Stanford theorists generally allow that information can be generated by reliable relations other than causal ones (e.g., entailment relations). These considerations don't, however, affect the point in the text.

8. As Georges Rey remarks, "The viability of a ceteris paribus clause depends not upon the actual specification or realizability of the idealization, but rather upon whether the apparent exceptions to the law to which it is attached can be explained as due to independently specifiable interference. It is a check written on the banks of independent theories, which is only as good as those theories and *their* independent evidence can make it. So the question . . . is not whether the ceteris paribus clause can be replaced, but rather: Can all the errors be explained as indpendent interference?" (Rey, ms.) It's worth spelling out an implication of Rey's point: To know what, in general, the consequence of satisfying a ceteris paribus condition would be, we would have to know what would happen if none of the sources of "independent interference" were operative. And to know *that*, we'd have to know, at a minimum, what the sources of independent interference *are*; we'd have to know which other laws can interact with the ceteris paribus law under examination. But, of course, it's never possible to know (much) of this under the conditions actually operative in scientific theory construction; what interactions between L and other laws are possible depends not just on how L turns out, but also on *how the rest of science turns out*.

9. This counterfactual is, of course, by no means vacuous. It claims, in effect, that our capacities to add are bounded *only* by the limitations of our working memory; in particular, they aren't bounded *by what we know about how to add numbers*. Such claims are, to put it mildly, often nonobvious. For example, as of this date nobody knows whether it's true that, but for memory constraints, a normal English speaker could parse every sentence of his language. ("Garden path" sentences appear to offer counterexamples.) As it turns out, the resolution of some rather deep issues in linguistics depend on this question.

10. For example, Steven Wagner's "Theories of Mental Representation" (ms) criticizes one version of the view I'll be proposing by remarking that it "has the *wildly*

implausible consequence that there are worlds remotely like ours in which cows could not be mistaken for horses." In fact, what I hold is only that if "cow" means *cow* and not *horse* then it must be nomologically possible to tell any cow from a horse; which doesn't sound all *that* wild after all. (Actually, there's a version of my story that requires still less; see the discussion of verificationism below.) You get the consequence that Wagner denounces only if you conjoin my story about semantics to the story about modals that says that if P is nomologically possible, then there is a world in which it's the case that P. So much the worse for that story about modals.

11. To be sure, this can't be the *only* way that asymmetric dependence gets its foothold. For example: if, as I'm claiming, the use of linguistic symbols to effect mislabelings, false predications, and the like is asymmetrically dependent on their being applied correctly, that asymmetry can't arise from linguistic practices in anything like the way that the asymmetric dependence of pagings on namings does; there's a *convention* for paging, but not for mislabeling. And, of course, we have no linguistic practices (no conventions) at all with respect to our mental representations. Patience, dear Reader; all in good time.

12. I'll use "concept" ambiguously; sometimes it refers to a mental representation (thus following psychological usage) and sometimes to the intension of a mental representation (thus following philosophical usage). The context will often make clear which reading is at issue. When I wish to name a concept, I'll use the corresponding English word in caps; hence, "COW" for the concept cow.

13. Roughly, a symbol is syntactically primitive iff it has no semantically evaluable proper parts.

14. Baker raises her problem for tokens of Mentalese, but nothing turns on this, and English is easier to spell.

15. There may be readers who demand a semantics that makes the first "cat" token come out false (i.e., who demand that it mean *robot-cat*). I beg a temporary suspension of their disbelief. We'll see further on how the theory could be revised to accommodate them.

16. I think these sorts of cases throw some interesting side light on the standard Twin Earth examples. It's usual in the literature to take the moral of the Twin cases to be the significance of context in determining content: "Water" means H_2O because there isn't any XYZ on earth. But Dretske's case opens the possibility of super-Twins: creatures who have not only type-identical neural structures, but who also share a context (in some reasonable sense), but whose intentional states nevertheless differ in content: the extension of A's term "water" includes XYZ and the extension of B's term "water" does not because it's fortuitous for A but not for B that he has encountered no samples of XYZ.

Apparently, then, the content of your term may differ from the content of mine if there's something that prevents tokens of your term from being caused by instantiations of a property whose instantiations could (i.e., really could, not just nomologically possibly could) cause tokenings of mine. This might be true even of two creatures who live in the same world if, as it happens, they live in different parts of the wood. If the nearest XYZ to me is so far away that I can't possibly get there in a lifetime, then, I suppose, "water" means something nondisjunctive in my mouth. Whereas, if the nearest XYZ to you is so close that it's just an accident that you haven't come across any, then, I suppose, "water" does mean something disjunctive in yours.

Does any of this matter? If so, to what?

17. The hyphens are because nobody could think that the frog has the disjunctive concept FLY OR BEE BEE (just as nobody could think that *S* has the disjunctive concept CAT OR ROBOT CAT in the Baker case discussed above). The issue, rather, is whether the frog has the concept FLY or the concept of a certain visible property which, de facto, flies and bee bees both exhibit.

18. It's crucial that this claim be read *synchronically* since, presumably, frogs wouldn't develop a disposition to snap at black dots in worlds where the black dots have *never* been flies. The semantically relevant sort of asymmetric dependence is a relation among an organism's *current* dispositions. Take real-world frogs and put them in possible worlds where the black dots are bee-bees and they'll snap away, happy as the day is long. But real-world frogs in possible worlds where the flies aren't black dots are ipso facto snapless.

19. Cf: "Is this a dagger which I see before me . . ./ Come, let me clutch thee./I have thee not, and yet I see thee still./ Art thou not, fatal vision, sensible/ To feeling as to sight? or art thou but/ A dagger of the mind, a false creation,/ Proceeding from the heat-oppressed brain?" Macbeth's morals were, no doubt, reprehensible, but his epistemology was spot on.

20. I've thus far made a point of not distinguishing two theses: (a) if *X* and *Y* are distinct concepts, then there must be a world in which *x*s but not *y*s cause "*X*"s; (b) if *X* and *Y* are distinct concepts *and xs and ys both cause* "*X*"*s in* this *world* then there must be a world in which *x*s but not *y*s cause "*X*"s. The (b) story is markedly less verificationist than the (a) story and some philosophers may prefer it on that ground. We'll come to this presently; but suffice it for now that both stories say the same things about what frogs snap at and about what Macbeth means by "dagger."

21. For further discussion of the analogy between the function of theories and of instruments of observation in mediating the symbol/world relations upon which content depends, see chapter 3 (especially fn.4); also Fodor, *Psychosemantics*, chapter 4.

22. The case is a little different when states of the central nervous system (as opposed, e.g., to retinal states) are proposed as the intentional objects of the thoughts that cows causally occasion. I suppose it might turn out that there are specifiable, *non*disjunctive states of the brain upon whose tokening the connection of cow-occasioned thoughts to cows asymmetrically depend. Such a discovery would not, however, require us to say that the intentional object of one's cow thoughts are brain states. Rather, we could simply take the brainstate tokens to be tokens of the Mentalese term for cow.

23. I say that one *might* rule out proximal referents for mental representations by appeal to the principle that open disjunctions aren't projectible. But one could also take the high ground and rule them out by stipulation: just as primitive symbols aren't allowed to express necessarily uninstantiated properties, so too they aren't allowed to express proximal properties. If this seems arbitrary, remember that we're looking for (naturalistically) *sufficient* conditions for representation.

24. And not vice versa. But where the asymmetry of the dependence is not germane to the point at issue I'll leave this clause out to simplify the exposition.

25. I take it that, but for the talk about intentions and policies, the same sort of line applies to kind-concepts. What makes something a kind-concept, according to his view, is what it tracks in worlds where instances of the kind to which it applies are distinguishable from instances of the kinds to which it doesn't

26. "E.g." rather than "i.e." because, for present purposes, we're not attending to the distinction between disjunctive predicates and ambiguous ones.

27. Boghossian isn't the only critic who has objected to the verificationist implications of the sort of treatment I've been proposing. Cf. Cummins (1989) and Wagner (ms).

28. For those keeping score: The information and asymmetric dependence conditions are clauses in a (putatively) sufficient condition for "X" expressing X; i.e., they are severally necessary and jointly sufficient conditions for the satisfaction of a sufficient condition.

29. Dretske is himself not faithful to purely informational semantics; his proposal for dealing with the disjunction problem requires that facts about the history of acquisition of a concept are relevant to determining its extension (see chapter 3). There's nothing unreasonable about this—there's no a priori argument that pure informational theories are better than impure ones. But, as we've seen, Dretske's way of adding a dash of causal history to his purely informational story doesn't get him where he wants to go.

30. A world where there is H_2O but not XYZ (or vice versa) doesn't count, because although only H_2O controls the *actual* WATER tokenings in worlds where there is only H_2O, XYZ controls *counterfactual* WATER tokenings in those worlds assuming that the connection between XYZ and WATER tokens is nomic. Remember unicorns: there can be laws about uninstantiated properties.

31. By contrast, He could tell just by looking in your head which of your mental states are in the ranges and domains of which of your mental processes. At least, He could if He's a methodological solipsist, which I'm sure He is.

32. I don't have a story about the difference between ambiguity and disjunctiveness that I feel like telling here so the "disjunction" problem is really the "disjunction or ambiguity" problem, as per note 26.

33. Strictly speaking, of course, the claim is only that if c-tokenings do mean Twins, then it must be in virtue of the satisfaction of some semantic condition other than the one we've been discussing. We've seen, as we've gone along, several reasons why our condition, though it is arguably sufficient for content, can't possibly be necessary.

34. Searle argues that consciousness must come in because nothing else suggests itself as distinguishing "derived" intentionality from the real thing. However, if the present story is right, this isn't so. Roughly, X's intentionality is real if it depends on X's satisfying conditions 1 to 3; X's intentionality is derived if it derives from Y's satisfying conditions 1 to 3, where $Y \neq X$.

35. Compare: "The crux of Kripke's reading of Wittgenstein may be put like this. It is of the essence of meaning an expression in a certain way, that meaning it that way determines how the expression would have to be used if it is to be used correctly. . . . Any proposed candidate for being the property in virtue of which an expression has meaning must be such as to ground the 'normativity' of meaning. . . ." (Boghossian, 1989, pp. 83–84.)

    I say that I am *sort of* sympathetic. The trouble is that requiring that normativity be grounded suggests that there is more to demand of a naturalized semantics than that it provide a reduction of such notions as, say, *extension*. But what could this 'more' amount to? To apply a term to a thing in its extension *is* to apply the term correctly; once you've said what it is that makes the tables the extension of "table"s, there is surely no *further* question about why it's *correct* to apply a "table" to a table. It thus seems that if you have a reductive theory of the semantic relations, there is no job of grounding normativity left to do.

In short, I'm not clear how—or whether—'open question' arguments can get a grip in the present case. I am darkly suspicious that the Kripkensteinian worry about the normative force of meaning is either a nonissue or just the reduction issue over again; anyhow, that it's not a *new* issue. In the text, however, I've surpressed these qualms.

Chapter 5

Making Mind Matter More

An outbreak of epiphobia (the fear that one is turning into an epi-phenomenalist) appears to have much of the philosophy of mind community in its grip. Though it is generally agreed to be compatible with physicalism that intentional states should be causally responsible for behavioral outcomes, epiphobics worry that it is *not* compatible with physicalism that intentional states should be causally responsible for behavioral outcomes *qua intentional*. So they fear that the very successes of a physicalistic (and/or a computational) psychology will entail the causal inertness of the mental. Fearing this makes them unhappy.

In this chapter, I want to argue that epiphobia is a neurotic worry; if there is a problem, it is engendered not by the actual-or-possible successes of physicalistic psychology, but by two philosophical mistakes: (a) a wrong idea about what it is for a property to be causally responsible, and (b) a complex of wrong ideas about the relations between special-science laws and the events that they subsume.[1] Here's how I propose to proceed: First, we'll have a little psychodrama; I want to give you a feel for how an otherwise healthy mind might succumb to epiphobia. Second, I'll provide a brief, sketchy, but I hope good-enough-for-present-purposes account of what it is for a property to be causally responsible. It will follow from this account that intentional properties are causally responsible if there are intentional causal laws. I'll then argue that (contrary to the doctrine called "anomalous monism") there is no good reason to doubt that there are intentional causal laws. I'll also argue that, so far as the matter affects the cluster of issues centering around epiphenomenalism, the sorts of relations that intentional causal laws can bear to the individuals they subsume are much the same as the sorts of relations that *non*intentional causal laws can bear to the individuals that *they* subsume. So then everything will be all right.

Causal Responsibility

There are many routes to epiphobia. One of them runs via two premises and a stipulation.

1. Premise of Supervenience of Causal Powers: The causal powers of an event are entirely determined by its physical properties. Suppose two events are identical in their physical properties; then all causal hypotheticals true of one event are true of the other. If, for example, $e1$ and $e2$ are events identical in their physical properties, then all hypotheticals of the form "if e1 occurred in situation S, it would cause. . . ." remain true if "$e2$" is substituted for "$e1$", and vice versa.

2. Premise of Property Dualism: Intentional properties supervene on physical properties, but no intentional property is identical to any physical property. (A physical property is a property expressible in the vocabulary of physics. Never mind for now what the vocabulary of physics is; just assume that it contains no intentional terms.)

3. Stipulation: A property is "causally responsible" iff it affects the causal powers of things that have it. And (also by stipulation) all properties that aren't causally responsible are epiphenomenal.

But then, consider the mental event m (let's say, an event which consists of you desiring to lift your arm) which is the cause of the behavioral event b (let's say, an event which consists of you lifting your arm). m does, of course, have certain intentional properties. But, according to premise 2, none of its intentional properties is identical to any of its physical properties. And, according to 3, m's physical properties fully determine its causal powers (including, of course, its power to cause b). So, it appears that m's being the cause of your lifting your arm doesn't depend on its being a desire to lift your arm; m would have caused your lifting of your arm even if it hadn't had its intentional properties, so long as its physical properties were preserved.[2] So it appears that m's intentional properties don't affect its causal powers. So it appears that m's intentional properties are causally inert. Clearly, this argument iterates to *any* intentional property of the cause of any behavioral effect. So the intentional properties of mental events are epiphenomenal. Epiphobia!

Now, the first thing to notice about this line of argument is that it has *nothing to do with intentionality as such.* On the contrary, it applies equally happily to prove the epiphenomenality of *any* nonphysical property, so long as property dualism is assumed. Consider, for example, the property of being a mountain; and suppose (what is surely plausible) that being a mountain isn't a physical property.

(Remember, this just means that "mountain" and its synonyms aren't items in the lexicon of physics.) Now, untutored intuition might suggest that many of the effects of mountains are attributable *to their being* mountains. Thus, untutored intuition suggests, it is because Mount Everest is a mountain that Mount Everest has glaciers on its top; and it is because Mount Everest is a mountain that it casts such a long shadow; and it is because Mount Everest is a mountain that so many people are provoked to try to climb it . . . and so on. But not so, according to the present line of argument. For, surely the causal powers of Mount Everest are fully determined by its physical properties, and we've agreed that *being a mountain* isn't one of the physical properties of mountains. So then, Mount Everest's being a mountain doesn't affect its causal powers. So then—contrary to what one reads in geology books—the property of being a mountain is causally inert. Geoepiphobia!

No doubt there will be those who are prepared to bite this bullet. Such folk may either (a) deny that property dualism applies to mountainhood (because, on reflection, *being a mountain* is a physical property after all) or (b) assert that it *is* intuitively plausible that *being a mountain* is causally inert (because, on reflection, it is intuitively plausible that it's not *being a mountain* but some other of Mount Everest's properties—specifically, some of its physical properties—that are causally responsible for its effects). So be it; I do not want this to turn into a squabble about cases. Instead, let me emphasize that there are lots and lots and *lots* of examples where, on the one hand, considerations like multiple realizability make it implausible that a certain property is expressible in physical vocabulary; and, on the other hand, claims for the causal inertness of the property appear to be wildly implausible, at least prima facie.

Consider the property of being a sail. I won't bore you with the fine points (terribly tempted, though I am, to exercise my hobbyhorse[3]). Suffice it that sails are *airfoils* and there is quite a nice little theory about the causal properties of airfoils. Typically, airfoils generate lift in a direction, and in amounts, that is determined by their geometry, their rigidity, and many, many details of their relations to the (liquid or gaseous) medium through which they move. The basic ideas is that lift is propagated at right angles to the surface of the airfoil along which the medium flows fastest, and is proportional to the relative velocity of the flow. Hold a flat piece of paper by one edge and blow across the top. The free side of the paper will move *up* (i.e., toward the air flow), and the harder you blow, the more it will do so. (Ceteris paribus.)

Now, the relative velocity of the airfoil may be increased by forcing the medium to flow through a "slot" (a constriction, one side of which is formed by the surface of the airfoil.) The controlling law is that the narrower the slot the faster the flow. (On sailboats of conventional Bermuda rig, the slot is the opening between the jib and the main. But perhaps you didn't want to know that.) Anyhow, airfoils and slots can be made out of all sorts of things; sails are airfoils, but so are keel-wings, and airplane wings, and bird's wings. Slots are multiply realizable too: you can have a slot both sides of which are made of sailcloth, as in the jib/mainsail arrangement, but you can also have a slot one side of which is made of sailcloth and the other side of which is made of *air*. (That's part of the explanation of why you can sail toward the wind even if you haven't got a jib). So then, if one of your reasons for doubting that *believing that P* is a physical property is that believing is multiply realizable, then you have the same reason for doubting that *being an airfoil* or *being a slot* counts as a physical property.

And yet, of course, it would seem to be quite mad to say that *being an airfoil* is causally inert. Airplanes fall down when you take their wings off; and sailboats come to a stop when you take down their sails. Everybody who isn't a philosopher agrees that these and other such facts are explained by the story about lift being generated by causal interactions between the airfoil and the medium. If that *isn't* the right explanation, what keeps the plane up? If that *is* the right explanation, how could it be that *being an airfoil* is causally inert?

Epiphobics primarily concerned with issues in the philosophy of mind might well stop here. The geological and aerodynamic analogies make it plausible that if there's a case for epiphenomenalism in respect of psychological properties, then there is the same case for epiphenomenalism in respect of *all* the nonphysical properties mentioned in theories in the special sciences. I pause, for a moment, to moralize about this:

Many philosophers have the bad habit of thinking about only two sciences when they think about sciences at all, these being psychology and physics. When in the grip of this habit, they are likely to infer that if psychological theories have some property that physical theories don't, that must be because psychological states (qua psychological) are intentional and physical states (qua physical) are not. In the present case, if there's an argument that psychological properties are epiphenomenal and no corresponding argument that physical properties are epiphenomenal, that must show that there is something funny about intentionality.

But we now see that it shows no such thing since, if the causal inertness of psychological properties is maintained along anything like the lines of 1–3, there are likely to be parallel arguments that *all properties are causally inert except those expressed by the vocabulary of physics*. In which case, *why should anybody care* whether psychological properties are epiphenomenal? All that anybody could reasonably want for psychology is that its constructs should enjoy whatever sort of explanatory/causal role is proper to the constructs of the special sciences. If beliefs and desires are as well off ontologically as mountains, wings, spiral nebulas, trees, gears, levers, and the like, then surely they're as well off as anyone could need them to be.

But, in fact, we shouldn't stop here. Because, though it's true that claims for the epiphenomenality of mountainhood and airfoilhood and, in general, of any nonphysical-property-you-like-hood, will follow from the same sorts of arguments that imply claims for the epiphenomenality of beliefhood and desirehood, it's also true that such claims are prima facie absurd. Whatever you may think about beliefs and desires and the other paraphrenalia of intentional psychology, it's a fact you have to live with that there are all these *non*intentional special sciences around; and that many, many—maybe even all—of the properties that figure in their laws are nonphysical too. Surely something *must* have gone wrong with arguments that show that all these properties are ephiphenomenal. How could there be laws about airfoils (notice, laws about *the causal consequences of something's being an airfoil*) if airfoilhood is epiphenomenal? How could there be a science of geology if geological properties are causally inert?

It seems to me, in light of the foregoing, that it ought to be a minimal condition upon a theory of what it is for something to be a causally responsible property that it does not entail the epiphenomenality of winghood, mountainhood, gearhood, leverhood, beliefhood, desirehood, and the like. I'm about to propose a theory which meets this condition and thereby commends itself as a tonic for epiphobics. This theory isn't, as you will see, very shocking or surprising or anything; actually it's pretty dull. Still, I need a little stage setting before I can tell you about it. In particular, I need some caveats and some assumptions.

Caveats
First, curing epiphobia requires making it plausible that intentional properties can meet sufficient conditions for causal responsibility; but one is not also required to show that they can meet *necessary and sufficient* conditions for causal responsibility. This is just as well, since necessary and sufficient conditions for causal responsibility might be sort of hard to come by (necessary and sufficient conditions for

anything tend to be sort of hard to come by) and I, for one, don't claim to have any.

Second, the question, "What makes a property causally responsible?" needs to be distinguished from the probably much harder question, "What determines which property is responsible in a given case when one event causes another?" Suppose that $e1$ causes $e2$; then, trivially, it must do so in virtue of some or other of its causally responsible properties; i.e., in virtue of some or other property in virtue of which it is able to be a cause. (Or, perhaps, in virtue of several such properties.[4]) But it may be that $e1$ has many—perhaps many, many—properties in virtue of which it is able to be a cause. So it must not be assumed that if $e1$ is capable of being a cause in virtue of having a certain property P, then P is ipso facto the property in virtue of which $e1$ is the cause of $e2$. Indeed, it must not even be assumed that if $e1$ is capable of being a cause *of $e2$* in virtue of its having P, then P is ipso facto the property in virtue of which $e1$ causes $e2$. For again it may be that $e1$ has many—even many, many— properties in virtue of which it is capable of being the cause of $e2$, and it need not be obvious which one of these properties is the one in virtue of which it actually *is* the cause $e2$. At least, I can assure you, it need not be obvious to me.

It is, to put all this a little less pedantically, one sort of success to show that it was in virtue of its intentional content that your desire to raise your hand made something happen. It is another, and lesser, sort of success to show that *being a desire to raise your hand* is the kind of property in virtue of which things *can* be made to happen. Curing epiphobia requires only a success of the latter, lesser sort.

Assumptions

I assume that singular causal statements need to be covered by causal laws. That means something like:

4. *Covering principle:* If an event $e1$ causes an event $e2$, then there are properties F, G such that:

>   4.1. $e1$ instantiates F
>   4.2. $e2$ instantiaties G

and

>   4.3. "F instantiations are sufficient for G instantiations" is a causal Law.[5]

When a pair of events bears this relation to a law, I'll say that the individuals are each *covered* or *subsumed* by that law and I'll say that the law *projects* the properties in virtue of which the individuals are subsumed by it. Notice that when an individual is covered by a law, it will always have some property in virtue of which the law subsumes it. If, for example, the covering law is that Fs cause Gs, then individuals that get covered by this law do so either in virtue of being Fs (in case they are subsumed by its antecedent) or in virtue of being Gs (in case they are subsumed by its consequent). This could all be made more precise, but I see no reason to bother.

OK, I can now tell you my sufficient condition for a property to be causally responsible:

5. *Condition*: P is a causally responsible property if it's a property in virtue of which individuals are subsumed by causal laws; equivalently:

> 5.1. P is a causally responsible property if it's a property projected by a causal law.

Or equivalently (since the satisfaction of the antecedent of a law is ipso facto nomologically sufficient for the satisfaction of its antecedent):

> 5.2. P is a causally responsible property if it's a property in virtue of the instantiation of which the occurrence of one event is nomologically sufficient for the occurrence of another.[6]

If this is right, then intentional properties are causally responsible in case there are intentional causal laws; aerodynamic properties are causally responsible in case there are aerodynamic causal laws; geological properties are causally responsible in case there are geological causal laws . . . and so forth. To all intents and purposes, on this view the question whether the property P is causally responsible *reduces to* the question whether there are causal laws about P. To settle the second question *is* to settle the first.

I don't mind it if you find this proposal dull, but I would be distressed if you found it circular. How, you might ask, can one possibly make progress by defining "*causally* responsible property" in terms of "covering *causal* law"? And yet it's unclear that we can just drop the requirement that the covering law *be* causal because there are *non*causal laws (e.g., the gas law about pressure and volume varying inversely) and perhaps an event's being covered by those sorts of laws *isn't* sufficient for its having a causally responsible property.

I can think of two fairly plausible ways out of this. First, it may be that any property in virtue of which some law covers an individual will be a property in virtue of which some causal law covers an individual;[7] i.e., that no property figures *only* in noncausal laws. This is, I think, an interesting metaphysical possibility; if it is true, then we can just identify the causally responsible properties with the properties in virtue of which individuals are covered by laws.

And, even if it's not true, it may be that what makes a law causal can itself be specified in noncausal terms; perhaps it involves such properties as covering temporal successions, being asymmetric, and the like. In that case it would be OK to construe "causally responsible" in terms of "causal law" since the latter could be independently defined. Barring arguments to the contrary, I'm prepared to suppose that this will work.

We're now in a position to do a little diagnosis. According to the present view, the properties projected in the laws of basic science are causally responsible, and so too are the properties projected in the laws of the special sciences. This is truistic since the present view just is that being projected is sufficient for being causally responsible. Notice, in particular, that even if the properties that the special sciences talk about are supervenient upon the properties that the basic sciences talk about, that does *not* argue that the properties that the special sciences talk about are epiphenomenal. Not, at least, if there are causal laws of the special sciences. The causal laws of the special sciences and causal laws of basic sciences have it in common that they *both* license ascriptions of causal responsibility. Or so, at least, the present view would have it.

This is not, however, to deny that there are metaphysically interesting differences between special science laws and basic science laws. Let me introduce here a point that I propose to make a fuss of later.

Roughly, the satisfaction of the antecedent of a law is nomologically sufficient for the satisfaction of its consequent[8] (I'll sometimes say that the truth of the antecedent of a law *nomologically necessitates* the truth of its consequent.). But a metaphysically interesting difference between basic and nonbasic laws is that, in the case of the latter but not the former, there always has to be *a mechanism in virtue of which* the satisfaction of its antecedent brings about the satisfaction of its consequent. If 'Fs cause Gs' is basic, then there is no answer to the question *how* do Fs cause Gs; they just do, and that they do is among the not-to-be-further-explained facts about the way the world is put together. Whereas, if 'Fs cause Gs' is *non*basic, then there is always a story about what goes on when—and in virtue of which—Fs cause Gs.

Sometimes it's a microstructure story (meandering rivers erode their outside banks; facts about the abrasive effects of particles suspended in moving water explain why there is erosion; the Bernoulli effect explains why it's the *outside* banks that get eroded most). Sometimes there's a story about chains of macrolevel events that intervene between F-instantiations and G-instantiations (Changes in CO_2 levels in the atmosphere cause changes in fauna. There's a story about how CO_2 blocks radiation from the Earth's surface; and there's a story about how the blocked radiation changes the air temperature; and there's a story about how changes in the air temperature cause climactic changes; and there's a (Darwinian) story about how climactic changes have zoological impacts. I try to be as topical as I can.)

Or, to get closer home, consider the case in computational psychology. There are—so I fondly suppose—intentional laws that connect, for example, states of believing that P & $(P \rightarrow Q)$ to states of believing that Q. (Ceteris paribus, of course. More of that latter.) Because there are events covered by such laws, it follows (trivially) that intentional properties (like *believing that P & (P →Q)* are causally responsible. And because nobody (except, maybe, panpsychists; whom I am prepared not to take seriously for present purposes) thinks that intentional laws are basic, it follows that there must be a mechanism in virtue of which believing that P & $(P \rightarrow Q)$ *brings it about* that one believes Q.

There are, as it happens, some reasonably persuasive theories about the nature of such mechanisms currently on offer. The one I like best says that the mechanisms that implement intentional laws are computational. Roughly, the story goes: believing (etc.) is a relation between an organism and a mental representation. Mental representations have (inter alia) syntactic properties; and the mechanisms of belief change are defined over the syntactic properties of mental representations. Let's not worry, for the moment, about whether this story is right; let's just worry about whether it's epiphobic.

Various philosophers have supposed that it is. Steven Stich, for example, has done some public hand-wringing about how anybody (a fortiori, how I) could hold *both* that intentional properties are causally responsible *and* the ("methodologically solipsistic") view that mental processes are entirely computational (/syntactic). And Norbert Hornstein[9] has recently ascribed to me the view that "the generalizations of psychology, the laws and the theories, are stated over syntactic objects, i.e., it is over syntactic representations that computations proceed." But: *the claim that mental processes are syntactic does not entail the claim that the laws of psychology are syntactic.* On the contrary, *the laws of psychology are intentional through and through.*

This is a point to the reiteration of which my declining years seem somehow to have become devoted. What's syntactic is not the laws of psychology but the mechanisms by which the laws of psychology are implemented. Cf.: The mechanisms of geological processes are (as it might be) chemical and molecular; it does not follow that chemical or molecular properties are projected by geological laws (on the contrary, it's geological properties that are projected by geological laws); and it does not follow that geological properties are causally inert (on the contrary, it's because Mount Everest is such a very damned big mountain that it's so very damned cold on top.)

It is, I should add, not in the least unusual to find that the vocabulary that's appropriate to articulate a special-science law is systematically different from the vocabulary that's appropriate to articulate its implementing mechanism(s). Rather, shift of vocabulary as one goes from the law to the mechanism is the *general* case. If you want to talk laws of inheritance, you talk recessive traits and dominant traits and homozygotes and heterozygotes; if you want to talk mechanisms of inheritance, you talk chromosomes and genes and how the DNA folds. If you want to talk psychological law, you talk intentional vocabulary; if you want to talk psychological mechanism, you talk syntactic (or maybe neurological) vocabulary. If you want to talk geological law, you talk mountains and glaciers; if you want to talk geological mechanism, you talk abrasion coefficients and cleavage planes. If you want to talk aerodynamic law, you talk airfoils and lift forces; if you want to talk aerodynamic mechanism, you talk gas pressure and laminar flows. It doesn't follow that the property of being a belief or an airfoil or a recessive trait is causally inert; all that follows is that *specifying the causally responsible macroproperty isn't the same as specifying the implementing micromechanism.*

It's a confusion to suppose that, if there's a law, then there needn't be an implementing mechanism; and it's a confusion to suppose there if there's a mechanism that implements a law, then the properties that the law projects must be causally inert. If you take great care to avoid both these confusions, you will be delighted to see how rapidly your epiphobia disappears. You really will. Trust me.

Intentional Laws

According to the position just developed, the question whether a property is causally responsible reduces to the question whether it is a property in virtue of which individuals are subsumed by covering causal laws. So in particular, if there are intentional laws, then it follows that intentional properties aren't epiphenomenal. But maybe there aren't intentional laws; or, if there are, maybe they can't cover individual causes in the way that causal laws are supposed to cover the events that they subsume. The view that this is so is widespread in recent philosophy of mind. Clearly, if intentional covering doesn't actually happen, the question whether it would be sufficient for the causal responsibility of the mental if it were to happen is academic even by academic standards. And the treatment for epiphobia that I prescribed above won't work. The rest of the paper will be devoted to this issue.

There seems to be some tension between the following three principles, each of which I take to be prima facie sort of plausible:

6. Strict covering: Just like 4 except with the following in place of 4.3:

> "Pl instantiations are causally sufficient for P2 instantiations" is a *strict* causal law.

7. Anomia of the mental: The only strict laws are laws of physics. Specifically, there are no strict 'psychophysical' laws relating types of brain states to types of intentional states; and there are no strict 'psychological' laws relating types of mental events to one another or to types of behavioral outcomes.

8. Causal responsibility of the mental: Intentional properties aren't epiphenomenal.

Principle 6 means something like this: Causal transactions must be covered by exceptionless laws; the satisfaction of the antecedent of a covering law has to provide literally nomologically sufficient conditions for the satisfaction of its consequent so that its consequent is satisfied in every nomologically possible situation in which its antecedent is satisfied.

Principle 7 means something like this: The laws of physics differ in a characteristic way from the laws of the special sciences (notably including psychology). Special science laws are typically hedged with 'ceteris paribus' clauses, so that whereas physical laws say what has to happen come what may, special science laws only say what has to happen all else being equal.[10]

How we should construe principle 8 has, of course, been a main concern throughout; but, according to the account of causal responsibility that I've been trying to sell you, it effectively reduces to the requirement that mental causes be covered by intentional laws. So now we can see where the tension between the three principles 6 through 8 arises. The responsibility of the mental requires covering by intentional laws. But given the revised notion of covering, according to which causes have to be covered by *strict* laws, it must be *physical* laws, and not intentional ones, that cover mental causes. So it turns out that the intentional properties are causally inert even according to the count of causal responsibility commended above.[11]

Something has to be done, and I assume it has to be done to principles 6 or 8 (or both) since 7 would seem to be OK. It is quite generally true about special science laws that they hold only 'barring breakdowns', or 'under appropriately idealized conditions', or 'when the effects of interacting variables are ignored'. If even geological laws have to be hedged—as indeed they do—then it's more than plausible that the 'all else equal' proviso in psychological laws will prove not to be eliminable. On balance, we had best assume that 7 stays.

What about 8, then? Surely we want 8 to come out true on *some* reasonable construal. I've opted for a robust reading: mental properties are causally responsible because they are properties in virtue of which mental causes are subsumed by covering laws; which is to say that mental properties are causally responsible because there are intentional generalizations which specify nomologically sufficient conditions for behavioral outcomes. But this reading of 8 looks to be incompatible with 7. Principle 7 suggests that there *aren't* intentionally specifiable sufficient conditions for behavioral outcomes since, at best, intentional laws hold only ceteris paribus. So, maybe the notion of causal responsibility I've been selling is too strong. Maybe we could learn to make do with less.[12]

This is, more or less explicitly, the course that LePore and Loewer recommend in "Mind Matters" (1987): If the causal *responsibility* of the intentional can somehow be detached from its causal *sufficiency* for behavioral outcomes, we could then maybe reconcile causal responsibility with anomicness. In effect, L and L's idea is to hold on to principles 6 and 7 at the cost of not adopting a nomological subsumption reading of 8. Prima facie, this strategy is plausible in light of a point that L and L emphasize (in their discussion of Sossa): the very fact that psychological laws are hedged would seem to rule out any construal of causal responsibility that requires mental causes qua mental to be nomologically sufficient for behavior. If it's only true ceteris paribus that someone who wants a drink reaches for the locally salient glass of water, then it's epiphobic to hold that desiring is causally responsible for reaching only if literally everyone who desires would thereupon reach. After all, quite aside from what you think of principle 6, it's simply not coherent to require the antecedents of hedged laws to provide literally nomologically sufficient conditions for the satisfaction of their consequents.

That's the stick; but L and L also have a carrot to offer. They concede that, if the only strict laws are physical, then instantiations of intentional properties are not strictly sufficient for determining behavioral outcomes. But they observe that granting principles 6 and 7 *doesn't* concede that the *physical properties of mental events are necessary* for their behavioral effects. To see this, assume an event *m* which instantiates the mental property *M* and the physical property *P*. Assume that *m* has the behavioral outcome *b*, an event with the behavioral property *B*, and that it does so in virtue of a physical law which strictly connects the instantiation of *P* with the instantiation of *B*. LePore and Loewer point out that all this is fully compatible with the truth of the counterfactual: $-Pm \ \& \ Mm \rightarrow Bb$ (i.e., with it being the case that *m* would have caused *Bb* even if it hadn't been *P*.) Think of the case where *M* events are "multiply realized," e.g., not just by *P* instantiations but also by P^* instantiations. And suppose that there's a strict law connecting P^* events with *B* events. Then $Mm \rightarrow Bb$ will be true not only when *m* is a *P* instantiation, but also in when *m* is a P^* instantiation. The point is that *one* way that $-Pm \ \& \ Mm \rightarrow Bb$ can be true is if there are strict psychological laws; i.e., if being an *M* instantiation is strictly sufficient for being a *B* instantiation. But the counterfactual could also be true on the assumption that *B* instantiations have *disjoint physically sufficient conditions*. And that assumption can be allowed by someone who claims that only physical laws can ground mental causes (e.g., because he claims that only physical laws articulate strictly sufficient conditions for behavioral outcomes.)

In short, LePore and Loewer show us that we can get quite a lot of what we want from the causal responsibility of the mental without assuming that intentional events are nomologically sufficient for behavioral outcomes (i.e., without assuming that intentional laws nomologically necessitate their consequents; i.e., without denying that the mental is anomic). Specifically, we can get that the particular constellation of physical properties that a mental cause exhibits needn't be necessary for its behavioral outcomes. I take LePore and Loewer's advice to be that we should settle for this; that we should construe the causal responsibility of the mental in some way that doesn't require mental events to be nomologically sufficient for their behavioral consequences. In effect, given a conflict between principle 6 and a covering law construal of principle 8, LePore and Loewer opt for 6. They keep the idea that causes have to be strictly covered, and give up on the idea that the causal responsibility of the mental is the nomological necessitation of the behavioral by the intentional.

Now, this may be good advice, but I seem to detect a not-very-hidden agenda. Suppose, just for the sake of argument, that there *is* some way of providing intentionally sufficient conditions for behavioral outcomes. Then this would not only allow for an intuitively satisfying construal of the causal responsibility of the mental (viz., mental properties are causally responsible if mental causes are covered by intentional laws, as described above), it would also undermine the idea that mental causes have to be covered by *physical* laws. If the laws of psychology have it in common with the laws of physics that both strictly necessitate their consequents, then presumably either would do equally well to satisfy the constraints that principle 6 imposes on the laws that cover mental causes. But the idea that mental causes have to be covered by physical laws is the key step in the famous Davidsonian argument from the anomia of the mental to physicalism. It may be that LePore and Loewer would like to hang onto the Davidsonian argument; it's pretty clear that Davidson would.

I take Davidson's argument to go something like this:

9.1 Mental causes have to be covered by some strict law or other. (Strict covering)

9.2 But not by intentional laws because intentional laws aren't strict; the satisfaction of their antecedents isn't nomologically sufficient for the satisfaction of their consequents. (Anomia of the mental.)

9.3 So mental causes must be covered by physical laws.

9.4 So they must have physical properties. Q.E.D.

But if there are intentionally sufficient conditions for behavioral outcomes you lose step 9.2; and if you lose step 9.2, you lose the argument. It appears that the cost of an intuitively adequate construal of mental responsibility is that there's no argument from mental causation to physicalism.

Well, so much for laying out the geography. Here's what happens next. First, I'll try to convince you that your intuitions really do cry out for some sort of causal sufficiency account of causal responsibility; something like that if it's m's being M that's causally responsible for b's being B, then b is B in all nearby worlds where m is M. (This is, to repeat, a consequence of defining causal responsibility in terms of strictly covering laws, since it is a defining property of such laws that the satisfaction of their antecedents necessitates the satisfaction of their consequents.) I'll then suggest that, appearances to the contrary, it really isn't very hard to square such an account with the admission that even the best psychological laws are very likely to be hedged. In effect, I'm claiming that, given a conflict between principles, 6 and 8, there's a natural replacement for 6. At this point the question about physicalism becomes moot since it will no longer be clear why hedged psychological laws can't ground mental causes; and, presumably, if hedged psychological laws can, then strict physical laws needn't. It still might turn out, however, that you can get a physicalist conclusion from considerations about mental causation, though by a slightly different route from the one that Davidson follows; a route that doesn't require the subsumption of causes by strict laws as a lemma.

My first point, then, is that notwithstanding L and L to the contrary, the notion of the causal responsibility of the mental that your intuitions demand is that Ms should be a nomologically sufficient condition for Bs. Accept no substitutes, is what I say. I'm not, however, exactly sure how to convince you that this is indeed what your intuitions cry out for; perhaps the following considerations will seem persuasive.

There aren't, of course, any reliable procedures for scientific discovery. But one might think of the procedures that have sometimes been proposed as, in effect, codifying our intuitions about causal responsibility. For example, it's right to say that Pasteur used the "method of differences" to discover that contact with stuff in the air—and not spontaneous generation in the nutrient—is responsible for the breeding of maggots. This is not, however, a comment on how Pasteur went about thinking up his hypotheses of his experiments. The method of differences doesn't tell you *how* to find out what is causally responsible. Rather, it tells you *what* to find out to find out what's causally responsible. It says, thrash about in the nearby nomologically possible worlds and find a property such that you get the maggots just when you get that property instantiated. *That* will be the property whose instantiation is causally responsible for the maggots.

I'm claiming that Pasteur had it in mind to assign causal responsibility for the maggots, and that, in doing so, it was preeminently reasonable of him to have argued according to the method of differences. Viz., if the infestation is airborne, then fitting a gauze top to the bottle should get rid of the maggots, and taking the gauze top off the bottle should bring the maggots back again. Assigning causal responsibility to contact with stuff in the air involved showing that such contact is necessary *and sufficient* for getting the maggots; that was what the method of differences required, and that was what Pasteur figured out how to do. If those intuitions about causal responsibility were good enough for Pasteur, I guess they ought to be good enough for you and me.

So then, I assume that the method of differences codifies our intuitions about causal responsibility. But this implies that assigning causal responsibility to the mental requires the truth of more counterfactuals than L and L are prepared to allow. Intuitively, what we need is that m's being M is what *makes the difference* in determining whether b is B, hence that 'Bb whenever Mm' is true in all nearby worlds. If the method of differences tells us what causal responsibility is, then what it tells us is that causal responsibility requires nomological sufficiency.[13] So the causal responsibility of the mental must be the nomological sufficiency of intentional states for producing behavioral outcomes.

The first—and crucial—step is getting what a robust construal of the causal responsibility of the mental requires is to square the idea that Ms are nomologically sufficient for Bs with the fact that psychological laws are hedged. How can you have it *both* that special laws only necessitate their consequents ceteris paribus *and* that we must get Bs *whenever* we get Ms? Answer: you can't. But what you can have is just as good: viz., that if it's a law that $M \rightarrow B$ ceteris paribus, then it follows that you get Bs whenever you get Ms *and the ceteris paribus conditions are satisfied.*[14] This shows us how ceteris paribus laws can do serious scientific business, since it captures the difference between the (substantive) claim that Fs cause Gs ceteris paribus, and the (empty) claim that Fs cause Gs except when they don't.

So, it's sufficient for M to be a causally responsible property if it's a property in virtue of which Ms causes Bs. And here's what it is for M to be a property in virtue of which Ms causes Bs:

10.1. Ms causes Bs.

10.2. '$M \rightarrow B$ ceteris paribus' is a law.[15]

10.3. The ceteris paribus conditions are satisfied in respect of some Ms.

I must say, the idea that hedged (including intentional) laws necessitate their consequents when their ceteris paribus clauses are discharged seems to me to be so obviously the pertinent proposal that I'm hard put to see how anybody could seriously object to it. But no doubt somebody will.

One might, I suppose, take the line that there's no fact of the matter about whether, in a given case, the ceteris paribus conditions on a special science law are satisfied. Or that, even if there is a fact of the matter, still one can't ever know what the fact of the matter is. But, surely that would be mad. After all Pasteur did demonstrate, to the satisfaction of all reasonable men, that ceteris paribus you get maggots when and only when the nutrients are in contact with stuff in the air. And presumably he did it *by* investigating experimental environments in which the ceteris paribus condition was satisfied and known to be so. Whatever is actual is possible; what Pasteur could do in fact, even you and I can do in principle.

I remark, in passing, that determining that ceteris paribus stuff in the air causes maggots did not require that Pasteur be able to *enumerate* the ceteris paribus conditions, only that he be able to recognize some cases in which they were in fact satisfied. *Sufficient* conditions for the satisfaction of ceteris paribus clauses may be determinate and epistemically accessible even when *necessary and sufficient* conditions for their satisfaction aren't. A fortiori, hedged laws whose ceteris paribus conditions cannot be enumerated may nevertheless be satisfied in particular cases. Perhaps we should say that M is causally responsible only if Ms cause Bs in *any* world in which the ceteris paribus clause of '$M \rightarrow B$ all else equal' is discharged. This would leave it open, and not very important, whether '*all and only* the worlds in which the ceteris paribus conditions are discharged' is actually well defined. It's not very important because what determines whether a given law can cover a given event is whether the law is determinately satisfied by the event. It is not also required that it be determinate whether the law would be satisfied by arbitrary other events (or by that same event in arbitrary other worlds). It seems to me that the plausibility of Davidson's assumption that hedged laws can't ground causes may depend on overlooking this point.

Finally, it might be argued that, although the ceteris paribus conditions on other special science laws are sometimes known to be satisfied, there is nevertheless something peculiar about *intentional* laws, so that their ceteris paribus conditions can't be. I take it that Davidson thinks that something of this sort is true; but I have never been able to follow the arguments that are supposed to show that it is. And I notice (with approval) that LePore and Loewer are apparently not committed to any such claim.

Where does all this leave us with respect to the classical Davidsonian argument that infers physicalism from the anomalousness of the mental? It seems to me that we are now lacking any convincing argument for accepting principle 6.

Suppose it's true that causes need to be covered by laws that necessitate their consequents; it doesn't follow that they need to be covered by *strict* laws. Hedged laws necessitate their consequents in worlds where their ceteris paribus conditions are satisfied. Why, then, should mental causes that are covered by hedged intentional laws with satisfied antecedents and satisfied ceteris paribus conditions require *further* covering by a strict law of physics?

The point till now has been that if strict laws will do to cover causes, so too will hedged laws in worlds where the hedges are discharged. I digress to remark that hedged laws can play the same role as strict ones in covering law explanations, so long as it's part of the explanation that the ceteris paribus conditions are satisfied.

When the antecedent of a strict law is satisfied you are *guaranteed* the satisfaction of its consequent, and the operation of strict laws in covering law explanations depends on this. What's typically in want of a covering law explanation is some such fact as that an event *m* caused an event *b* (and not, N.B., that an event *m* caused an event *b* ceteris paribus. Indeed, it's not clear to me that there are facts of this latter sort. Hedged generalizations are one thing; hedged singularly causal statements would be quite another.).[16] Well, the point is that strict laws can explain *m*'s causing *b* precisely because if it's strict that *M*s cause *B*s and it's true that there is an *M*, then it *follows* that there is an *M*-caused *b*. 'You got a *B* because you had an *M*, and it's a law that you get a *B* *whenever* you get an *M*'. But if that sort of explanation is satisfying, then so too ought to be: 'You got a *B* in world *w* because you had an *M* in world *w*, and it's a law that ceteris paribus you get a *B* whenever you have an *M*, and the ceteris paribus conditions were satisfied in world *w*.'

The long and short is: one reason why you might think that causes have to be covered by strict laws is that covering law explanations depend on this being so. But they don't. Strict laws and hedged laws with satisfied ceteris paribus conditions operate alike in respect of their roles in covering causal relations and in respect of their roles in covering law explanations. Surely this is as it should be: strict laws are just the special case of hedged laws where the ceteris paribus clauses are discharged *vacuously*; they're the hedged laws for which 'all else' is *always* equal.

Still, I think that there is *something* to be said for the intuition that strict physical laws play a special role in respect of the metaphysical underpinnings of causal relations, and I think there may after all be a route from considerations about mental causation to physicalism. I'll close by saying a little about this.

In my view, the metaphysically interesting fact about special science laws isn't that they're hedged; it's that they're *not basic*. Correspondingly, the metaphysically interesting contrast isn't between physical laws and special science laws; it's between basic laws and the rest. For present purposes, I need to remind you of a difference between special laws and basic laws that I remarked on earlier in this chapter;: If it's nonbasically lawful that Ms cause Bs, there's always a story to tell about how (typically, by what transformations of microstructures) instantiating M brings about the instantiation of B. Nonbasic laws want implementing mechanisms; basic laws don't. (That, I imagine, is what makes them basic).

It is therefore surely no accident that *hedged* laws are typically—maybe always—*not* basic. On the one hand, it's intrinsic to a law being hedged that it is nomologically possible for its ceteris paribus conditions not to be satisfied. And, on the other hand, a standard way to account for the failure of a ceteris paribus condition is to point to the breakdown of an intervening mechanism. Thus, meandering rivers erode their outside banks ceteris paribus. But not when the speed of the river is artificially controlled (no Bernoulli effect); and not when the river is chemically pure (no suspended particles); and not when somebody has built a wall on the outside bank (not enough abrasion to overcome adhesion). In such cases, the ceteris paribus clause fails to be satisfied *because* an intervening mechanism fails to operate. By contrast, this strategy is unavailable in the case of *non*basic laws; basic laws don't rely on mechanisms of implementation, so if they have exceptions that must because they're nondeterministic.

We see here one way in which ceteris paribus clauses do their work. Nonbasic laws *rely on* mediating mechanisms which they do not, however, *articulate* (sometimes because the mechanisms aren't known; sometimes because As can cause Bs in many different ways, so that the same law has a variety of implementations). Ceteris paribus clauses can have the effect of existentially quantifying over these mechanisms, so that 'As cause Bs ceteris paribus' can mean something like 'There exists an intervening mechanism such that when it's intact, As cause Bs.' I expect that the ceteris paribus clauses in special science laws can do other useful things as well. It is a scandal of the philosophy of science that we haven't got a good taxonomy of their functions.

However, I digress. The present point is that:

11. Nonbasic laws require mediation by intervening mechanisms,

and

12. There are surely no basic laws of psychology.

Let us now make the following bold assumption: all the mechanisms that mediate the operation of nonbasic laws are eventually physical.[17] I don't, I confess, know exactly what this bold assumption means (because I don't know exactly what it *is* for a mechanism to be physical as opposed, say, to spiritual); and I confess that I don't know exactly why it seems to me to be a reasonably bold assumption to make. But I do suspect that if it could be stated clearly, it would be seen to be a sort of bold assumption for which the past successes of our physicalistic worldview render substantial inductive support.

Well, if all the mechanisms that nonbasic laws rely on are eventually physical, then the mechanisms of mental causation must be eventually physical too. For, on the current assumptions, mental causes have their effects in virtue of being subsumed by psychological laws and, since psychological laws aren't basic, they require mediation by intervening mechanisms. However, it seems to me that to admit that mental causes must be related to their effects (including, notice, their *mental* effects) by physical mechanisms *just is* to admit that mental causes are physical. Or, if it's not, then it's to admit something so close that I can't see why the difference matters.

So, then, perhaps there's a route to physicalism from stuff about mental causation that *doesn't* require the claim that ceteris paribus laws can't ground mental causes. If so, then my story gives us both physicalism and a reasonable account of the causal responsibility of the mental; whereas Davidson's story gives us at most the former.[18] But if we *can't* get both the causal responsibility of the mental and an argument for physicalism, then it seems to me that we ought to give up the argument for physicalism. I'm not really convinced that it matters very much whether the mental is physical; still less that it matters very much whether we can prove that it is. Whereas, if it isn't literally true that my wanting is causally responsible for my reaching, and my itching is causally responsible for my scratching, and my believing is causally responsible for my saying . . . , if none of that is literally true, then practically everything I believe about anything is false and it's the end of the world.

Acknowledgment

This paper is a revised and extended version of some remarks presented at an APA symposium on December 30, 1987, in reply to Ernest LePore and Barry Loewer's "Mind Matters" (1987). I am grateful to LePore and Loewer and to Brian McLaughlin for much stimulating conversation on these and related issues.

Notes

1. I shall more or less assume in what follows that events are the individuals that causal laws subsume and to which causal powers are ascribed. Nothing will turn on this; it's just that it's a bore to always be having to say "events, or situations, or things, or whatever. . ."

2. It facilitates the discussion not to worry about which of their properties events have essentially. In particular, I shall assume that we can make sense of counterfactuals in which a certain mental event is supposed to have no intentional content or physical constituency different from its actual content or constituency. Nothing germane to the present issues hangs on this since, as far as I can tell, the same sorts of points I'll be making about counterfactual properties of events could just as well be made about relations between events and their counterparts.

3. What follows is a very crude approximation to the aerodynamic facts. Enthusiasts will find a serious exposition in Ross, 1975.

4. There is, I suppose, no guarantee that there is a unique property of $e1$ in virtue of which it causes $e2$. In fact, according to the account of causal responsibility I'll propose, both macroproperties and microproperties of the events will typically be implicated. This seems to me to be intuitively plausible; one resists choosing between, say, his being tall and his having tall genes as 'the' property of John's in virtue of which he has tall children.

5. The covering principle is generally in the spirit of proposals of Donald Davidson's, except that, unlike Davidson, I'm prepared to be shameless about properties.

6. 5.2 is in the text to emphasize that the nomological subsumption account of the causal responsibility of the mental is closely connected to the idea that mental events are nomologically sufficient for behavioral outcomes. We will thus have to consider how to square the nomological subsumption story with the fact that the antecedents of psychological laws generally do *not* specify nomologically sufficient conditions for the satisfaction of their consequents (because, like the laws of the other special sciences, the laws of psychology typically have essential ceteris paribus causes.) See the section on Intentional Laws.

7. I'm leaving statistical laws out of consideration. If some laws are irremediably statistical, then the proposal in the text should be changed to read: "any property in virtue of which some deterministic law covers an individual will be a property in virtue of which some causal law covers an individual."

8. But this will have to be hedged to deal with ceteris paribus laws. The second part of this chapter (Intentional Laws) is about what's the right way to hedge it.

9. Hornstein (1988), p. 18.

10. Special science laws are unstrict not just de facto, but in principle. Specifically, they are characteristically *"heteronomic"*: you can't convert them into strict laws by elaborating their antecedents. One reason why this is so is that special science laws typically fail in limiting conditions, or in the case of conditions where the idealizations presupposed by the science aren't approximated; and generally speaking, you have to go outside the vocabulary of the science to say what these conditions are. Old rivers meander, but not when somebody builds a levee. Notice that "levee" is not a *geological* term. (Neither, for that matter, is "somebody.")

   I emphasize this point because it's sometimes supposed that heteronomicity is a proprietary feature of *intentional* laws qua intentional. Poppycock.

11. It could no doubt be said that accepting principle 6 doesn't really make the mental properties drop out of the picture; even if mental causes have to be covered by

physical laws, it can still be true that they are *also* covered by intentional laws, viz., in the old (4.3) sense of "covering" that didn't require covering laws to be strict. As Brian McLaughlin (unpublished) has rightly pointed out, it's perfectly consistent to hold that covering by strict laws is necessary and sufficient for causal relations *and also to hold that covering by loose laws is necessary, or even sufficient, for causal relations,* so long as you are prepared to assume that every cause that is loosely covered is strictly covered too.

However, it is not clear that this observation buys much relief from epiphobia. After all, if mental properties really are causally active, why isn't intentional covering *all by itself* sufficient to ground the causal relations of mental events? I've been urging that intentional properties are causally responsible if mental causes are covered by intentional laws. But that seems plausible only if mental events are causes *in virtue of* their being covered by intentional laws. But how could mental causes be causes qua intentionally covered if, in order to *be* causes, they are further required to be subsumed by nonintentional laws? Taken together, principles 6 and 7 make it look as though, even if mental events are covered qua intentional, they're causes only qua physical. So again it looks like the intentional properties of mental events aren't doing any of the work.

12. I'm doing a little pussyfooting here, so perhaps I'd better put the point exactly: on the view that I will presently commend, there *are* circumstances in which instantiations of mental properties nomologically necessitate behavioral outcomes. What isn't, however, quite the case is that these circumstances are fully specified by the antecedents of intentional laws. In my view, only *basic* laws have the property that their antecedents fully specify the circumstances that nomologically necessitate the satisfaction of their consequents (and then only if they're deterministic).

13. It will be noticed that I'm stressing the importance of causal sufficiency for causal responsibility, whereas it was causal necessity that Pasteur cared about most. Pasteur was out to show that contact with stuff in the air and *only* contact with stuff in the air is causally responsible for maggots; specifically that contact with stuff in the air accounts for *all* of the maggots, hence that spontaneous generation accounts for none. I take it that it is *not* among our intuitions that a certain mental property is causally responsible for a certain behavior only if that sort of behavior can have no other sort of cause.

14. So, what I said above—that a law is a hypothetical the satisfaction of whose antecedent nomologically necessitates the satisfaction of its consequent—wasn't quite true since it doesn't quite apply to hedged laws. What *is* true is that a law is a hypothetical the satisfaction of whose antecedent nomologically necessitates the satisfaction of its consequent *when its ceteris paribus conditions are satisfied.*

15. If it's a strict law, then the ceteris paribus clause is vacuously satisfied.

16. To put it another way: Suppose you're feeling Hempelian about the role of covering laws in scientific explanations. Then you might worry that:

(i)   Ceteris paribus As cause Bs

together with

(ii)   Aa

yields something like

(iii)   Ceteris paribus Bb

which isn't strong enough to explain the datum (*Bb*). 'Ceteris paribus *Bb*' doesn't look to have the form of a possible data statement. I wonder in the text whether it even has the form of a possible truth.

17. "Eventually" means: Either the law is implemented by a physical mechanism, or its implementation depends on a lower-level law which is itself either implemented by a physical mechanism or is dependent on a still lower-level law which is itself either implemented by a physical mechanism or . . . etc. Since only finite chains of implementation are allowed, you have to get to a physical mechanism "eventually."

    We need to put it this way because, as we've been using it, a "physical" mechanism is one whose means of operation is covered by a physical law, i.e., by a law articulated in the language of physics. And though presumably physical mechanisms implement every high-level law, they usually do so via lots of levels of intermediate laws and implementations. So, for example, intentional laws are implemented by syntactic mechanisms that are governed by syntactic laws that are implemented by neurological mechanisms that are governed by neurological laws that are implemented by biochemical mechanisms that . . . and so on down to physics.

    None of this really matters for present purposes, of course. A demonstration that mental events have neural properties would do to solve the mind/body problem since nobody doubts that neural events have physical properties.

18. On the other hand, I don't pretend to do what Davidson seems to think he can, viz., get physicalism *just* from considerations about the constraints that causation places on covering laws together with the truism that psychological laws aren't strict. That project was breathtakingly ambitious but maybe not breathtakingly well advised. My guess is, if you want to get a lot of physicalism out, you're going to have to put a lot of physicalism in. What I put in was the independent assumption that the mechanism of intentional causation is physical.

Chapter 6

Substitution Arguments and the Individuation of Beliefs

Introduction

The older I get, the more I am inclined to think that there is nothing at all to meaning except denotation; for example, that there is nothing to the meaning of a name except its bearer and nothing to the meaning of a predicate except the property that it expresses.

The popular alternative to the view that there is nothing to meaning except denotation is that meaning is a composite of denotation and *sense*. And ever since Wittgenstein (or maybe since Saussure) it has been widely assumed that the sense of an expression is to be understood as somehow emerging from its *use*. Practically everybody who's anybody in modern Anglo-American philosophy has held some or other version of this sense-cum-use doctrine. Still, as I say, I'm increasingly inclined to think that it's a dead end and that there is nothing at all to meaning except denotation.

What I most want to do in this paper is reconsider a main argument that's supposed to show that there *must* be something more to meaning than denotation. So I don't propose to spend much time reviewing the general considerations that lead me to think that the sense/use story is no good. Roughly, however, nobody has succeeded in making it clear just *how* the sense of an expression is supposed to emerge from its use; not, at least, if use is taken as something that is nonsemantically and nonintentionally specifiable. (And if it's not, it's hard to see what the interest of a reduction of sense to use would be.)

At a minimum, a use theory of meaning ought to be a function from uses onto meanings. There are, however, precisely no candidates for the formulation of such a function. Wittgenstein, in the *Investigations* (1953), imagines a "primitive language game" in which one guy is disposed to bring a slab when another guy says (i.e., *utters*) "Slab!" Presumably the fact that utterances of "Slab!" have compliance conditions in this game (and that it's bringing a slab that counts as complying) reduces to the fact that the people playing the game have the dispositions that they do. But how does this reduction go? Why does the fact that one guy brings a slab when the other says "Slab!" constitute "Slab!" meaning *bring me a slab* and not, as it might be, *meet me at the Algonquin* or *two is a prime number*? It is, after all, easy enough to dream up a story in which a guy brings a slab when you say "Slab!" *because* he takes "Slab!" to mean *meet me at the Algonquin*. Imagine, for example, someone whose practice it is to bring you a slab whenever he intends to meet you there. It may be that you could get the Wittgensteinian version of the reduction of sense to use to go through if you threw in a little behaviorism. The which, however, Heaven forfend. (These remarks also apply, mutatis mutandis, to versions of sense/use semantics according to which the sense of an expression is a construct out of its role in a theory, assuming that 'role' is construed causally or syntactically—anyhow not inferentially or intentionally or otherwise question-beggingly.)

Second, the sense/use theory invites semantic holism via a line of argument that is by now too well known to bother recapitulating in detail. Briefly, there appears to be no atomistic way of individuating uses; hence no atomistic way of individuating senses; hence nowhere to stop short of identifying the units of sense with entire belief systems (or "ways of life" or whatever). When pursued in this direction, however, the sense/use story is not a theory of meaning but the reductio ad absurdum of the possibility of such a theory. On the holistic account of content individuation, it hardly ever turns out that two tokens of a symbol have the same sense. And what's the good of a suicidal semantics?

Whereas, by contrast, a sense-less account of meaning looks to be in better shape in both these respects (assuming that it can be made to satisfy "internal" conditions of adequacy that a semantic theory ought to meet, like assigning the right truth conditions, exhibiting compositional structure, and so forth). Whereas nothing is known about how sense arises from use, there has been some glimmer of progress in attempts to reduce denotation to causation. (See recent work by Dretske, Stampe, Fodor, etc.) And, while the use of a symbol is generally assumed to be at least partly constituted by its intralinguistic relations, denotation is presumably a word/world relation purely.[1] There is thus some hope that an extensional semantics can avoid the holism that plagues use theories. (For more discussion of both these points, see Fodor, 1986).

So tell me again: why does there have to be sense as well as denotation? What's wrong with the idea that denotation is all that there is to meaning?

The Substitution Argument.

Here's what's supposed to be wrong. The expressions "Jocasta" and "Oedipus' Mother"[2] are coreferential *and must therefore be synonyms if denotation is all that there is to meaning*. But it's true that Oedipus believed that Jocasta was eligible and it's false that Oedipus believed that Oedipus' Mother was eligible. So the expressions "Jocasta" and "Oedipus' Mother" are not freely substitutable *salve veritate*. So they are not synonyms. So denotation can't be all that there is to meaning.

I'll call this kind of argument a "substitution argument" (and I'll call the implied test for content identity the "substitution test"). I think that substitution arguments are—and have been since Frege— a lot of what's behind the idea that there must be something more to meaning than denotation. But the older I get, the more I wonder whether substitution arguments are any damned good. I therefore propose to have a good look at substitution arguments. Starting now.

On the face of it, substitution salve veritate in belief contexts doesn't *look* to be a test for identity of content. What it looks to be is a test for identity of *belief-state*.[3] If 'O believes E' is true and 'O believes E'' is false, then it must be that believing E and believing E' are different states. In the present case, if believing J to be eligible and believing O's M to be eligible were the same state, then it would be both true and false that O was in it, and that is not allowed. But it's one thing to admit that believing that J is eligible is a different state than believing that O's M is eligible; it would seem to be quite another thing to admit that 'J' and 'O's M' are nonsynonymous. And it is, decisively, the latter conclusion that we need to be able to draw if we're to infer from the facts about Oedipus that there is more to meaning than denotation.

Recap:

(i) What's granted is that if the expression E fails to substitute for the expression E' salve veritate in the context 'believes that . . .', then believing that E is a different state from believing that E'.

(ii) What's claimed is that if the expression E fails to substitute for the expression E' salve veritate in the context 'believes that . . .', then E and E' differ in semantic value.

Required: an argument that gets from what's granted to what's claimed. The older I get, the more I am inclined to doubt that there is one.

I now propose to run through a couple of candidate arguments, neither of which strikes me as very convincing. I then want to tell you a story about the individuation of beliefs that makes it clear why the inference from *(i)* to *(ii)* shouldn't be expected to go through and that is, I think, not implausible on independent grounds.

Argument 1

Premise 1: If 'believes E' is sometimes true when 'believes E'' is false, then E and E' are not freely substitutable salve veritate.

Premise 2: Synonyms are freely substitutable salve veritate.

Conclusion: E and E' aren't synonyms if 'believes E' is sometimes true when 'believes E'' is false.

Comment: Premise 1 is common ground, but why should we believe premise 2?

Certainly 2 is false as stated; as everybody and his grandmother points out, substitution of synonyms clearly fails in quotation contexts (like "uttered '. . . .'"); maybe it fails in belief contexts too. How are we to tell?

I'd prefer to avoid a vulgar squabble over intuitions. For what it's worth, however, it seems to me (as it seemed to Mates' 1952) that it is possible for me to doubt (/deny) that everybody who believes that Oedipus is a bachelor believes that Oedipus is an unmarried man even though I don't doubt (/deny) that everybody who believes that Oedipus is a bachelor believes that Oedipus is a bachelor. At a minimum, it's surely possible for it *to seem to me* that [it's possible for me to doubt (/deny) that everybody who believes that Oedipus is a bachelor believes that Odeipus is an unmarried man] even though it doesn't seem to me that [it's possible for me to doubt (/deny) that everybody who believes that Oedipus is a bachelor believes that Oedipus is a bachelor]. For, as a matter of fact, it does seem to me that it seems to me that all of this is so; and I would seem to be in about as good a position as anyone can be to say how things seem to me to be, *nicht wahr*? So maybe substitution of synonyms salve veritate fails in the context 'it seems to me that . . . .', or in iterations of that context. In which case, the failure of 'J' and 'O's M' to substitute in such contexts would not show that they aren't synonyms.

In rather similar spirit, it seems to me certain that my daughter, when she was three years old, believed me to be her father. But I really do have my doubts about whether she believed me to be her male parent. Introspection suggests (again, for what it's worth) that the reason I really do doubt this is that I doubt that three-year-olds *have the concept* PARENT, and I'm inclined to hold that you can't believe that someone is your male parent unless you do have the concept PARENT. Merely having the concept FATHER—a concept that's *definable in terms of* PARENT—strikes me as not good enough.

The Mates sort of argument throws doubt on the claim that failures of substitution salve veritate in belief contexts are ipso facto arguments for nonsynonymy. Reflection on Kripke's example about Pierre (1979) makes this claim seem still more questionable—at least if you're prepared to believe that *translation* is a test for synonymy.[4] For our purposes a stripped down version of the example will do. Pierre is a French/English bilingual who has come across tokens of the type 'Londres' in French texts and tokens of the type 'London' in English texts. He understands that 'London' and 'Londres' both refer to cities, but he doesn't realize that they both refer to the same city; for simplicity, we can assume that he takes it that they don't. So the intuition seems to be that "Pierre believes that Londres is pretty" is true and "Pierre believe that London is pretty" is false. (It is an argument for this intution that if you say to him: "Pierre, do you believe that London is pretty?" Pierre says "But no!", whereas if you say to him "Pierre, do you believe that Londres is pretty?" he says "But yes!") However, 'London' translates as 'Londres' if anything translates as anything. So, if translations are ipso facto synonyms, it would seem that there's at least one case where you can't infer difference of meaning from failure of substitution.[5] But that was the very form of inference that we required in order to get from 'O believed . . . J . . .' and 'O didn't believe . . . O's Mom . . .' to '"J" and 'O's Mom' mean different things'. Why is sauce for Pierre's goose not sauce for Oedipus' gander? Since there are cases where the substitution test fails when the translation test is satisfied, the right conclusion would seem to be that if translation tests for sense, substitution doesn't.

But, as I say, all this relies a lot on intuitions, over which I do not wish to squabble. All I ask for at this stage is a Scotch verdict. It turns out that, given a story about the individuation of quotations together with a story about how embedded formulas function in contexts like 'uttered ". . ."', we can see how substitution of synonyms could fail in quotation contexts. So maybe there could be a story about the individuation of beliefs that, together with a story about how embedded formulas function in contexts like 'believes that . . .', would show us how substitution of synonyms could fail in belief contexts too. We'll return to this presently.

Argument 2

Premise 1: Distinct intentional states must differ either in their *mode* (e.g., in the way that believing that P differs from desiring that P) or in their *content* (e.g., in the way that believing that P differs from believing that Q).[6]

Premise 2: Believing that J is eligible is an intentional state distinct from believing that O's M is eligible (the failure of the substitution test shows this; see above).

These states do not differ in mode (they're both belief-states);

- So they differ in contents (they have different propositional objects);
- So 'J is eligible' and 'O's M is eligible' are nonsynonymous (they express different propositions).
- So 'J' and 'O's M' are nonsynonymous (by the principle that if nonsynonymous formulas differ only in that one has constituent C where the other has constitutent C', then C and C' are non-synonymous. I propose to grant this for the sake of argument.).
- So denotation can't be all that there is to meaning.

Comment: Excellent, except that why should we believe premise 1? Specifically, why shouldn't there be cases where beliefs that are tokens of different state types nevertheless have the same propositional object?

I now propose to tell you a story about belief individuation, and about how embedded formulas function in belief attributions. The relevant peculiarity of this story is that it permits distinct belief-states to have the same contents (the same propositional objects). The point of telling you this story is that since such cases are allowed, the proposition that J is eligible might turn out to be identical to the proposition that O's M is eligible *even though* believing the one proposition is a different state from believing the other. But if these propositions might be the same then we have, so far, no reason to doubt that 'J' and 'O's M' are synonyms. Which is to say that, at least so far as the facts about Oedipus are concerned, we have no reason to doubt that denotation is all that there is to meaning.

Let's start with belief individuation, leaving the issues about belief attribution till later. The standard story about believing is that it's a two-place relation, viz., a relation between a person and a proposition. My story about believing is that it's a four-place relation, viz., a relation between a person, a proposition, a vehicle, and a functional role. According to my story, if all you know is that two of a guy's belief-states differ, then all you can infer is that they differ *either* in content *or* in vehicle *or* in functional role. Since, in particular, you can't infer that they differ in content, argument 2 is invalid if my story about the individuation of belief-states is true.

A vehicle is a symbol. A symbol (token) is a spatiotemporal particular which has syntactic and semantic properties and a causal role. Vehicles, like other symbols, are individuated with respect to their syntactic and semantic properties, but *not* with respect to their causal roles. In particular, two vehicle tokens are type distinct if they are syntactically different or if they express different propositions. But type-identical vehicle tokens can differ in their causal roles because the role that a token plays depends not just on which type it's a type of, but also on the rest of the world in which its tokening transpires. (This is true of the causal roles of symbols because it's true of the causal roles of everything. Roughly, your causal role depends on what you are, what the local laws are, and what else there is around.)

I assume, finally, that vehicles can be type distinct but synonymous; distinct vehicles can express the same proposition. So much for the individuation of vehicles.

If you like language of thought stories, then the typical vehicle of believing is a formula of Mentalese. If you don't like language of thought stories, then let it be a formula of anything you please. What's essential to my story is that believing is never an *unmediated* relation between a person and a proposition. In particular, nobody "grasps" a proposition except insofar as he is appropriately related to a token of some vehicle that expresses the proposition. (I think this not only because it strikes me as metaphysically plausible, but also because it is required for a story I like about how graspings of propositions—more specifically, tokenings of propositional attitudes—can eventuate in the behavioral consequences that they do. But I've told that story elsewhere and I don't propose to repeat it here; see Fodor 1975 and 1978.)

I can now tell you my story about Oedipus, which is that he had two different ways of relating to the proposition that J was eligible (and, mutatis mutandis, to its denial). One way was via tokens of some such vehicle as 'J is eligible' and the other way was via tokens of some such vehicle as 'O's M is eligible'. Since difference of vehicles implies (or, more precisely, *can* imply; see below) correspondingly different mental states, it was possible for Oedipus to have two beliefs with the same content; i.e., two beliefs both of whose object was the proposition that can be expressed as either *Jocasta is eligible* or *Oedipus' Mother is eligible*.

My story about Oedipus is, no doubt, tendentious. It's notoriously possible to hang onto the idea that distinct belief-states imply distinct belief contents by distinguishing between two propositions that extensionalists take to be identical: the proposition that O's M is eligible and the proposition that J is. Since it thus appears that you can tell the story about O either way, O's case doesn't distinguish between my view of belief individuation and the standard view.

But, as we've seen, Pierre is a horse of a different color. In Pierre's case, as in O's, you get the failure of substitution of coextensive expressions ('London'/'Londres'; 'J'/'O's M'). But in the Pierre example it's implausible that the explanation of the substitution failure is that the expressions mean different things. 'London'/'Londres' is bad news for Frege's strategy of explaining failures of substitution by positing differences of sense. But if it's not difference in sense that explains the substitution failure (as apparently it's not) and if failure of substitution is a test for distinctness of belief-state (as apparently it is), then it must be that distinct belief-states can have the same content. I.e., there must be more to the identity of an attitude than its content and its mode. The vehicle by means of which the content is presented does rather suggest itself since, in Pierre's case, differences in their vehicles seem to be all that's *left* to distinguish his London-beliefs from his Londres ones.

A very rough theory of belief individuation might make do with *just* a person, a vehicle, and a content. You get a rather sharper picture if you also allow in a functional role for the vehicle. Loosely speaking, I mean by the functional role of a vehicle the role that it plays in inference; more strictly speaking, I mean its causal role in (certain) mental processes. It seems to me plausible that you can have two beliefs with the same object and the same vehicle, where the difference between the beliefs comes from differences in the inferential/causal roles that the vehicles play. This happens when, for example, two guys who use the same vehicle to express the same content differ in their background theories; specifically, in the identity statements that they hold true.

Let's suppose—what is plausible the case—that I know that Janet is my wife. What belief am I expressing when I say "I'm expecting my wife to phone at 3"? It seems to me merely captious to insist that it's the belief that my wife will phone at 3 *and not the belief that Janet will*. On the other hand, what belief is *acquired* by the guy who heard me say what I did but who *doesn't* know about Janet being my wife? Clearly *not* the belief that Janet will phone; clearly only the belief that my wife will. The intuitions get still clearer if you run the example on 'Janet' and 'Janet D. Fodor'; my believing that Janet will call *is* my believing that Janet D. Fodor will. But if you don't know about Janet being JDF, then your acquiring the one belief isn't your acquiring the other. Or so it seems to me.[7] I admit that this is all the merest intuition-mongering; but if you accept the intuitions, what it looks like we have is: one format ('Janet will call'), one proposition (extensionalist principles are assumed to be operative), but two beliefs depending on differences in the background of cognitive commitment.[8]

So much for the belief-state *individuation* according to my revisionist account. What is the story about belief-state *attribution* going to be?

Consider the expression 'believes that E' where it is used to attribute to some agent the state of believing that E. How does it go about doing what it is used to do? How, in particular, does the "E" part work?

First off, E needs somehow to pick out the propositional object of the belief; it has to specify the content of the belief ascribed. I think this works in the following simple and aesthetically satisfying fashion. The proposition that is the object of the belief-state that is *attributed by* using the formula 'believes E' is the very same proposition that is *expressed by* using the unembedded formula E. So, for example, the expression 'believes that it's raining' is used to attribute a belief-relation to the proposition that it's raining; and this is the very same proposition that the unembedded formula 'it's raining' is used to express.

It follows, on my semantic principles, that the function of 'believes J is eligible' in 'O believes J is eligible' is to attribute to O a belief-relation to the proposition that is expressed both by the unembedded formula 'J is eligible' and by the unembedded formula 'O's M is eligible'. It doesn't, of course, follow that believing that O's M is eligible and believing that J is eligible are the same belief-state since, on my metaphysical principles, the identity of a propositional attitude is not determined by specifying a mode and an object. You must also specify (inter alia) a vehicle; and this is the other thing that the embedded formula in 'believes E' can function to do. It does it, to put it roughly, by *displaying* the vehicle; or to put it slightly less roughly, it does it by displaying a formula that is, to one or another degree, structurally isomorphic to the vehicle. I may, for example, wish to distinguish (see above) between beliefs about one's father and beliefs about one's male parent. I can do so by distinguishing between attributions via the formula 'believes . . . father . . .' and via the formula 'believes . . . male parent . . .'. Similarly, *mutatis mutandis*, I can distinguish between '. . . O's M . . .' beliefs and '. . . J . . .' beliefs; or between '. . . Janet . . .' beliefs and '. . . my wife . . .' beliefs. In each case, according to my story about belief individuation, it's the vehicle, not the content, that distinguishes the belief-states. And, in each case, the intended distinction is signaled by a choice among (coextensive but structurally distinct) formulas embedded to the 'believes' predicate.

It bears emphasis that a cost of accepting this sort of view is abandoning the principle of strict compositionality of reference: i.e., the principle that its denotation is *all* that a referring expression contributes to fixing the denotation of the referring expressions of which it is a constituent. On the present view, the reason that 'the belief that O's M is eligible' picks out a diffent mental state from the one picked out by 'the belief that J is eligible' *despite* the denotational equivalence of 'J' and 'O's M' is that the denotations of expressions like 'the belief that . . .' are determined by *both* the denotation *and* the form of their constituents.

However, strict composition of reference never was a particularly attractive story about opaque contexts. Classical Fregian semantics preserves it only by endorsing the not wildly plausible view that, although 'J' and 'O's M' both refer in both opaque and transparent contexts, and although they both refer to the same thing in transparent contexts, they nevertheless refer to *different* things when they occur embedded to verbs like 'believes'. (Specifically, 'O's M' refers to the sense *O's M* and 'J' refers to the sense *J*. *O's M* and *J* are *different* senses since 'O's M' and 'J' are, by assumption, nonsynonymous.) It's arguable that, as between giving up the strict compositionality of reference and giving up what Davidson has called "semantic innocence" (the principle that, in general, words mean the same in opaque contexts as they do in transparent ones), there doesn't seem to be much to choose. In particular, it's not a priori obvious that strict compositionality of reference is worth having if it's going to cost that much.

Actually, the situation is rather worse than this suggests. If referring expressions denote their senses in opaque contexts, and if strict compositionality of reference holds, then belief clauses that differ only in synonyms must corefer; synonymous expressions which denote their senses ipso facto denote the same thing. But then, it's hard to see how 'Pierre's belief that Londres is pretty' could fail to refer to the same mental state as 'Pierre's belief that London is pretty'. But if they do refer to the same state, how *could* it be that Pierre has one of the beliefs and not the other? (Similar arguments could, of course, be constructed from Mates cases.) It appears that if, as Pierre suggests, substitution sometimes does fail for synonyms, and if, as everyone supposes, synonyms corefer, then it must not be supposed that terms that fail to substitute have ipso facto got different referents.[9]

It's plausible, given all of this, that a term may contribute not just its referent, but also its vehicle, to fixing the referents of the expressions in which it occurs. How much, then, of the structure of the vehicle of a belief is the embedded formula in a belief-state-attributing expression required to display in order that the attribution should be univocal? In the case of the first of the functions of the embedded formula—specifying the propositional object of the attributed belief—the matter is clear: the embedded formula must express *the very proposition* that the 'believes' predicate attributes. I think, however, that it is otherwise with the specification of the vehicle; here everything is slippery and pragmatic. Roughly, what's required is a degree of isomorphism to the vehicle that is appropriate to the purposes at hand; and there isn't any purpose-independent specification of how much isomorphism is enough.

I say: 'Baby believes that Santa Claus will come down the chimney'. My intention is to specify a belief that is individuated, in part, by reference to a vehicle in which the expression 'Santa Claus' occurs essentially. On the other hand, I say: 'I believe that Bill Smith will come down the chimney dressed as Santa Claus' and here it's probably *not* essential that 'Bill Smith' occur in the vehicle ('he' or 'Mary Smith's husband' would perhaps do as well). Similarly, I say 'Some folks believed FDR to be the incarnation of the devil'; here practically nothing about the vehicle of the attributed belief matters to the success of the attribution. It doesn't matter, for example, that the folks in question thought of FDR via the formula 'the SOB in the White House' or that they thought of the empty set via the vehicle 'Old Nick' or 'the archfiend' (it does matter, however, that they didn't think of it it via the vehicle 'the empty set'). I don't, in short, generally require that my belief attributions be univocal; I am generally satisfied to pick out any of a class of belief-states that have their propositional objects and certain features of their vehicles in common. And do not send to know *just how* vehicle-independent my belief attributions are required to be, for there is no precise answer. Good enough for the purposes at hand is generally all I have in mind.

There also isn't an answer to the request for a form of embedded expressions that is *guaranteed* to specify the vehicle of an attitude uniquely. This is to say that there isn't, in ordinary belief/desire talk, anything that corresponds to the canonical description of a belief or a desire. To put it another way, it's not that there are de dicto attributions and de re attributions; it's rather that there is a continuum along which an embedded expression can be explicit about the vehicle of an attributed belief. If there's a rule in play, it's a rule of conversation: 'Kindly so construe my embedded formulas that my belief attributions come out plausible on the assumption that my utilities are rational'. If I say that John believes that Cicero was Tully, I *must* be trying to specify John's vehicle; what would be the point of my telling you something that would be true in virtue of John's believing that Cicero is Cicero? On the other hand, if I tell you that the English wanted to seize New York from the Dutch, I couldn't possibly be wanting to specify *their* vehicle; everybody called the place New Amsterdam at the time.

Here's the box score: beliefs are relations between persons, contents, vehicles, and functional roles. We have a precise semantics for the attributions of beliefs insofar as their identity depends upon their contents. We have a less precise, but serviceable, semantics for individuating beliefs insofar as their identity depends upon their vehicles: when it matters, and to the extent that it matters, you can indicate the vehicle of a belief by choosing an embedded formula that is more or less structurally isomorphic to it.

There is, however, no parameter of a 'believes' formula whose function is to signal the functional role of the vehicle of a belief. Typical cases of belief attribution involve people who share, more or less, the ideology of the believer. When this isn't so, the 'believes that E' format breaks down and even a reasonable degree of univocality of attribution may involve telling quite a long story.

Conclusion

I suppose that my polemical strategy must now be embarrassingly clear. Suppose—contrary to what the substitution test assumes—that difference of belief-state does *not* imply difference of belief content. Then I'm prepared to accept practically anything that practically anyone has ever said about content attribution; even, if you like, that it's pragmatic, holistic, hermenutic, ich/du-istic, and so forth. Except that I claim that it's *belief-state* attribution and *not* content attribution that all that stuff is true of, and from truths about the one nothing much of interest follows about the other.

Thus as we've seen there are people who say that the substitution test is a test for content identity; what I say is that they are almost right except that what it tests for is not identity of content but identity of belief-state. In similar spirit there are such things as functional-role semanticists, and they say that functional roles makes content. And they are almost right because functional role does make belief-state; it's just that belief-state doesn't make content, so content needn't be a functional notion even if belief-state is.

Or, again, there are Kuhnians out there, and they say that differences in cognitive background are sometimes tantamount to content differences. That's OK with me too, except that it's differences in belief-state that differences in cognitive background make and *not* differences in content, so it distinguishes my view from Kuhn's that I'm not committed to the "incommensurability" of radically different theories. The Greeks thought that stars are holes in the sky; I think that they are not. If theoretical background makes content, it's hard to see how the Greeks and I could agree about (e.g.) how many visible stars there are. But differences of theoretical background *don't* make differences of content; all there is to content is denotation.

On the other hand, differences of theory do (can), on my view, make differences of belief-state, so how does it come out of the story I've been telling that what I believe about the cardinality of the visible stars agrees what the Greeks believed? All that's required for agreement is that the *propositional objects* of the belief-states are the same: if x believes that P, and y believes that P, then x and y agree, *whether or not x and y are in the same belief-state*; and what they agree about is true iff it's the case that P. Similarly, if x believes that P and Y believes that $-P$, then they disagree regardless of consideration of vehicles and roles; and x is right iff P and y is right iff $-P$. This is a reasonable way to assess disputes since what's at issue in a clash of beliefs is, after all, the truth of their propositional objects; and the identity of the propositional objects of a belief-state is independent of its vehicle and functional role, assuming that vehicle and functional role don't make content.

Also, there are Davidsonians out there, and Davidsonians say that the attribution of content is constrained by conditions of rationality. For example, we have to distinguish between O's believing that *J is not his mother* and his believing that *his mother is not his mother* on pain of uncharitably ascribing to O a belief that is manifestly self-contradictory *and thereby violating the very conditions of intentional ascription.*

Well, maybe Davidsonians are right too. Only in my view the rationality conditions constrain *belief-state* attribution, not *content* attribution; and, once again, differences of belief-state don't make differences of content. This, surely, is the right end of the stick; it isn't remotely plausible that 'principles of charity' constrain intentional attributions per se, however much they may be supposed to constrain attributions of belief-states. In particular, it couldn't conceivably be required that the *propositional objects* of all the attitudes attributed to a guy at any one time should be to any extent mutually consistent: There's nothing wrong with hoping that *P* while fearing that *not-P*; and believing that *P* while wishing that *not-P* practically defines the human condition. If there are rationality contraints on propositional-attitude attributions, they apply to relations among the attitudes, not to relations among their propositional objects.[10]

We can put all this in a nutshell: in my view, the most that the standard skeptical arguments about content actually show is that belief individuation is plausibly pragmatic and holistic. But this implies nothing about the individuation of content unless you accept 'different beliefs → different propositional objects'. Which I don't. What strikes me as especially attractive about this strategy is that it allows me to distinguish between two questions that are invariably confused in the philosophical literature: the question about the scientific status of *propositional-attitude* psychology and the question about the scientific status of *intentional* psychology. A word about this to close the discussion.

The predictive and explanatory success of commonsense belief/desire psychology strikes me as the second most remarkable fact about the intellectual history of our species. (The first most remarkable fact about the intellectual history of our species is the predictive and explanatory success of commonsense middle-sized-object ontology.) For, here is this delicate and elaborate—and largely inexplicit—psychological theory that we seem, in several respects, to get for free. It is presumably prehistoric in origin; it is culturally universal; and it is assimilated practically instantaneously and without explicit instruction by every normal child. And, by all reasonable empirical criteria, this theory that we seem to get for free appears to be *true*: its predictive adequacy is not susceptible to serious doubt, and it has repeatedly proven superior to such rival theories as have sought to replace it (e.g., behavioristic theories and pie-in-the-sky neuroscience of the San Diego sort). So impressive are the successes of grandmother psychology that the rational strategy for an empirical approach to the mind is surely to co-opt its apparatus for service as explicit science. This has in fact been the strategy of modern intentional realists from Freud to Chomsky, and it seems to me perfectly obvious that it has produced all the best psychology we've got. It would be barely hyperbolic to claim that it has produced all the only psychology we've got.

But having said all these reactionary and antirevisionist things, I nevertheless want to distinguish between two versions of intentional realism, one of which is merely conservative, and the other of which is die-hard. The merely conservative view is that the best hope for psychology is the exploitation of intentional categories, just as Granny has always said. The die-hard line, by contrast, is that the intentional categories that we want for science ought to include belief, desire, and the other taxa of commonsense propositional attitudinizing. It's here that I (and, by the way, Freud and Chomsky) finally part company with Granny.

If much of what I've been saying about belief individuation is true, then the identity conditions for belief-states are vague and pragmatic in practice; perhaps they are ineliminably so. On the one hand, there are no guaranteed-univocal descriptors for picking them out. And, on the other, belief-state individuation appears to depend on the individuation of functional roles; where are we to look for identity criteria for these? But we needn't care if it turns out that believing and desiring are ineliminably infected with vagueness and holism. A conservative intentional realist who is not a diehard can contemplate with equanimity the abandonment of belief/desire psychology strictly socalled, so long as the apparatus of *intentional* explanation is itself left intact. So, two take-home questions:

1. How much, if any, of the skeptical argumentation about grandmother psychology is effective against *intentional* realism *as opposed to belief/desire realism*?

and

2. How much, if any, of the predictive/explanatory success of grandmother psychology depends on *belief/desire* realism *as opposed to intentional realism*?

It would be a comfort to aging intentional realists like me if the answer to both these questions turned out to be "None."

Notes

1. Putnam (1983) remarks (plausibly) that ". . . determining the extension of a term always involves determining the extension of other terms." (p. 149) But of course it wouldn't follow that any term's *having* an extension depends on any other term's having one. Epistemic dependence is one thing, metaphysical dependence is quite another.
2. The reader would do me a kindness if he were to take "Oedipus' Mother" as a name rather than a description. (Like "the Iron Duke" or "the Big Apple.")
3. I'm talking in this funny hyphenated way because it's important to my present purposes to avoid state/object ambiguities. 'The belief that P' is notorious for

equivocating between the *state of believing* that P and the *proposition* that P. I'm using "belief-state" to indicate the former.

4. It's not self-evident that translation *is* a test for synonymy; whereas 'synonymy' is presumably an equivalence relation, 'translates' is arguably intransitive, and translations of the same expression need not translate one other. I make this point in light of the tendency of writers like Putnam, Davidson, and Quine to just take it for granted that the constraints (epistemic, metaphysical, or whatever) on semantic theories can be just read off from the constraints on translation. However, I doubt that these general considerations about translation bear on the moral I want to draw from the Pierre case.

5. I can imagine somebody arguing that this isn't a bona fide failure of substitution on the grounds that since 'London' is an English word and 'Londres' is a French word, they can't contrast in the (English) frame "Pierre believes . . . is pretty" or, mutatis mutandis, in the (French) frame "Pierre croit que . . . . est jolie". I say pooh to this. "Do you believe that Londres is pretty?" is a question that Pierre perfectly well understands and is perfectly well prepared to answer; the evidence that the form of words "Londres is pretty" expresses a belief that he holds is every bit as good as the evidence that the form of words "London is pretty" expresses a belief that he doesn't.

6. It goes without saying that this claim is made on behalf of state *types*, not state tokens. It will be the individuation of types rather than tokens that's at issue throughout the following discussion, except where the contrary is explicit.

7. If you're prepared to accept that encapsulated 'subdoxastic' states qualify as bona fide belief-states, then they offer further cases where belief-states that are identical in content, vehicle, and format are distinguished by their functional roles. For discussion, see Fodor, 1986.

8. I'm claiming that you can have difference of functional role (hence belief-state) without difference of vehicle; but does it go the other way around as well? Otherwise, we can do without specifying vehicles in belief individuation; all we need is functional roles.

   I'm inclined to think that Mates-type considerations show that there are at least some contexts in which you can slice belief-states as thin as you can slice quotations. Since it's hard to imagine a useful criterion for individuation of functional roles that doesn't slice *them* pretty thick, it seems plausible that 'vehicle' and 'functional role' are, at least in principle, independent parameters in the individuation of beliefs.

9. I'm indebted to Barry Loewer for a discussion that prompted the preceding three paragraphs.

10. Correspondingly, according to the present view, questions of *rationality* are assessed with respect to the vehicle of a belief as well as its content; whereas questions of *truth* are assessed with respect to content alone (see above). It's because the vehicle of his belief that his mother was eligible was, say, "J is eligible" rather than, say, "Mother is eligible" that O's seeking to marry his mother was not irrational in face of his abhorrence of incest. (I've heard it claimed that this won't do because appeals to merely morphosyntactic differences among vehicles *can't* rationalize differences in behavior; only appeals to differences in the *content* can do that. But the Pierre case looks to be a counterexample.)

Chapter 7

Stephen Schiffer's Dark Night of The Soul:

A Review of *Remnants of Meaning*

Stephen Schiffer used to believe in a theory—or better, in a theory schema, or better still, in a research program—that he calls "Intention-based Semantics" (IBS). But he doesn't believe in it any more, and it's the old story: you lose your faith, you have an existential crisis; you have an existential crisis, you write a book. ". . . [Are my views] *despairing?* That is a . . . difficult question to answer, and one that I care very much about. I do not want to think that my career is to show the fly the way out of the fly-bottle. I wish that I could go on from here to raise new questions. . . . But I have not been able to define those questions. I would like to think that I have not *yet* succeeded. Maybe the answer lies in some alliance with cognitive science" (Schiffer, 1987, 271). You can read *Remnants of Meaning* as a philosopher's *8 1/2*, an analytical *Baby, Its Cold Outside*; imagine *Either/ or* rewritten by Tarski, and you'll have the feel of it. However you read it, it's a super book: richly detailed, beautifully argued, and with a comprehensive geographer's sense of the lay of the landscape. This is, I think, the best attack on Intentional Realism that has ever been written. What it isn't, however, is convincing. Thank Heaven, since, of course, Intentional Realism is true.

Two doctrines distinguish IBS from other species of Intentional Realism. These are (i) the idea that the semantic properties of natural language expressions (the meaning of words and sentences, for example) should reduce to the intentional properties of the mental states of speaker/hearers (I'll call this Grice's Program), and (ii) the idea that there should be something *naturalistically specifiable* that is— as Schiffer likes to put it—*what makes it the case* that someone believes that *P* (I'll call this the Naturalization Program). If the Gricean program and the Naturalization program can be carried through, then IBS will have solved one of the Great Metaphysical Problems: it will have found a place for meaning in the natural order. It would certainly be nice to solve a Great Metaphysical Problem; philosophy could do with a success or two.

But, as remarked above, Schiffer has lost his faith in IBS. It's not that he thinks it suffers from internal incoherence; rather he has come to doubt that IBS can cash its checks. Neither the Gricean nor the Naturalistic reduction can, in Schiffer's view, be carried out. His book surveys all the proposals for doing so that he has found in the literature, together with all the other options that he's been able to think of, with arguments to show that none of them will work.

Now, the trouble with this way of arguing is that it's convincing only if you have a cat for every mousehole. It's open to the committed advocate of IBS to claim that Schiffer has failed to consider all the options; or that some of the options that he does consider are in fact in better shape than he supposes. A predictable reaction to Schiffer's polemic is, "Well, he's right about everybody's kind of IBS *except mine.*" I must confess to reacting in something like this way. There are, I think, paths through the thicket that Schiffer hasn't shown to be dead ends. And I think that he underestimates the empirical—as opposed to the logico-semantical—motivations for IBS. IBS *must* be right because there are facts about intentionality that nothing else will explain. Or so it seems to me. The rest of this discussion is devoted to the elaboration of these themes.

1. *Intentional Properties.*

Schiffer often has it that the main issue is whether intentional psychological states are *relational*; standard versions of IBS treat belief as a relation between a believer and a thing of a certain kind, where the content of one's belief depends on *which* thing of that kind one is belief-related to. To put the same idea in the formal mode, "believes that P" expresses a relation between a believer and something—an object of belief—that "that P" names. Qua Intentional Realists, IBS theorists have to hold that the "that P" position in "believes that P" is subject to 'objectual', as opposed to merely 'substitutional' quantification. Qua Gricean Reductionists, IBS theorists have to hold that the facts about these putative objects of the attitudes are ontologically independent of any semantical facts about natural languages since the semantical facts about natural languages are themselves supposed to depend on the facts about propositional attitudes. And, qua naturalists, IBS theorists have to hold that the object of the belief relation and the conditions for bearing that relation to one of these objects are specifiable in nonsemantic and nonintentional vocabulary.

When he is in the mood to set things up this way, Schiffer's argument is that there simply aren't any candidates for objects of the attitudes that will meet these conditions. Propositions, sets of worlds, mental representations, modes of presentation, prototypes, and so forth are examined and dismissed, sometimes for familiar reasons, often for reasons that are new and strikingly insightful.

Now, the claim that propositional attitudes are relations equivocates between a metaphysical thesis and a thesis about logical form. You could imagine a version of IBS that runs like this: Semantic facts about natural languages reduce to facts about the intentional states of speaker/hearers (as above). An intentional state is a state of instantiating an intentional property. The Naturalistic Program requires providing naturalistically specified conditions for having such properties and it *may* be that some or all of these conditions are relational. (Maybe they involve having a sentence of Mentalese in your belief box; or being causally connected to the world in the right sort of way, etc.) But it's left open, so far as questions of *logical form* are concerned, whether "*x* believes that *P*" is notated as *R(x, that P)* or just as *Fx*. In particular, it's left open whether "that *P*" is a referring expression in "believes that *P*" and what, if it is, it denotes.

Consider, for example, informational versions of IBS. According to them, the basic semantic properties are species of *carrying the information that P*, and the conditions for a thing's having these properties are spelled out by reference to (actual and counterfactual) causal relations. To a zero-ith approximation, "*x* carries the information *that a if F*" comes out, after Naturalization, as something like "*x* is in a state that is reliably caused by *a*'s being *F*." The question of the denotational (or otherwise) status of "*that a is F*" in "carries the information *that a is F*" is moot, since nothing corresponding to this expression is left in the Naturalized version of the theory; "that *a* is *F*" translates out, like the reference to the average man in "the average man's income." (Schiffer doesn't actually say much about informational theories of content. He seem to think that they have an insuperable problem in making sense of error; and I agree that this problem is insuperable if going teleological (à la recent proposals by Dennett, Millikan, Papineau, and Stalnaker, for example) is the only way to supe it. But this may be one of those cases of too many mouseholes for too few cats (see chapter 3).

Anyhow, insofar as IBS is defined by its commitment to Realism, Griceanism, and Naturalism, it's unclear to me that it also needs to endorse any particular doctrine about the logical form of attitude sentences; or, indeed, any logico-semantic theses about attitude sentences whatever. What really matters to Intentional Realism—hence to IBS—is not whether psychological properties are relational, but just whether there *are* any psychological properties; and whether, if there are, any of them are instantiated.

From the IBS theorist's perspective, there may be a strategic point to this shift of emphasis. The argument that "that-" clauses refer (to propositions, as it might be) is motivated, almost entirely, by semantical and epistemological considerations. One needs a story about what it is for a sentence to mean what it does; one needs a story about what it is to grasp the meaning of a sentence; one needs a solution of Frege's problem; and one needs a reading of belief sentences that quantify over contents. Propositions and the like are tailor-made—arguable all *too* tailor-made—to give one what one needs. But none of this will impress a guy who is already dubious about the status of the alleged semantic facts. Complain to Quine that there are no truths about meaning unless "that-"clauses denote, and he will tell you that, sure, the myth about propositions is of a piece with the myth of content; and so much the worse for both. Schiffer is clearly inclined to see this Quine's way: the real charge is less that IBS doesn't work than that it isn't motivated. It's only because you are *already* committed to a misguided sort of semantical Realism that the IBS agenda seems pressing. "The questions that now define the philosophy of language seem to have false presuppositions" (p. 269) so the cure for IBS is to stop asking the questions it's supposed to answer. Stop asking, "What do 'that-' clauses refer to?" and "What, beside people, does *everybody believes something* quantify over?"—for two examples.

But however that may be, Realism about psychological states and properties seems to be motivated independent of tendentious semantical assumptions. All the evidence suggests that there are intentional psychological *laws*. On the one hand, laws are relations among properties, so there can't be psychological laws unless there are psychological properties; on the other hand, individuals are subsumed by psychological laws in virtue of the psychological states they're in, so if there are psychological laws there must be psychological states to fall under them.[1] I wouldn't for the world be taken as suggesting that Schiffer has failed to notice this way of running IBS. But I do think he substantially underestimates its resilience, and I now propose to harp on this.

Schiffer offers two different lines of argument:

(*i*)   There aren't really any psychological laws, so psychological properties aren't, after all, required for psychological laws to hold among.

(*ii*)   If there are psychological properties, they must be reducible to physical properties. But there are no such reductions. So there are no psychological properties.[2]

Let's have a look at this, starting with argument (*ii*).

First off I propose to give Schiffer his premise that psychological states/properties aren't *reducible* to physical states/properties. For one thing, nothing ever seems to reduce to anything, as Schiffer often reminds us, and why should intentionality prove the exception? Indeed, the standard attempts to provide a reduction—behaviorism, type physicalism, and functionalism—are all pretty clearly bankrupt. It may be, for example, that intentional states have some of their functional properties essentially; but, like Schiffer, I doubt there's any chance that they have their semantical properties *in virtue of* their functional properties, which is what a functionalist reduction of *believing that P* would require.

Notice, however, that conceding this doesn't give the game away to anti-Naturalists. There isn't a *reductive* account of *being a mountain*, but nobody doubts that *mountainhood* is as real as any property gets. If nothing ever reduces to anything, that just shows that reduction is the wrong thing for Naturalists in psychology to demand. What's wanted—for the geological properties as well as the psychological properties—is just that we be able to understand *how purely physical things can have them*. In the case of mountains, we want to know how anything made entirely of electrons, protons, quarks, and the like could obey the laws that geology says apply to mountains. In the case of beliefs and desires, we want to know how anything made entirely of electrons, protons, quarks, and the like could obey the laws that psychology says apply to intentional states. In neither case do general strictures against *reduction* show that we can't have this.

All of which amounts to saying that if you're a Realist about psychological properties, you had better be prepared to be a (Property) Dualist about them. But then, if Schiffer is right and IBS requires property monism—if it requires, specifically, the identity of psychological properties with physical ones—then IBS is in deep trouble. So, what is Schiffer's case for property monism?

Schiffer has it in mind to run a sort of overdetermination argument (see circa p. 151); it's a variant of the currently fashionable worry that either psychological properties are physical properties, or they are epiphenomenal. Here's how this argument goes: Nobody doubts—well, almost nobody doubts—that the etiology of human behavior, like the etiology of everything else, falls under physical laws. So if there are also irreducibly *psychological* laws—as presumably there will be if there are irreducibly psychological properties—it must be, according to Schiffer, that "there is overdetermination at the level of *causal laws*. That is to say, there is one causal law [L] containing [neural/physical property] *P* and another [causal law] L' containing [psychological/intentional property] *B*; subsumption under either law is sufficient to explain [an event] *n*'s being a cause of [some behavior], and *n* is covered by both laws by virtue of having *P* and *B*." Schiffer thinks that property dualism thus implies "a sort of overdetermination [that] is in danger of being as difficult to believe in as the [*substance* dualism] that postulate[s] an overdetermination of actual causes, and for pretty much the same reason: superfluousness with respect to independent application. Because all bodily movements have complete explanations in wholly physical terms, L' would never explain a sequence of events except when that sequence was already explained by an *L*-style law."

Now I admit to being not much moved by this, and for reasons that Schiffer himself goes on to recite: "A reasonable version of the unity of science would hold that the laws of no special science have application independently of the laws of physics. . . . This could be viewed as a kind of acceptable 'overdetermination' at the level of causal laws, and it is imaginable that the [property] dualist . . . would try to claim that his overdetermination was acceptable in the same way." Quite so. Special-science laws (psychological laws of course included) are always *nonbasic*; this is to say that there are invariably *physical mechanisms* the operation of which connects the satisfaction of the antecedents of such laws with the satisfaction of their consequents. And, of course, the operation of these physical mechanisms is governed by the laws of physics. This is arguably all that "overdetermination at the level of causal laws" comes to *in psychology or elsewhere in the special sciences*. But if this sort of overdetermination isn't an argument against Boyle's Law, why is it an argument against the Weber-Fechner law? Schiffer Unfair to Working Psychologists! Shop Elsewhere!

For my kind of IBS, this is a critical juncture in the argument; my own particular mouse lives *right here*. I am therefore relieved to report a substantial absence of cat. Schiffer says that the difficulty is in seeing how the Property Dualist could suggest assimilating intentional overdetermination to the routine overdetermination of special science laws given that the "[psychological] property B was [assumed to be] irreducible and given his denial that its causal efficacy could be explained in terms of [neurophysical properties]. . . . Although I do not have a theory of acceptable intertheoretic relations to offer, it does seem clear that the onus is on the [Property Dualist] to defeat the assumption that his overdetermination would not fit into the acceptable mold" (p. 151).

I'm not at all sure what's going on here. Since "nothing reduces to anything" applies to mountainhood inter alia, the irreducibility of psychological properties is no worse than the irreducibility of geological properties. (At least it hasn't been *shown* to be worse). So, if Schiffer is prepared to live with overdetermination in the case of irreducible geological laws about mountainhood, why is he not prepared to live with overdetermination in the case of irreducible psychological laws about beliefhood? And correspondingly, if there's a sense in which the causal efficacy of psychological properties can't be explained by appeal to the physical properties of organisms, that's just to say that there *really are* psychological laws, and we really do need them to explain the way that organisms behave. But then, in *that* sense, the causal efficacy of mountainhood can't be explained by appealing to the physical properties of mountains. That's just to say that there *really are* geological laws, and we really do need them to explain the way that mountains behave. If we didn't need them, I suppose we'd stop doing geology and do just physics.

These are, no doubt, deep waters; but the proliferation of special sciences (for evidence of which, see any university catalogue) does suggest a certain metaphysical speculation: It appears that matter is subsumed by reliable, counterfactual supporting generalizations *at many levels of aggregation*. Correspondingly, if scientists want to capture these generalizations, they need to be Realist about the properties of matter *at many levels of aggregation*. That is, arguably, what the explanatory irreducibility of special-science laws and properties comes to in psychology *and* geology. So why is Schiffer worried about the one but not about the other?

Schiffer's flagship argument for intentional property monism is overdetermination; but I think that what's really driving his intuitions is just skepticism about there being psychological laws at all. Intentional laws aren't able to be taken seriously, and *that's* why the metaphysical morals suggested by *real* special sciences don't apply to psychology. (That Schiffer's book should, in spite of this, close with the hope that an alliance with cognitive science may revive the theory of intentionality only shows the depths of his existential despair). Well, what does this skepticism about intentional laws actually come to? Here Schiffer's polemics turn uncharacteristically old hat: Putative psychological laws have ceteris paribus clauses that can't be filled in; when one tries to state the laws precisely they degenerate into tautologies.

> For suppose that Ava stepped back because she saw that a car
> was coming. . . . If there is *any* "law" that applies to the mental
> causation of her act, it is surely some belief/desire generalization,
> some generalization that refines and completes, and otherwise
> makes respectable, the platitude that if a person desires to avoid
> a certain result (say, getting run over by a car), believes that she
> will avoid that result by doing an act of a certain type (say,
> stepping back to the curb), believes that she is able to perform
> an act of that type, does not believe that there is any better, or
> equally good, way of avoiding that result [etc., then] . . . she
> will perform an act of that type. What is problematic here is that,
> first, it is by no means clear that this "generalization" has any
> true completion, and, second, to the extent that we can fill it
> out, to that extent it begins to look more and more analytic, more
> and more expressive of truths constitutive of our propositional-
> attitude concepts, and thus less and less like a contingent causal
> law. (p. 148)

Now, in the first place, if "many [philosophers] have commented on
the analytic, or quasi-analytic, nature of belief desire generalizations"
(p. 286), equally many have commented on the "analytic, or quasi-
analytic" nature of the deepest laws in *any* empirical theory; and
Quine has suggested—completely convincingly, in my view—that
they were all wrong to do so. What seems to be the *analyticity*,
(conventionality, etc.) of these laws is just their *centrality* misper-
ceived; the doctrine that "$F=MA$" (as it might be) is quasi-analytic
postulates a semantic fact where there is only an epistemic one. But
if this is true of the putative analyticity of the basic laws of mechanics,
why shouldn't it also be true of the putative analyticity of the basic
decision-theoretic laws that relate beliefs and desires to one another
and to actions?

In the second place, it is unclear why the elimination of ceteris
paribus clauses—the replacement of ceteris paribus laws by "some
generalization that refines and completes [them]"—is required to
make such laws "respectable." Respectable laws do all sorts of useful
things—they back singularly causal statements; they play a crucial
role in Hempelian explanations; they secure counterfactuals, and so
forth. Presumably, the respectability of a law *just is* its availability for
these sorts of functions. Well, I know of no argument why ceteris
paribus laws can't do these things, even assuming—what, indeed, I
do assume—that their ceteris paribicity is typically ineliminable. Indeed, it had better be that ceteris paribus laws can be respectable

qua ceteris paribus laws; because, as usual, Schiffer's complaints about intentional psychology apply, whole cloth, to the *un*tendentious special sciences. The laws of geology are *also* ceteris paribus laws ineliminably; i.e., they can't be "completed" *in the vocabulary of geology*. (I suppose that they can be "completed" in the vocabulary of physics; but I suppose this of psychological laws too.) But the laws of geology are, surely, OK? I mean, like, they're respectable even by philosophy's stringent standards?

And, finally, what about all the *other* psychological laws? For example, what about the law that, ceteris paribus, the probability of recalling an item from a list of otherwise unstructured stimuli is a nonmonotonic function of its ordinal position. Or the law that, ceteris paribus, the apparent change of intensity of a stimulus is a power function of its change in physical intensity. Or the law that, ceteris paribus, the apparent prosody of a sentence is a function of its constituent structure. Unlike the practical syllogism, these laws typically quantify—not just *over* contents, but also *into*—content clauses.[3] (For example, laws about prosody say things like: *For certain prosodic features X, there are certain structural features Y such that, for many positions Z, if a sentence has Y at Z, then the sentence will be heard as having X at Z*. Prima facie, these generalizations quantify into the intentional context "heard . . . as . . ."). But psychological generalizations that quantify into content clauses exhibit no tendency to look more "more and more analytic" as they are stated with increasing precision. This is hardly surprising; such a law applies to a belief state not qua belief state but, as it might be, qua state of believing *that a is F*. So it's hard to see how it could be analytic *of belief* ("constitutive of our propositional attitude concepts") even if, for example, the practical syllogism turns out to be.

The practical syllogism *may* analyze to a platitude (though I doubt it; if nothing reduces to anything, nothing analyzes to anything either). But, I promise you, the serial position curve isn't going to. It's contingent all the way through. And it's intentional all the way through. Because there are many, many such examples, I take it that the prima facie evidence strongly favors contingent and irreducible intentional laws. So I take it that the argument from irreducible intentional laws to intentional Property Dualism remains intact. So I take it that there's at least one intact argument for Intentional Realism. And, as Schiffer agrees, an intact argument for Intentional Realism is an intact argument for IBS, since IBS is the only kind of Intentional Realism that has a chance to work.

I conclude that Schiffer is short at least one cat.

2. *Compositional Semantics*

Schiffer holds that, if there is to be a compositional semantics for belief predicates, that alone requires that believing must be relational: Just by assuming compositional semantics, you get, if not IBS, then at least Intentional Realism. ". . . I have argued that . . . the relational theory of propositional attitudes [is false] and the falsity of the theory would seem to be inconsistent with the proposition that natural languages have a compositional semantics . . . the only feasible way of accommodating propositional-attitude verbs within a compositional semantics is as *relational* predicates that relate, in the case of 'believes', a believer to what he believes." Schiffer is prepared to bite this bullet: Since propositional attitudes are not relational, the semantics of natural languages is not compositional. Schiffer's argument that it is independently plausible that the semantics of natural languages is not compositional is among the most striking features of his book. Here's how that argument goes:

To begin with, it's untendentious that speaker-hearers (of English, say) are able to understand utterances of novel expressions in their language. This would be comprehensible if English did have a compositional semantics. For, in effect, a compositional semantics for L is a procedure which determines the meaning of any formula of L given the meaning and syntactic arrangement of its lexical constituents. The speaker-hearer's ability to grasp novel expressions is explained on the assumption that he knows such a procedure.

Schiffer's reply to this, set out in detail in chapter 8, strikes me as exactly right and is intrinsically interesting *however* things turn out for IBS. What Schiffer says, considerably boiled down, amounts to this: assume the standard story according to which speaker-hearers are computational systems whose mental processes are defined over the formulas in some language of thought (call it M[entalese]). Then you can think of understanding natural language expressions as a matter of *translating* them into M. To understand a sentence of English on this account *just is* to compute its M-translation.

Now, presumably you have to know the syntax of English in order to compute its M-translations because the M-translation of an English expression depends not just on its lexical content but on its syntax as well. (The M-translation of "John loves Mary" has to come out different from the M-translation of "Mary loves John," etc.). But it's far from obvious that you have to know the *semantics* of an English expression to determine its M-translation; on the contrary, the translation algorithm might well consist of operations that deliver Mentalese expressions under syntactic description as output given

English expressions under syntactic description as input *with no se-mantics coming in anywhere* except, of course, that if it's a good trans-lation, then semantic properties will be preserved. That purely syntactic operations can be devised to preserve semantic properties is the philosophical moral of proof theory.

So then, there's at least one way it might work out that the theory of language understanding does not presuppose a compositional semantics for the language understood. As I remarked above, this observation is extremely important, regardless of the present meta-physical issues. It is very widely assumed, among cognitive scientists at least, that semantics is *a level of linguistic description,* just like syntax or phonology; specifically, that the same sorts of arguments that suggest that speaker-hearers have to know the syntax of their lan-guage also suggest that they have to know its semantics. (To see this assumption at work, look at books like Jackendoff's *Semantic Inter-pretation in Generative Grammar.*) But in fact this is all wrong, and for precisely the reason that Schiffer points out. It's entirely natural to run a computational story about the attitudes together with a trans-lation story about language comprehension; and there's no reason to doubt, so far at least, that the sort of translation that's required is an exhaustively syntactic operation. That you know the semantics of your language *does not follow* from the fact that you can understand the indefinitely many sentences of your language; it doesn't follow even by argument to the best explanation.

There is, in short, a way of developing the computational picture in philosophy of mind that suggests much the same moral as recent 'externalist' speculations in philosophy of language: Syntax is about what's in your head, but semantics is about how your head is con-nected to the world. Syntax is part of the story about the mental representation of sentences, but semantics isn't. I like this very much. I suspect in fact, that I like it even more than Schiffer does.

However, back to work. Arguing against a compositional semantics for English is, of course, no good for Schiffer's purpose of under-mining Intentional Realism, unless one is also prepared to argue against a compositional semantics for Mentalese. And here, it seems to me, Schiffer had trouble. He says, correctly, that ". . . if there's a reason for thinking M needs a compositional semantics, then that reason cannot have anything to do with understanding public-lan-guage utterances" (p. 206). That is, so far as the story about under-standing English is concerned, it's coherent to assume that *neither* English *nor* Mentalese has a compositional semantics. We don't need a combinatorial semantics for English because, though using English requires understanding its sentences, we can identify understanding

English sentences with translating them into Mentalese (see above). And, appearances to the contrary notwithstanding, this need not generate a regress. In particular, we don't need a combinatorial semantics for Mentalese because *using a productive language as a medium of computation doesn't require access to its semantics*; by definition, computational processes are exhaustively syntactic, and it's not in dispute that Mentalese has a combinatorial *syntax*. Making the syntactic character of computation clear was Turing's foundational contribution to the philosophy of mind. Turing's way of getting mental processes to be symbolic without having to postulate a regression of understanders is what the idea of computation *buys you* in the philosophy of mind.

OK so far. However, there are at least two other kinds of considerations—considerations that *don't* derive from facts about how we understand English—that argue for a compositional semantics for Mentalese. Schiffer considers only one of these, and I find what he says about it unconvincing.

Schiffer thinks that you don't need to assume a compositional semantics for M to account for the role that its formulas play as—to put it a little misleadingly—the 'immediate objects' of beliefs. This requires some unpacking. The standard language of thought story—the one that Schiffer requires for his account of understanding English as translation into Mentalese—is that believing P is being in a certain relation to a formula of M. Formulas of M are the immediate objects of belief in the sense given by S:

> S: (u) (EP) (if u is a sentence of M and u is in one's belief-box, then one believes that P). (p. 218)

So the present question is: does S presuppose a compositional semantics for M? No, according to Schiffer, because "we could discover this [i.e., that S is true] via a mapping of formulae of M onto English content sentences (i.e., those that occur in "that"-clauses)—in effect, a translation from M into English—together with the understanding we already have of English." (p. 218). This is a little cryptic, but I guess the idea is that if we know which part of Herbert is his belief box (this means, near enough, 'if we know what causal role u_i plays in Herbert's mental life'), then we could find out, empirically, that u_i is in Herbert's belief box if a certain English sentence (say the sentence "Herbert believes there's a cat on Granny's mat") is true. And that *would be* finding out what u_i means; viz., that it means that there's a cat on Granny's mat.

Now, I'm more than just a little doubtful about this. Schiffer puts his claim epistemologically: "We could discover that [S is true] . . .

etc." But what has to be the case for us to discover that S is true isn't to the point. What's to the point is what has to be the case for S to *be* true. And what has to be the case for S to be true can't, on pain of circularity, be something about the relation between M and English.

Schiffer thinks that the sentences of English have their semantical properties (specifically, their "saying potentials") in virtue of their "processing roles," where, in effect, the processing role of a sentence is its relation to its translation in M. (For Schiffer's elaboration of this story, see especially chapter 8, section 2). Well, the worry is that it can't both be that:

(i)   English sentences have their semantical properties in virute of their relation to sentence of Mentalese

and that:

(ii)   *What makes it the case* that u_i is the immediate object of, say, the belief that there's a cat on Granny's mat, is that u_i is the formula that translates the English sentence "there's a cat on Granny's mat" (i.e., u_i is the formula that translates the English sentence whose "saying potential" is *that* there's a cat on Granny's mat).

You can't *both* derive the semantical properties of English sentences from those of their Mentalese translations *and* derive the semantical properties of Mentalese formulas from those of their English translations. At least, I don't *think* you can.

I suppose Schiffer might respond with a charge of begging the question; viz., that, on the current deflationary view, there is *nothing* that "makes it the case" that Mentalese formulas mean what they do. But I don't think I'm having this. My point isn't, after all, that Schiffer has failed to provide a *reductive* account of the meaning of formulas in Mentalese; that complaint *would* be question begging in the present context. But it's one thing to say there is no reductive story about Mentalese semantics; it's quite another thing to say there is no story at all; that it is, as it were, just a brute fact that a certain Mentalese formula means that it's raining and not that the cat is on the mat. That a symbol means what it does *can't* be a brute fact; it's not the right *kind* of fact to be brute. So, a story is wanted about what makes the symbols of Mentalese mean what they do. And, as far as I can see, either Schiffer has no such story, or he's got one that swallows its own tail by embracing both (*i*) and (*ii*), thereby committing circularity. Either way, I doubt that Schiffer has what he admits he needs: a case that *S* doesn't require a compositional semantics for M.

Anyhow Schiffer ignores a straightforward and indeed familiar argument that Mentalese must have a compositional semantics; one which seems to me as decisive as anything ever gets in this part of the woods. I'll close with a word on this.

Mentalese must itself be productive. The reasoning is, as I say, familiar: on the one hand, propositional attitudes derive their semantical properties (their intentional contents) from the semantics of the Mentalese expressions that are their immediate objects (as per S). And, on the other hand, there are infinitely many psychologically possible, semantically distinct, propositional attitudes (of which *the belief that Granny has a cat on her mat, the belief that Granny has two cats on her mat, the belief that Granny has three cats on her mat,* etc., provide an extendible subset.) It follows that there are infinitely many formulas of Mentalese.

Notice—and this is crucial—that this infinity of Mentalese expressions is not to be accounted for simply by assuming that M has a recursive *syntax*. What needs to be explained is that (synonymy aside) each of the syntactically distinct expressions of M has its distinctive truth condition. The point is not just that what corresponds in M to the English "Granny has a cat" has to be *morphosyntactically* distinct from what corresponds in M to the English "Granny has two cats"; it also has to come out that each of these morphosyntactically distinct M expressions has a truth condition different from the other. And, on the one hand, on pain of circularity, the buck has to stop at Mentalese; these facts about the meanings of M expressions can't be parasitic on semantic facts about English. And, on the other hand, nobody has the slightest idea how M could be semantically productive unless it has a compositional semantics.

I take it, and I take it that Schiffer grants it, that the metaphysical consequences of postulating a compositional semantics for Mentalese would not be interestingly different from the metaphysical consequences of postulating a compositional semantics for English. In particular, if (theory) *T* is the correct compositional semantics for M, then *T* must entail infinitely many formulas of the form *F means that P*, where *F* is a quoted formula of M and *P* is a formula semantically equivalent to *F*. And now we're in the soup again; we need a theory to explain how merely physical things like tokens of *F* could have semantical properties like *meaning that P*; the very sort of theory that Schiffer doubts that we can have.

(I pause to remark parenthetically, for those who are not prepared to idealize to an infinity of psychologically possible attitudes, or who are prepared to accept the idealization only in the case of verbal organisms, that an analog to the productivity argument can be run on the *systematicity* of the attitudes; systematicity is a property that finite minds—indeed, quite small finite minds—can have. See Fodor, 1987; Fodor and Pylyshyn, 1988.)

So, here's the story in a nutshell. Schiffer is right; we don't know how IBS *could* be true. But IBS is the metaphysics we require to explain how there could be intentional laws, and it's the metaphysics that the computational theory of the mind presupposes. So we know that IBS *must* be true. So we know that IBS *is* true. So, there's no need to throw an existential fit; *everything is going to be all right,* many current appearances to the contrary notwithstanding.

It doesn't follow, of course, that everything is going to be all right *in the near future.* In the meantime, faith is the evidence of things unseen.

Notes

1. The implications of this issue about whether there are psychological laws reverberate through the whole architecture of Schiffer's argument. Thus, it's part of Schiffer's "no-theory theory" of meaning (see his chapter 10) that there aren't substantive answers to questions like "In virtue of what does someone have the belief that P?" (*Non*substantive, "pleonastic" answers include "in virtue of believing that P" and the like). But this line is plausible only on the assumption that "believes that P" isn't a natural-kind predicate (i.e., that there are no laws about creatures that believe that *P* qua creatures that believe that *P*.) Schiffer is quite aware that, where we do have (nonbasic) natural kinds (like, say, *water*), we expect substantive answers to "in virtue of what" questions (answers like "something is water in virtue of its being H$_2$O").

2. What's at issue here isn't, of course, Nominalism. Somebody who doesn't doubt that there are properties can nevertheless doubt that there are mental properties that are irreducibly nonphysical (where a physical property is, let's say, one in virtue of which individuals are subsumed by the laws of an appropriately ideal physics.)

3. It's a little unfortunate that when philosophers have wanted examples of good candidates for intentional laws, they've generally chosen ones like the practical syllogism or "ceteris paribus, if you believe *P* and you believe if *P* then *Q*, then you believe *Q*" and so forth. The point about these sorts of examples is that they are indifferent to the content of the mental states that they apply to; relations of identity and difference of content are all that they care about.

   It is, however, a bad idea to run your philosophical psychology on the assumption that all intentional laws are like this. The examples in the text are counterinstances; and there are very many others.

PART II

Modularity

You have to have the facts before you can pervert them.
—Mark Twain

Chapter 8
Précis of *The Modularity of Mind*

Everybody knows that something is wrong. But it is uniquely the achievement of contemporary philosophy—indeed, it is uniquely the achievement of contemporary *analytical* philosophy—to have figured out just what it is. What is wrong is not making enough distinctions. If only we made all the distinctions that there are, then we should all be as happy as kings. (Kings are notoriously *very* happy.)

The Modularity of Mind (henceforth *Modularity*) is a monograph much in the spirit of that diagnosis. I wanted to argue there (and will likewise argue here) that modern Cognitivism failed, early on, to notice a certain important distinction: roughly, a distinction between two ways in which computational processes can be "smart." Because it missed this distinction, Cognitivism failed to consider some models of mental architecture for which a degree of empirical support can be marshaled, models that may, indeed, turn out to be true. If these models *are* true, then standard accounts of the nature of cognition and perception—and of the relations between them—are seriously misled, with consequences that can be felt all the way from artificial intelligence to epistemology. That was my story, and I am going to stick to it.

"What," you will ask, "was this missed distinction; who missed it; and how did missing it lead to these horrendous consequences?" I offer a historical reconstruction in the form of a fairy tale. None of what follows actually happened, but it makes a good story and has an edifying moral.

So then: Once upon a time, there was a Wicked Behaviorist. He was, alas, a mingy and dogmatic creature of little humor and less poetry; but he did keep a clean attic. Each day, he would climb up to his attic and throw things out, for it was his ambition eventually to have *almost nothing in his attic at all*. (Some people whispered that this was his *only* ambition, that the Wicked Behaviorist was actually just a closet Ontological Purist. For all I know, they were right to whisper this.)

Anyhow, one day when the Wicked Behaviorist was upstairs clean-
ing out his attic, the following Very Interesting Thought occurred to
him. "Look," he said to himself, *"I can do without perceptual processes."*
(Because he had been educated in Vienna, the Wicked Behaviorist
usually thought in the formal mode. So what actually occurred to
him was that he could do without a *theory* of perceptual processes.
It comes to much the same thing.) "For," it continued to occur to
him, "perceptual identification reduces without residue to discriminative responding. And discriminative responding reduces without
residue to the manifestation of conditioned (as it might be, operant)
reflexes. And the theory of conditioned reflexes reduces without
residue to Learning Theory. So, though learning is one of the things
that there are, perceptual processes are one of the things there aren't.
There also aren't: The True, or The Beautiful, or Santa Claus, or
Tinkerbell; and unicorns are metaphysically impossible and George
Washington wore false teeth. So there. Grrr!" He really was a *very*
Wicked Behaviorist.

Fortunately, however, in the very same possible world in which
the WB eked out a meager existence as a value of a bound variable
(for who would call that living?), there was also a Handsome Cognitivist. And whereas the WB had this preference for clean attics and
desert landscapes, the HC's motto was: "The more the merrier, more
or less!" It was the HC's view that almost nothing reduces to almost
anything else. To say that the world is full of a number of things
was, he thought, putting it mildly; for the HC, every day was like
Christmas in Dickens, ontologically speaking. In fact, far from wishing to throw old things out, he was mainly interested in turning new
things up. "Only collect," the HC was often heard to say. Above
all—and this is why I'm telling you this story—the HC wanted mental
processes in general, and perceptual processes in particular, to be
part of his collection.

Moreover, the HC had an argument. "Perceptual processes," he
said, *"can't"* be reflexes because, whereas reflexes are paradigmatically
dumb, perceptual processes are demonstrably smart. Perception is
really a part of cognition; it involves a kind of *thinking*."[1]

"And what demonstrates that perceptual processes are smart?"
grumbled the Wicked Behaviorist.

"I will tell you," answered the Handsome Cognitivist. "What demonstrates that perceptual processes are smart is *poverty of the stimulus
arguments*". (A poverty of the stimulus argument alleges that there
is typically *more information* in a perceptual response than there is in
the proximal stimulus that prompts the response; hence perceptual
integration must somehow involve the *contribution* of information by

the perceiving organism. No one knows how to quantify the relevant notion of information, so it is hard to show conclusively that this sort of argument is sound. On the other hand, such phenomena as the perceptual constancies have persuaded almost everybody—except Gibsonians and Wicked Behaviorists—that poverty of the stimulus arguments have to be taken very seriously. I shall assume, in what follows, that this is so.) "Poverty of the stimulus arguments," continued the HC, "show that perceptual identifications can't be reflexive responses to proximal stimulus invariants. In fact, poverty of the stimulus arguments strongly suggest that perceptual identifications depend on some sort of *computations*, perhaps on computations of quite considerable complexity. So, once we have understood the force of poverty of the stimulus arguments, we see that there probably are perceptual processes after all. And," the HC added in a rush, "I believe that here are Truth and Beauty and Santa Claus and Tinkerbeil too (only you have to read the existential quantifier leniently). And I believe that for each drop of rain that falls / A flower is born. So *there*." (Some people whispered that the Handsome Cognitivist, though he was *very* handsome, was perhaps just a little wet. For all I know, they were right to whisper that, too.) End of fairy tale.

My point is this: Modern Cognitivism starts with the use of poverty of the stimulus arguments to show that perception is smart, hence that perceptual identification can't be reduced to reflexive responding. However—and I think this is good history and not a fairy tale at all—in their enthusiasm for this line of argument, early Cognitivists failed to distinguish between two quite different respects in which perceptual processes might be smarter than reflexes. Or, to put it the other way around, they failed to distinguish between two respects in which perception might be similar to cognition. It is at precisely this point that *Modularity* seeks to insert its wedge.

Reflexes, it is traditionally supposed, are dumb in two sorts of ways: they are *noninferential* and they are *encapsulated*.[2] To say that they are noninferential is just to say that they are supposed to depend on "straight-through" connections. On the simplest account, stimuli elicit reflexive responses directly, without mediating mental processing. It is my view that the HC was right about perceptual processes and reflexive ones being different in *this* respect. Poverty of the stimulus arguments do make it seem plausible that a lot of inference typically intervenes between a proximal stimulus and a perceptual identification.

By contrast, to describe reflexes as encapsulated is to say that they go off largely without regard to the beliefs and utilities of the behaving organism; to a first approximation, all that you need to do to evoke a reflex is to present the appropriate eliciting stimulus. Here's how *Modularity* put this point:

> Suppose that you and I have known each other for many a long year . . . and you have come fully to appreciate the excellence of my character. In particular, you have come to know perfectly well that under no conceivable circumstances would I stick my finger in your eye. Suppose that this belief of yours is both explicit and deeply felt. You would, in fact, go to the wall for it. Still, if I jab my finger near enough to your eyes, and fast enough, you'll blink. . . . [The blink reflex] has no access to what you know about my character or, for that matter, to any other of your beliefs, utilities, [or] expectations. For this reason the blink reflex is often produced when sober reflection would show it to be uncalled for. . . . (p. 71)

In this respect, reflexes are quite unlike a lot of "higher cognitive" processes, or so it would certainly seem. Chess moves, for example, aren't elicited willy-nilly by presentations of chess problems. Rather, the player's moves are determined by the state of his utilities (is he trying to win? or to lose? or is he, perhaps, just fooling around?) and by his beliefs, including his beliefs about the current state of the game, his beliefs about the structure of chess and the likely consequences of various patterns of play, his beliefs about the beliefs and utilities of his opponent, his beliefs about his opponent's beliefs about *his* beliefs and utilities, and so on up through ever so many orders of intentionality.

So, then, cognition is smart in two ways in which reflexes are dumb. Now the question arises: What is *perception* like in these respects? *Modularity* offers several kinds of arguments for what is, really, a main thesis of the book: Although perception is smart like cognition in that it is typically inferential, it is nevertheless dumb like reflexes in that it is typically encapsulated. Perhaps the most persuasive of these arguments—certainly the shortest—is one that adverts to the persistence of perceptual illusions. The apparent difference in length of the Mueller-Lyer figures, for example, doesn't disappear when one learns that the arrows are in fact the same size. It seems to follow that at least *some* of one's perceptual processes are insensitive to at least some of one's beliefs. Very much wanting the Mueller-Lyer illusion to go away doesn't make it disappear either; it seems to follow that at least some of one's perceptual processes are insensitive to at least some of one's utilities. The ecological good sense of this arrangement is surely self-evident. Prejudiced and wish-ful seeing makes for dead animals.

This sort of point seems pretty obvious; one might wonder how Cognitivist enthusiasm for "top down," "cognitively penetrated" per-ceptual models managed to survive in face of it. I think we have already seen part of the answer: Cognitivists pervasively confused the question about the encapsulation of perception with the question about its computational complexity. Because they believed—rightly—that poverty of the stimulus arguments settled the second question, they never seriously considered the issues implicit in the first one. You can actually *see* this confusion being perpetrated in some of the early Cognitivist texts. The following passage is from Bruner's "On Perceptual Readiness":

> Let it be plain that no claim is being made for the utter indistin-guishability of perceptual and more conceptual inferences. . . . I may know that the Ames distorted room that looks so rectan-gular is indeed distorted, but unless conflicting cues are put into the situation . . . the room still looks rectangular. So too with such compelling illusions as the Mueller-Lyer: In spite of knowl-edge to the contrary, the line with the extended arrowheads looks longer than the equal-length line with arrowheads inclined inward. *But these differences, interesting in themselves, must not lead us to overlook the common feature of inference underlying so much of cognitive activity.* (Bruner 1973, p. 8; emphasis added)

The issue raised by the persistence of illusion is not, however, whether some inferences are "more conceptual" than others—what-ever, precisely, that might mean. Still less is it whether perception is in some important sense inferential. Rather, what's at issue is: How rigid is the boundary between the information available to cognitive processes and the information available to perceptual ones? How much of what you know/believe/desire actually does affect the way you see? The persistence of illusion suggests that the answer must be: "at most, less than all of it."

So far, my charge has been that early Cognitivism missed the distinction between the inferential complexity of perception and its cognitive penetrability. But of course it's no accident that it was just that distinction that Cognitivists confused. Though they are inde-pendent properties of computational systems, inferential complexity and cognitive penetrability are intimately related—so intimately that, unless one is *very* careful, it's easy to convince oneself that the former actually entails the latter.

What connects inferential complexity and cognitive penetrability is the truism that inferences need premises. Here's how the argument might seem to go: poverty of the stimulus arguments show that the organism must contribute information to perceptual integrations; "perceptual inferences" just *are* the computations that effect such contributions. Now, this information that the organism contributes—the premises, as it were, of its perceptual inferences—must include not just sensory specifications of current proximal inputs but also "background knowledge" drawn from prior experience or innate endowment; for what poverty of the stimulus arguments show is precisely that sensory information alone underdetermines perceptual integrations. But, surely, the availability of background knowledge to processes of perceptual integration *is* the cognitive penetration of perception. So if perception is inferentially elaborated, it *must* be cognitively penetrated. Q.E.D.

What's wrong with this argument is that it depends on what one means by cognitive penetration. One might mean the availability to perceptual integration of some information not given in the proximal array. Because poverty of the stimulus arguments show that some such information must be available to perceptual integration, it follows that to accept poverty of the stimulus arguments is to accept the cognitive penetrability of perception *in this sense*. But one might also mean by the cognitive penetrability of perception that *anything that the organism knows, any information that is accessible to any of its cognitive processes,* is ipso facto available as a premise in perceptual inference. This is a much more dramatic claim; it implies the *continuity* of perception with cognition. And, if it is true, it has all sorts of interesting epistemic payoffs (see Fodor, 1984). Notice, however, that this stronger claim does not follow from the inferential complexity of perception.

Why not? Well, for the following boring reason. We can, in principle, imagine three sorts of architectural arrangements in respect of the relations between cognition and perception: *no* background information is available to perceptual integration; *some but not all* background information is available to perceptual integration; *everything one knows* is available to perceptual integration. Because poverty of the stimulus arguments imply the inferential elaboration of perception, and because inferences need premises, the first of these architectures is closed to the Cognitivist. But the second and third are still open, and the persistence of illusions is prima facie evidence that the second is the better bet.

We arrive, at last, at the notion of a psychological module. A module is, inter alia, an informationally encapsulated computational system—an inference-making mechanism whose access to background information is constrained by general features of cognitive architecture, hence relatively rigidly and relatively permanently constrained. One can conceptualize a module as a special-purpose computer with a proprietary database, under the conditions that (a) the operations that it performs have access *only* to the information in its database (together, of course, with specifications of currently impinging proximal stimulations), and (b) at least some information that is available to at least some cognitive process is *not* available to the module. It is a main thesis of *Modularity* that perceptual integrations are typically performed by computational systems that are informationally encapsulated in this sense.

Modularity has two other main theses which I might as well tell you about now. The first is that, although informational encapsulation is an essential property of modular systems, they also tend to exhibit other psychologically interesting properties. The notion of a module thus emerges as a sort of "cluster concept," and the claim that perceptual processes are modularized implies that wherever we look at the mechanisms that effect perceptual integration we see that this cluster of properties tends to recur. The third main thesis is that, whereas perceptual processes are typically modularized—hence encapsulated, hence stupid in one of the ways that reflexes are—the really "smart," really "higher" cognitive processes (thinking, for example) are not modular and, in particular, not encapsulated. So *Modularity* advocates a *principled distinction* between perception and cognition in contrast to the usual Cognitivist claims for their continuity.

Since *Modularity* goes into all of this in some detail, I don't propose to do so here; otherwise, why would you buy the book? But I do want to stress the plausibility of the picture that emerges. On the one hand, there are the perceptual processes; these tend to be input driven, very fast, mandatory, superficial, encapsulated from much of the organism's background knowledge, largely organized around bottom-to-top information flow, largely innately specified (hence ontogenetically eccentric), and characteristically associated with specific neuroanatomical mechanisms (sometimes even with specific neuroanatomical loci). They tend also to be domain specific, so that—to cite the classic case—the computational systems that deal with the perception/production of language appear to have not much in common with those that deal with, for example, the analysis of color or of visual form (or, for that matter, the analysis of nonspeech auditory signals). So strikingly are these systems autonomous that they often rejoice in their proprietary, domain-specific pathologies: compare the aphasias and agnosias. *Modularity* takes the view that it is high time to praise Franz Joseph Gall for having predicted the existence of psychological mechanisms that exhibit this bundle of properties. (Gall was approximately a contemporary of Jane Austen's, so you see how far we have come in cognitive psychology—and in the novel, for that matter.) It is precisely in the investigation of these "vertical faculties" that modern Cognitivism has contributed its most important insights, and *Modularity* suggests that this is no accident. Precisely because the perceptual mechanisms are encapsulated, we can make progress in studying them without having to commit ourselves about the general nature of the cognitive mind.

On the other hand, there are the true higher cognitive faculties. So little is known about them that one is hard-put even to say *which* true higher cognitive faculties there are. But "thought" and "problem solving" are surely among the names in the game, and here *Modularity*'s line is that these are everything that perception is not: slow, deep, global rather than local, largely under voluntary (or, as one says, "executive") control, typically associated with diffuse neurological structures, neither bottom-to-top nor top-to-bottom in their modes of processing, but characterized by computations in which information flows every which way. Above all, they are paradigmatically *un*encapsulated; the higher the cognitive process, the more it turns on the integration of information across superficially dissimilar domains. *Modularity* assumes that in this respect the higher cognitive processes are notably similar to processes of scientific discovery— indeed, that the latter are the former writ large. Both, of course, are deeply mysterious; we don't understand nondemonstrative inference in either its macrocosmic or its microcosmic incarnation.

If much of the foregoing is right, then mainstream Cognitive science has managed to get the architecture of the mind *almost exactly backwards*. By emphasizing the continuity of cognition with perception, it missed the computational encapsulation of the latter. By attempting to understand thinking in terms of a baroque proliferation of scripts, plans, frames, schemata, special-purpose heuristics, expert systems, and other species of domain-specific intellectual automatisms—jumped-up habits, to put it in a nutshell—it missed what is most characteristic and most puzzling about the higher cognitive mind: its nonencapsulation, its creativity, its holism, and its passion for the analogical. One laughs or weeps according to one's temperament. It was, perhaps, Eeyore who found precisely the right words: "'Pathetic,' he said, 'That's what it is, pathetic.'"

Well, yes, but *is* much of this right? I want at least to emphasize its plausibility from several different points of view. Perception is above all concerned with keeping track of the state of the organism's local spatiotemporal environment. Not the distant past, nor the distant future, and not—except for ecological accidents like stars—what is very far away. Perception is built to detect what is right here, right now—what is available, for example, for eating or being eaten by. If this is indeed its teleology, then it is understandable that perception should be performed by fast, mandatory, encapsulated, etc., systems that—considered, as it were, detection-theoretically—are prepared to trade false positives for high gain. It is, no doubt, important to attend to the eternally beautiful and to believe the eternally true. But it is more important not to be eaten.

Why, then, isn't perception even stupider, even less inferential than it appears to be? Why doesn't it consist of literally reflexive responses to proximal stimulations? Presumably because there is so much more variability in the proximal projections that an organism's environment offers to its sensory mechanisms than there is in the distal environment itself. This kind of variability is by definition irrelevant if it is the distal environment that you care about—which, of course, it almost always is. So the function of perception, from this vantage point, is to propose to thought a representation of the world from which such irrelevant variability has been effectively filtered. What perceptual systems typically "know about" is how to infer current distal layouts from current proximal stimulations: the visual system, for example, knows how to derive distal form from proximal displacement, and the language system knows how to infer the speaker's communicative intentions from his phonetic productions. Neither mechanism, on the present account, knows a great deal else, and that is entirely typical of perceptual organization. Perceptual systems have access to (implicit or explicit) theories of the mapping between distal causes and proximal effects. But that's all they have.

If the perceptual mechanisms are indeed local, stupid, and extremely nervous, it is teleologically sensible to have the picture of the world that they present tempered, reanalysed, and—as Kant saw—above all *integrated* by slower, better informed, more conservative, and more holistic cognitive systems. The purposes of survival are, after all, *sometimes* subserved by knowing the truth. The world's deep regularities don't show in a snapshot, so being bullheaded, ignoring the facts that aren't visible on the surface—encapsulation in short—is not the cognitive policy that one wants to pursue *in the long run*. The surface plausibility of the *Modularity* picture thus lies in the idea that Nature has contrived to have it both ways, to get the best out of fast dumb systems *and* slow contemplative ones, by simply refusing to choose between them. That is, I suppose, the way that

Nature likes to operate: "I'll have some of each"—one damned thing
piled on top of another, and nothing in moderation, ever.

It will have occurred to you, no doubt, that Cognitivism could
quite possibly have hit on the right doctrine, even if it did so for the
wrong reasons. Whatever confusions may have spawned the idea
that perception and cognition are continuous, and however plausible
the encapsulation story may appear to be a priori, there is a lot of
experimental evidence around that argues for the effects of background knowledge in perception. If the mind really is modular, those
data are going to have to be explained away. I want to say just a
word about this.

There are, pretty clearly, three conditions that an experiment has
to meet if it is to provide a bona fide counter-instance to the modularity of a perceptual system.

1. It must, of course, demonstrate the influence of background
information in some computation that the system performs. But,
more particularly, the background information whose influence it
demonstrates must be *exogenous* from the point of view of the module
concerned. Remember, each module has its proprietary database;
whatever information is in its database is ipso facto available to its
computations. So, for example, it would be no use for purposes of
embarrassing modularity theory to show that words are superior to
nonwords in a speech perception task. Presumably, the language
processing system has access to a grammar of the language that it
processes, and a grammar must surely contain a lexicon. What words
are in the language is thus one of the things that the language module
can plausibly be assumed to know consonant with its modularity.

2. The effect of the background must be distinctively perceptual,
not postperceptual and not a criterion shift. For example, it is of no
use to demonstrate that utterances of "implausible" sentences are
harder to process than utterances of "plausible" ones if it turns out
that the mechanism of this effect is the hearer's inability to believe
that the speaker could have said what it sounded like he said. No
one in his right mind doubts that perception interacts with cognition
somewhere. What's at issue in the disagreement between modularity
theory and "New Look" Cognitivism (e.g., Bruner 1957) is the *locus*
of this interaction. In practice, it usually turns out that the issue is
whether the recruitment of background information in perception is
predictive. Modularity theory says almost never; New Look Cognitivism says quite a lot of the time.

3. The cognitively penetrated system must be the one that shoul-
ders the burden of perceptual analysis in normal circumstances, and
not, for example, some backup, problem-solving type of mechanism

that functions only when the stimulus is too degraded for a module to cope with. Therefore, it is of no use to show that highly redundant lexical items are easier to understand than less redundant ones when the speech signal is very noisy—unless, of course, you can also show that the perception of very noisy speech really is bona fide speech perception.

So far as I know, there is very little in the experimental literature that is alleged to demonstrate the cognitive penetration of perception that meets all three of these conditions (to say nothing of replicability). This isn't to claim that such experiments cannot be devised or that, if devised, they might not prove that New Look Cognitivism is right after all. I claim only that, contrary to the textbook story, the empirical evidence for the continuity of perception with cognition is not overwhelming when contemplated with a jaundiced eye. There is, in any event, something for laboratory psychology to do for the next twenty years or so: namely, try to develop some designs subtle enough to determine who's right about all this.

"But look," you might ask, "why do you care about modules so much? You've got tenure; why don't you take off and go sailing?" This is a perfectly reasonable question and one that I often ask myself. Answering it would require exploring territory that I can't get into here and raising issues that *Modularity* doesn't even broach. But roughly, and by way of striking a closing note; The idea that cognition saturates perception belongs with (and is, indeed, historically connected with) the idea in the philosophy of science that one's observations are comprehensively determined by one's theories; with the idea in anthropology that one's values are comprehensively determined by one's culture; with the idea in sociology that one's epistemic commitments, including especially one's science, are comprehensively determined by one's class affiliations; and with the idea in linguistics that one's metaphysics is comprehensively determined by one's syntax. All these ideas imply a sort of relativistic holism: because perception is saturated by cognition, observation by theory, values by culture, science by class, and metaphysics by language, rational criticism of scientific theories, ethical values, metaphysical world-views, or whatever can take place only *within* the framework of assumptions that—as a matter of geographical, historical, or sociological accident—the interlocutors happen to share. What you can't do is rationally criticize the framework.

The thing is: I *hate* relativism. I hate relativism more than I hate anything else, excepting, maybe, fiberglass powerboats. More to the point, I think that relativism is very probably false. What it overlooks, to put it briefly and crudely, is the fixed structure of human nature.

(This is not, of course, a novel insight; on the contrary, the *malleability* of human nature is a doctrine that relativists are invariably much inclined to stress. See, for example, John Dewey in *Human Nature and Conduct*, 1922.) Well, in cognitive psychology the claim that there is a fixed structure of human nature traditionally takes the form of an insistence on the heterogeneity of cognitive mechanisms and on the rigidity of the cognitive architecture that effects their encapsulation. If there are faculties and modules, then not everything affects everything else; not everything is plastic. Whatever the All is, at least there is more than One of it.

These are, as you will have gathered, not issues to be decisively argued—or even perspicuously formulated—in the course of a paragraph or two. Suffice it that they seem to be the sorts of issues that our cognitive science ought to bear on. And they are intimately intertwined: surely, *surely*, no one but a relativist would drive a fiberglass powerboat.

Coming in our next installment: "Restoring Basic Values: Phrenology in an Age of License." Try not to miss it!

Notes

1. See, for example, Gregory (1970, p. 30): "perception involves a kind of problem-solving; a kind of intelligence." For a more recent and comprehensive treatment that runs along the same lines, see Rock (1983).
2. I don't at all care whether these "traditional assumptions" about reflexes are in fact correct, or even whether they were traditionally assumed. What I want is an ideal type with which to compare perception and cognition.

Chapter 9

Why Should the Mind Be Modular?

Danny Kaye once described the oboe as "an ill wind that nobody blows good." Much the same could be said—and with more justice—of teleological explanations in psychology. There is an irresistible temptation to argue that the organization that one's favorite cognitive theory attributes to the mind is the very organization that the mind ought to have, given its function. One knows that such arguments are, in the nature of the case, post hoc; one knows that the cognitive theories they presuppose invariably come unstuck, leaving the teleologist with a functional explanation for mental structures that don't exist; one knows that there are, in general, lots of mechanisms that can perform a given task, so that inferences from a task to a mechanism are up to their ears in affirmation of the consequent; one knows about the philosopher who, just before they discovered the ninth planet, proved from first principles that there have to be exactly eight. One knows all this; but the temptation persists.

In this chapter, I propose to offer some teleological excuses for the modular organization of perception. In particular, I'll raise some functional considerations that might favor modularity in perception even if—as I'm inclined to suppose—the organization of much of the rest of cognition is nonmodular in important ways. Some of the arguments for modularity that I've seen in the literature—for example, that modular processes are especially debuggable—don't do this; so they suggest that, insofar as teleology rules, the mind ought to be modular all over. My line, by contrast, is that given the specifics of what perception is supposed to do, and given internal constraints on processes that do that sort of thing, modular structure in perceptual systems is perhaps what you'd expect.

What *is* perception supposed to do? Psychologists have tended to disagree about this in ways that have deep consequences for the rest of what they say about cognition. There are, for example, those who take it for granted that the primary function of perception is to guide action. (Illustrious psychologists who have held this view include

Piaget, Gibson, Dewey, Vygotsky, and surely many others). It is no accident that such psychologists invariably take the reflex to be the primitive mode of psychological organization, to which cognitive functions must somehow be reduced (phylogenetically, ontogenetically, or otherwise).[1] In reflexes, specific perceptual events are lawfully connected to correspondingly specific behavioral outcomes. To take the reflex as the paradigm psychological process is thus to see perceptual mechanisms as detectors that function to monitor an organism's environment, looking for occasions on which the associated behavior is appropriately released.

I am going to assume (without argument, for the moment) that this picture is profoundly misled. In my view, behavior is normally determined decision-theoretically, viz., by the interaction of belief with utilities; in the interesting cases, perception is linked to behavior only via such interactions. Specifically, perception functions in belief fixation (in ways that we are about to explore), and perceptually fixed beliefs, like any others, may eventuate in behavioral outcomes. Whether they do so depends on what the organism wants and on the rest of its cognitive commitments. I was once told (by a Gibsonian) that this decision-theoretic understanding of the relation between perception and behavior won't do for flies, since it's plausible that their behaviors really are all reflexive. If this is true, it is another contribution to the accumulating evidence that flies aren't people. Perhaps minds started out as stimulus-response machines. If so, then according to the present view the course of evolution was to interpose a computer—programmed, as it might be, with the axioms of your favorite decision theory—between the identification of a stimulus and the selection of a response.

So my working assumption is that perception is a species of cognition; it's one of the psychological mechanisms whose main job is the fixation of belief. If, therefore, you are looking for a teleological story about the design of perceptual systems, the first step is to get clear about just what perception contributes to belief fixation. You can maybe then go on to show why mechanisms that make *that* contribution to belief fixation ought to be modular. That, in any event, is the game plan for what follows.

To get started, we need a general story about belief fixation within which to locate perception's role. Here's an old-fashioned story—assembled as much from epistemology as from psychology—that strikes me as reasonable as far as it goes. Beliefs have two main kinds of causes: other beliefs and organism-environment interactions. So, for example, one way that you may come to believe that Q is as a causal consequence of believing $P \rightarrow Q$ and P. Being in the first mental state is approximately causally sufficient for being in the second.[2] In principle, such chains of mental causation can be as long as you like, bounded only by the inferential capacities of the organism. But I suppose that, as a matter of fact, they rarely get *very* long. Its prior cognitive commitments impact upon an organism's present cognitive state; but so too do its causal transactions with the world. In consequence of such transactions, chains of thought are forever being supplemented by underived premises.

The typical nonmental cause of a belief is an interaction between the body of an organism and something in its environment. Bodily states register—and are thus informative about—the effects of local environmental causes in exactly the way that thermometers register ambient temperature and tidemarks register encroachments of the sea, in fact, in exactly the way that *any* effect registers—and is thus informative about—its cause. Changes in states of the retina, for example, register changes in the properties of incident light, which are in turn caused by alterations in the arrangement of the distal objects that radiate and reflect the light. To the extent that such proximal effects are specific to their distal causes, cognitive processes with access to the one have grounds for inference to the other.

So, the picture is that certain organic states register the proximal stimuli that cause them, and that certain cognitive processes infer the arrangement of local distal objects from the organic effects of these proximal stimulations. In particular, I assume that it's the function of perceptual mechanisms to execute such inferences.[3]

So much for the function of perception. The modularity thesis for perception is accordingly the claim that the mechanisms that perform this function are (a) dedicated, and (b) encapsulated. And the teleological question is whether there is something about inferences from representations of proximal stimuli to representations of distal layouts that makes dedicated and encapsulated devices especially appropriate for executing them. Before I turn to this question, however, I want to say a word about the thesis that perception is a species of inference—dedicated, encapsulated, or otherwise. The way that I've been setting things up, this thesis turns out to be next door to a truism; by contrast, some psychologists (and many philosophers) have taken it to be extremely tendentious.

Discussion of this issue in the cognitive science literature has tended to center—misleadingly, in my view—on the question whether "poverty of the stimulus" arguments are reliable. It's worth taking a moment to dissociate these issues.

The first step in developing a poverty of the stimulus argument for the inferentiality of perception is to claim, on empirical grounds, that proximal stimulation typically contains 'less information' than the perceptual beliefs that it engenders (sensation underdetermines perception, to put this in an older vocabulary). The phenomenon of perceptual ambiguity—Necker cubes and the like—is one sort of evidence for this premise. The second step is to note that this extra information has to come from somewhere; presumably it comes from the organism's store of background knowledge. The last step is to *identify* the claim that perception is inferential with the claim that it exploits cognitive background. In effect, the completed argument is that perception must be inferential because it is 'top down'. Correspondingly, psychologists who don't like the inferential story about perception have generally undertaken to show that proximal stimulation is actually informationally richer than poverty of the stimulus arguments suppose, and that—at least in 'ecologically valid' circumstances—there is, in principle, enough information in the light impinging at the retina (and hence enough information registered by the retinal effects that this impinging light produces) to determine a unique and correct perceptual analysis of the distal layout.[4]

Whatever one thinks of this argument, however, it is important to see that the claim that perception is inferential is distinguishable from the claim that it is underdetermined by its psychophysical basis. In particular, it is *not* required of an inference that its conclusion must be stronger than (that it must be 'underdetermined' by) its premises. Demonstrative inferences are, of course, all counterexamples; P and $Q \rightarrow P$ is a paradigm case of an inference, though, on any reasonable measure, P contains less information than P and Q. Similarly, the mental process that gets one from the thought that John is an unmarried man to the thought that he is a bachelor presumably counts as inferential, though in no sense is the second thought 'stronger than' the first. Similarly again for the perceptual case: even if the information in the proximal light uniquely determines the visible properties of the distal layout, the inferentiality of the mental process that proceeds from representing the one to representing the other would not be impugned.

The core argument for the inferentiality of perception derives from two considerations, both of which are quite independent of claims for underdetermination. On the one hand, perception fixes beliefs about *distal* objects, objects typically at some spatial remove from the perceiving organism.[5] On the other hand, there is no causal interaction at these distances; all the intentional effects of distal stimuli must be mediated by the organic effects of proximal stimuli (by retinal states and the like). I assume that, if these organic effects represent anything, then they represent their proximal causes (cf. note 3). On this assumption, it follows that perception is a process in which representations of proximal stimuli causally determine beliefs about distal layouts. But that *is* what's claimed when it's claimed that perception is inferential.

I am not, by the way, taking it for granted that every causal chain of intentional states is an inference; for example, associative chains aren't. But then, association doesn't eventuate in the fixation of belief, and perception does. Nor do I hold that perceptual inferences differ in *no* important ways from paradigms of explicit reasoning. For one thing, explicit reasoning is explicit; and that may be important. For another thing, in paradigm cases where *the thought that A*'s causing *the thought that B* counts as the agent's inferring B from A, the agent accepts the proposition *if A then B* in whatever sense he accepts the proposition A and B.[6] This is, however, unlikely to be true in perceptual inference, especially if perception proves to be modular. It's generally assumed that modular systems are "hardwired," i.e., that the principles of inference according to which they operate are "inexplicit": not just not conscious, but also not mentally represented. A hardwired system that 'accepts' the principle 'if A then B' may thus do so *only* in the sense that it is disposed to accept Bs when it accepts As. By contrast, the sense in which it accepts the As and Bs themselves is much stronger; it involves the tokening of representational states of which they are the intentional objects.

So there are these (and perhaps other) legitimate respects in which the causal chain from representations of proximal stimuli to representations of distal layouts may differ from paradigm cases of inferences. Whether this makes these chains noninferential depends on whether the missing properties are among those that are *essential* to inference. And, for us Realists, that depends in turn on what inferences *really are,* a question that only a developed cognitive science could reasonably be expected to answer. For present purposes, I propose to beg these sorts of issues. All I care about is that there are mental processes in which representations of proximal stimuli cause representations of local distal layouts. I treat it as a stipulation that perceptual inference is modular iff—or rather, to the extent that—these processes are executed by dedicated and encapsulated systems.

Why Should Perceptual Mechanisms Be Dedicated?

Why should perceptual inferences be carried out by specialized mechanisms? Or, to put it another way, why should the mind treat the problem of inferring local distal layouts from proximal stimulations as a different *kind* of computational task than the problem of figuring out the next chess move from the current board state, or the problem of figuring out your account balance from your check stubs, or the problem of diagnosing a disease from a display of its symptoms? For that matter, precisely *which* proximal-to-local-distal inferences are supposed to be executed by dedicated mechanisms? Perhaps, on noticing a sudden increase in the volume of the street noise, I infer that someone has opened a window. Surely there isn't a mental faculty that is dedicated to doing *that*?

I'm going to consider these questions first as they apply to the special case of language perception. I'll then say a little about how the morals might generalize to other perceptual capacities.

I assume that language perception is constituted by nondemonstrative inferences from representations of certain effects of the speaker's behavior (sounds that he produces; marks that he makes) to representations of certain of his intentional states. As a rough approximation, I'll say that such inferences run from premises that specify acoustic properties of utterance tokens to conclusions that specify the speaker's communicative intentions. A speaker makes a certain noise (e.g., the sort of noise that gets made when you pronounce the sentence "it's going to rain tomorrow"), and, in consequence of hearing the noise, one is somehow able to infer something about what the speaker intends that one should take him to believe (e.g., that he intends that one should take him to believe that it's going to rain tomorrow.) The question before us is, why should there be dedicated mechanisms devoted to the execution of such inferences?

I think the crucial consideration is that inferences from acoustic properties of utterance tokens to intentional properties of the speaker's mental state—unlike almost all of the rest of the mental processing that mediates the intentional interpretation of the behavior of one's conspecifics—are algorithmic. That is, they are effected by employing a mechanical computational procedure that is guaranteed to deliver a canonical description of a speaker's mental state given a canonical representation of his behavior.[7] (More precisely, you're guaranteed a canonical description of a communicative intention in exchange for a canonical description of the acoustic properties of a token of any expression in the language that the speaker and hearer share.) If the computations that mediate speech perception are indeed specialized in this way, then familiar teleological arguments for the computational division of labor would favor cognitive architectures in which they are implemented by dedicated processors.[8]

Whether there is an algorthm for inferring the mental state of a speaker from the acoustics of his speech clearly depends on which acoustic properties are specified in the premises and which intentional properties are specified in the conclusion. It may be that it's the speaker's desire to startle Granny that causes him to speak so loudly; but, patently, there is going to be no general form of inference that will connect that sort of acoustic property of an utterance to that sort of intentional property of a mental state. By contrast, there may be a routine procedure whereby someone who hears an utterance of the acoustic form "it's going to rain" can infer a description of the speaker as intending to communicate his belief that it's going to rain. If so, it would be natural to view the ability to execute this procedure as part of knowing English.[9]

Notice that, in this view, it is quite possibly a mistake to assume—as many psychologists like to do—that ". . . the function of [the language comprehension mechanisms] is to project the speech input onto a representation of the world—onto, for example, a mental model. . . ." (Marslen-Wilson & Tyler 1987, p. 58) No doubt, what the hearer wants from the speaker *in the long run* is news about the world; news that he can integrate with the rest of what he knows. But the way that he contrives to get the news, according to the present view, is by first effecting a more or less algorithmic construction of a canonical representation of *what the speaker said*. And the price of the algorithmicity of this construction may be precisely its encapsulation from information garnered from the preceding dialogue or, for that matter, from information garnered from any sources other than the speaker's phonetic output.

The idea, then, is that speech communication exhibits a trade-off in which the algorithmicity of a computational procedure is purchased at the price of severe constraints on the sorts of inferences that it can mediate. On the one hand, there are properties of the speaker's state of mind that can be inferred *just from the noises that he makes*; and the speaker has a guarantee that (ceteris paribus) *any* of his colinguals who hear the noises will be able to draw the inferences, *just in virtue of their being his colinguals.* That speakers *can* rely on this is really quite remarkable, considering how tricky inferences from behaviors to their mental causes are in the general case. One expects them to go wrong, often enough, even with the spouse of one's bosom. One expects them to go wrong proportionately more often where the background of shared experience is thinner. What is usually required in the intentional analysis of behavior is a kind of hermeneutic sophistication that's as far as can be from the execution of a rote procedure. The notable exception is inferring intentional content from utterance form. Show me an English speaker who utters "it's about to rain" and I'll show you an English speaker who is, in all likelihood, thinking about the weather. This sort of inference is enormously reliable even though its premises are strikingly exiguous. All you have to know about an English speaker is that he made a certain sort of noise, and the intentional interpretation of his behavior is immediately transparent.

On the other hand, one buys this transparency at a price. There appears to be something like a procedure from the intentional inter-pretation of verbal behavior; but all that executing the procedure gives you is a specification of the propositional object of a commu-nicative intention. The only intentional information about a speaker that his colinguals are ipso facto able to recover from his verbal behavior is the literal content of what he says. For all the other sorts of things that you might want to know about the speaker's state of mind ("Why did he say that?" "Did he mean it?" "What did he mean by it?" "Why does he believe it?" "What's he trying to get away with?") you're on your own; hermeneutic sophistication comes into play, mediated by heaven knows what problem-solving heuristics. The good news is that a shared language approximates a guaranteed channel along which a speaker may indicate the contents of his thoughts; the bad news is that it's a very narrow channel.

If much of this is right, it's clear why you might expect the mech-anisms of speech perception to be discontinuous from the mecha-nisms of cognitive problem solving at large. Real problem solving generally has two parts: first there's the business of figuring out how to solve the problem, and then there's the business of proceeding to solve it that way.[10] But speech perception has only part two; it con-sists entirely of executing an algorithim for the intentional analysis of verbal behavior. One doesn't have to invent the procedure before one applies it because one finishes inventing it when one finishes learning the language. One doesn't have to worry about whether to employ the procedure, because speech perception isn't voluntary. And one doesn't have to worry about what to do if the procedure fails, because its success is guaranteed (modulo notes 7 and 9). Speech perception really isn't thinking; it's just computing. Inferring communicative intentions from verbal behavior is a solved problem, so why should the mind treat it as problem solving?[11]

It's instructive to contrast the present treatment of language per-ception with the approach favored in Fodor, Bever, and Garrett, 1974. FB&G are enthusiastic about the analogy between perception and the process whereby a detective infers the identity of a criminal from his information about the clues. The force of the analogy is that both kinds of mentation involve nondemonstrative inferences from effects to causes; they're presumably both species of hypothesis formation and confirmation. But what FB&G missed—and now strikes me as important—is that the first sort of inference is plausibly algorithmic in a way that the second certainly isn't. Holmes has to *think* to figure out that it was Moriarty who did it; whereas in perception, you don't think, you just open your eyes and look. For the perceiver, but not for Holmes, the space of hypotheses that's available to be confirmed is determined a priori (it's just the set of well-formed canonical descriptions of distal objects); and, given the data as canonically described, the choice of one of these hypotheses is approximately mechanical. It's wrong to suppose that because perception is phenomenologically instantaneous it must be noninferential; but it's equally wrong to suppose that if perception is inferential, then it must be computationally just like thought.

We've been seeing that the teleological argument for a dedicated speech processor depends on the plausiblity of the claim that speech perception is algorithmic. And that might lead one to wonder about the generality of this line of argument. After all, if there's an algorithm for the perceptual analysis of utterances, that's presumably because speakers and hearers abide by the same conventions for correlating forms of utterance with mental states. None of this applies, however, to computing the correspondence between distal arrangements and proximal stimuli in, for example, vision. So why should one suppose perceptual mechanisms to be dedicated in the *non*linguistic cases?

But, in fact, the conventionality of language is inessential to the algorithmicity of speech perception. What really matters is this: *For any perceptually analyzable linguistic token there is a canonical description (DT) such that for some mental state there is a canonical description (DM) such that 'DTs cause DMs' is true and counterfactual supporting.* (For tokens of "it's raining," there is a canonical description—viz., "token of 'it's raining'"—such that "tokens of 'it's raining' are caused by intentions to communicate the belief that it's raining" is true and counterfactual supporting.)

Which is to say that speech perception can be algorithmic because certain of the acoustic properties of linguistic tokens bear regular relations to certain intentional properties of their mental causes. It happens, in the case of language, that this relation is largely supported by conventions. But it would work just as well if it were supported by natural laws.[12] As I suppose the corresponding relation often is in the case of other sorts of perceptual systems. For example, certain aspects of visual perceptual processing can be algorithmic because: *For any perceptually analyzable pattern of proximal excitation of the retina, there is a canonical description (RD) such that for some distal layout of visible objects there is a canonical description (DL) such that 'DLs cause RDs' is a law* (and hence true and counterfactual supporting).

Thus, there are laws relating the two-dimensional shape and orientation of retinal images to the three-dimensional shapes and orientations of their distal causes. Because, in such cases, the relation between being RD and being caused by a DL is quite regular, the procedure that infers DLs from RDs can be approximately fail-proof. And because there is a DL for *every* perceptually analyzable RD, it can be general. If, moreover, the function from RDs to DLs is mechanically computable, then the lawful relation between distal layouts and proximal arrays opens the way to an algorithmic solution to these aspects of visual perception.

All of this makes perception seem rather special among the varieties of problem solving that can effect belief fixation. In perception one is often guaranteed a description of the problem and a description of its solution such that given the former there is a mechanical procedure for computing the latter. And access to the data for this computation is itself nomologically guaranteed for any (normal) organism that bears the appropriate psychophysical relation to a distal stimulus. All you have to do is turn up the lights and point your eyes, and all the retinal information required for (e.g.) visual perception of three-dimensional shape is ipso facto available. For auditory perception you have to do still less; all that's required is (what they call on the Continent) *being there.*

Needless to say that nothing like this holds for cognitive problem solving at large. Thinking is *hard*: There need be no description of the terms of a problem from which a (nontrivial) specification of its solution follows mechanically. And, even if there is such a description, there need be no guaranteed procedure for getting access to it. So perception—but not thinking—can often be carried out by "canned" computational procedures. So, it wouldn't be very surprising if many perceptual mechanisms were dedicated. So, so much for that.

Why Should Perception Be Encapsulated?

An unencapsulated (or "penetrable"; see Pylyshyn, 1984) psychological mechanism is one that has unconstrained access to cognitive background. The limit of perceptual penetrability is reached when information that is available to *any* cognitive mechanism is ipso facto available as the premise of any perceptual inference. That perception actually approximates this limit has been a main tenet of most post-behaviorist cognitive science and of most post-positivist epistemology. The support for this view of the perception/cognition relation derives partly from empirical evidence, but also partly from a widely accepted teleological argument that is supposed to show that unencapsulated perception makes ecological good sense. Let's now consider this argument.

The *locus classicus* is Bruner's "On Perceptual Readiness" (1957), a psychological work so influential that even philosophers have heard of it. Here's the kernel of Bruner's teleological argument for the cognitive penetration of perception: "Where accessibility of categories reflects environmental probabilities, the organism is in the position of requiring less stimulus input, less redundancy of cues for the appropriate categorization of objects." (p. 19) That is, the more perception exploits the organism's background of cognitive commitments, the less proximal information the organism requires to identify a distal layout. Penetration buys shallow processing of proximal stimuli; shallow processing of proximal stimuli buys speed of perceptual identification; and speed of perceptual identification is a desideratum. Thus Bruner on the teleological argument for penetrated perception.

Whether this argument is any good, however, depends on a couple of empirical questions that Bruner largely ignores; and, unfortunately, answering these questions involves quantitative estimates that nobody is in a position to make.

What is the relative computational costs of processing the proximal stimulus vs processing the background information?

It's all very well to emphasize, as Bruner does, that penetration allows perceptual analysis to proceed with "fairly minimal" proximal information. But this is valuable only if it achieves a reduction of computational load *over all*; and whether it does so depends on how much processing is required to bring the cognitive background to bear.

The cost of computing the background depends on two unknowns:

1. *The cost of achieving access.* Background information must be *located* before it can be *applied*. Depending on the search mechanisms employed, this process may become more costly in proportion as the potentially available background gets larger. If it does, then—all else being equal—the prediction is that perception gets *slower* as cognitive penetrability increases.

This consequence may be avoidable on the assumption that cognitive background is accessed by "massively parallel" memory searches, as in associative networks. But here too the issues are unclear. In network systems, the computational cost of access is reduced because the possible search paths are fixed antecedently: they are determined by the character of the connectivity among the nodes in the network, which is in turn determined by the stochastic properties of the network's "training." In such architectures, memory search is cheap because it's quite insensitive to the details of the perceptual task in hand. (In particular, you don't get the recursive loops that are so characteristic of classical top-down models of perceptual processing; a candidate analysis of the input determines the initial direction of a search, which in turn modifies the analysis of the input, which in turn modifies the subsequent direction of search . . . until some success criterion is achieved.) The consequence—for all the network models so far proposed, at any rate—is that a lot of perceptual preprocessing is required to start them running; They achieve the cognitive penetration of perception by assuming the perceptual penetration of memory search. Nobody knows whether there is some optimal balance in which the right kind of preprocessor conjoined with the right kind of network memory produces computational savings relative to encapsulated perceptual systems. Unless there is, Bruner's speed argument for the penetration of perception looks to be unreliable.

  2. *The cost of computing confirmation levels.* Whatever background information is accessed must be applied to the analysis of the current proximal display. If you insist on the cognitive penetration of perceptual inference, you have to bear the cost of determining *how much confirmation* the background information that you recover bestows on your current perceptual hypothesis. The problem is that the more background information you access, the more such confirmation relations you will have to compute.

  This is rather different from the worry that the more cognitive background you have access to, the more expensive it may be to find the piece of information that you want. As we've just seen, the way out of *that* problem may be to fix the search paths antecedently and then explore them in parallel. But that kind of solution is implausible for the problem of computing confirmation relations. What degree of confirmation a given piece of background information bestows on a given perceptual hypothesis can't be decided ahead of time because it depends not just on what the information is and what the hypothesis is, but also on a bundle of local considerations that change from moment to moment.

  "Could the yellow stripy thing I've just glimpsed be a tiger?"
  "But this is the middle of New York."

"Yes, but the Bronx Zoo is in the middle of New York."

"Yes, but I can see the Empire State Building, and you can't see the Empire State Building from the Bronx Zoo."

"Yes, but tigers sometimes escape from zoos."

"Yes, but the Times would have mentioned it if a tiger had escaped from the Bronx Zoo."

So, *in some circumstances* it can matter to deciding whether a yellow stripy thing is a tiger that the Times really does tell all the news that's fit to print. In other circumstances—if I'm in Budapest, say, or if I'm in a yellow-stripy-chair store—the inductive relevances are quite different. The moral is that it's just about inconceivable that confirmation relations could be "hardened in" once and for all in the way that the structure of memory search might be. Our estimates of what confirms what change as fast as our changing picture of the world.

What, you might reasonably ask, is the bearing of all this on Bruner's argument? It's that if 1 and 2 are large with respect to the cost of bottom-up processing of proximal stimuli, *you may gain time by encapsulation.* This was, in fact, the line I took in *The Modularity of Mind,* where I argued that since perception is clearly specialized for the fixation of belief about local distal objects, and since it's the local distal objects that one eats and gets eaten by, it is biological good sense for perceptual systems to be fast. All that agrees with Bruner. But I then made the reverse assumption from his about the relative computational costs of bottom-up proximal analysis as compared to the exploitation of cognitive background; I took it for granted that memory searches and computations of confirmation relations cost a lot. I thus arrived at a teleological conclusion exactly opposite to Bruner's: *MOM* says that if you want speed, make perception as much like a reflex as possible.[13] That is, make it as encapsulated as you can. The real point, I suppose, is that *neither* Bruner's argument nor mine is empirically warranted in the current state of our science. How the teleology goes depends on estimating empirical tradeoffs about which, in fact, almost nothing is known.

What is the relative payoff for being fast when you're background assumptions are right vs. being accurate when they are wrong?

I've been saying that Bruner's teleological argument for the cognitive penetration of perception ignores the computation-theoretic costs of top-down processing. The next point is that it also ignores the game-theoretic costs of misperception.

To be sure, Bruner notices that "the more inappropriate the readiness, the greater the input or redundancy of cues required for appropriate categorizations to occur." (p. 20) I.e., if you let your expectations run away with your perceptions, then you're likely to do worse than an encapsulated perceiver when you're expectations are wrong (just as you're likely to do better than an encapsulated perceiver when they're right). What he doesn't notice, however, is the consequent tradeoff between speed and accuracy. Ceteris paribus, penetrated perceivers are relatively fast when their background beliefs are true but they're relatively inaccurate when their background beliefs are false; ceteris paribus, encapsulated perceivers are relatively accurate when their background beliefs are false, but they're relatively slow when their background beliefs are true. Assuming that the choice is exclusive, which sort of perceiver would you prefer to be?[14]

Alas, it's simply not possible to estimate which cognitive architecture is better over all; still less to guess which one would have bred most or lived longest in the conditions in which the brain evolved. Suffice it that it's easy to imagine cases in which the cautious—viz., encapsulated—nervous system clearly wins. Consider my belief that there *isn't* a tiger salivating in my word processor. This is a belief that I cleave to firmly; I haven't a doubt in the world that it's true. Do I want it to bias my perceptions? Well, what are the probable payoffs?

If I'm right about the tiger not being there, I'll get certain gains from cognitive penetration: If I'm looking for a tiger, I won't start by looking in my word processor; and, since there *isn't* a tiger in my word processor, this will save me time. Similarly, if I'm mucking around in my word processor, trying to figure out what's gone wrong with it, I will not entertain the hypothesis that the bug is a tiger; and that too will save me time. These gains are real but they are modest.

On the other hand I'm *wrong* about whether there's a tiger in the word processor, then what I want is for my tiger-perception to be accurate in spite of my expectations. In fact, I want my tiger-perceptions to *correct my expectations,* and I want this very much. Tiggers bounce, (as Pooh remarked) and they also bite (a point that Pooh failed to stress). For this sort of case, given an (exclusive) choice between a penetrated perceptual system that is fast when my biases are right and an encapsulated perceptual system that is accurate when my biases are wrong, I opt for encapsulation.

What's the situation when what I believe is that there *is* a salivating tiger in the word processor? Here, whether I'm right or wrong, neither perceptual speed nor perceptual accuracy buys me much.

That's because, unless one is absolutely bonkers, what one *doesn't* do if one believes that there is a salivating tiger in one's word processor is look and see. What you do instead is, you tiptoe *very quietly* out the door, which you then lock behind you. Then you run like stink.

The upshot is that in the pay-off matrix if you're a *possible edible*, the cell where penetration matters is the one where you think that there is *no* eater around and you're *wrong*. And what you want in that cell is encapsulation. As you might expect, the situation is roughly symmetrical, but with the signs reversed, if you're the tiger. In the pay-off matrix for *possible eaters* the cell that matters is the one where you think there *is* an edible around and you're *right*. What you want to be if you're in that cell is fast, since what you don't eat someone else is likely to.

As for the remaining possibilities: Perceptual accuracy in *discon*-firming the hypothesis that there's a local edible doesn't buy you much; you're just as hungry after you look as you were before. How much might perceptual accuracy buy you in the case where you think there are *no* edibles on offer and you're *wrong*? Probably not much because probably—as in the case where you wrongly believe that there's a tiger in the word processor—the more firmly you hold the belief, the more you don't bother to look.

So much for the payoff matrix. There's a case where it is very desirable to be fast if you're right even at the cost of not being accurate if you're wrong (i.e., you'd want your perception to be penetrated) and there's a case where it is very desirable to be accurate if you're wrong even at the cost of not being fast if you're right (i.e., you'd want your perception to be encapsulated.) Whether Bruner has a teleological argument for penetration depends primarily on the relative payoffs associated with these two conditions. The trouble is that what these payoffs are is not an a priori issue; it depends entirely on how the world is arranged. And neither I nor Bruner is in a position to estimate the relevant facts. Perhaps the only way to tell which architecture is worth more is to argue the other way 'round: infer the cost benefits by finding out which architecture selection actually endorsed.

It looks like the standard design arguments for penetrated percep-tion aren't actually very convincing; I propose presently to sail off on a different tack. First, however, a digression: Some epistemolo-gists have exhibited great enthusiasm for the perceptual penetration of observation in science, and this appears peculiar in light of the previous discussion. Here is Paul Churchland, (1988) for example, feeling quite rhapsodic about perceptual bias:

> . . . even the humblest judgement . . . is always a speculative
> leap. . . . In the case of perceptual judgements, what the senses
> do is cause the perceiver to activate some specific representation
> from the . . . conceptual framework . . . that has been brought
> to the perceptual situation by the perceiver. A perceptual judge-
> ment, therefore, can be no better, though it can be worse, than
> the broad system of representations in which it is consti-
> tuted. . . . The journey of the human spirit is essentially the
> story of our evolving conception of the world. . . . The human
> spirit will continue its breathtaking adventure of self reconstruc-
> tion, and its perceptual and motor capabilities will continue to
> develop as an integral part of its self-reconstruction. . . .

Well, if so then so be it. But one wonders *just* what it is that Churchland thinks perceptual bias buys for the scientist. We've seen that
the standard (Bruner) argument for penetration comes down to an
assumption about the relative payoffs in speed/accuracy trades. And
we've seen that it's perfectly conceivable that selection may have
favored speed in the conditions under which the nervous system
evolved (just as it's perfectly conceivable that it may have favored
accuracy). But surely there is no question about which to choose in
the circumstances that obtain in scientific investigations; surely what
one wants there is observational accuracy *even if accuracy takes a lot of
time*.[15] And what you *particularly* want is that your observations
should be accurate when your theories are wrong, because then your
observations can correct your theories. But if, in science, the smart
money is on observational accuracy, then it's an *encapsulated* perceptual psychology that a scientist should want to have. There's no point
trying to build bias out of scientific instruments if it's built into the
guy who reads them.[16]

The upshot seems to be that nature *may* have equipped us with
cognitively penetrated perceptual systems; but if she did, there is
nothing in that to gladden the heart of an epistemologist. On the
contrary, if we have an unencapsulated perceptual architecture, that's
just another respect in which we are not a species ideally endowed
for the scientific enterprise.

Encapsulation and Objectivity

We seem not to be getting anywhere; after all the talk about cost
accounting, we're still in want of a plausible teleological argument
for (or against) encapsulated perception. Let's, however, make one
last try.

Early on in this discussion, I endorsed what I called a 'decision-theoretic' account of the etiology of behavior, according to which behavior is caused by the interaction of beliefs and utilities. I remarked that this decision-theoretic picture is to be distinguished from the view that the model for the etiology of behavior is the reflex. On the reflex story, an organism's behavioral repertoire is made up of perception-action pairs. On the decision-theoretic story, by contrast, there is nothing special about the relation between perception and action; perception affects behavior in much the same way that other cognitive processes (e.g., thinking) do; viz., via the fixation of belief. (The only difference is that perception typically gives rise to beliefs about relatively *local* distal layouts, so—given reasonable utilities—the demands that perceptual beliefs make on action are likely to prove pressing. As I observed above, it's the local distal layouts that one eats and gets eaten by.)

Now, this difference between ways of understanding the perception-action relation implies corresponding differences in the way one understands the function of perception, and thus affects the status of teleological arguments from function to design. Presumably, an organism that is built to act on its beliefs will do best, on balance, if the beliefs that it acts on are *true*. If this is so, then a good way to illuminate the teleology of cognitive mechanisms might be to consider what design constraints the quest for true beliefs imposes on the process of belief fixation. The architectural organization of perception might then be understood by reference to its contribution to the truth-seeking process.

What, then, should the design of perception be if our perceptual inferences are generally to lead us from true premises to true conclusions? This way of framing the question suggests an approach to teleological arguments in which normative epistemology provides design hypotheses for theories of cognitive architecture. You tell me something about what good nondemonstrative inference is like and I'll tell you something about what the computational structure of cognition ought to be, assuming that the function of cognition is the fixation of true beliefs.

The trouble with this research strategy in practice is that very little is known about good nondemonstrative inferences. Still, there are some considerations on which practically everybody seems to be agreed, and I think these may bear on the teleological justification of perceptual encapsulation. So I propose first to enunciate a few epistemological truisms and then to see what support they may offer for the view that perception is modular.

First truism: A good empirical inference is subject to at least two constraints: *observational adequacy* and *conservatism*. On one the hand, one wants the hypotheses one accepts to be compatible with as much of one's data as possible; and, on the other hand, one wants accepting the hypothesis to do the least possible damage to one's prior cognitive commitments.

Second truism: Observational adequacy and conservatism are *independent* constraints on nondemonstrative inference. There is no guarantee that the hypothesis that fits most of the data will be maximally conservative or, conversely, that the maximally conservative hypothesis will be the one that fits most of the data. It's too bad that this is so; if the most conservative theory were always best confirmed, we'd never have the nuisance of having to change our minds.

Third truism: We have repeatedly remarked upon the special role that perception plays in the fixation of beliefs about the spatio-temporally local environment. But, it isn't, of course, the concern with locality per se that distinguishes perception from other processes of belief fixation; some of your beliefs about stars are perceptual and most of your beliefs about your appendix are not, though even the farthest appendixes are appreciably localer than even the nearest stars. The essential difference between perception and other modes of cognition is that perception provides the *data* for the inferences by which we construct our theories of the world; perception is our only source of underived, contingent premises for such inferences. If it isn't a truth of logic, and if it doesn't somehow follow from what you already know, then either perception tells you about it or you don't find out. If this be Empiricism, make the most of it.

So much for epistemological truisms. Now let's put this all together. We've got so far that the data for our empirical hypotheses—the underived contingent premises of our nondemonstrative inferences—are mostly information about the layout of spatio-temporally local distal stimuli; and these data are supplied largely or entirely by perception. And it is a constraint on rational belief fixation that the hypotheses that we select should be as compatible with these data as may be, consonant with a simultaneous and independent requirement to maximize conservatism. The following design question thus arises: According to what architecture should one construct a primate nervous system—considered, now, as a machine for drawing sound, nondemonstrative inferences—if one is concerned that empirical hypotheses should be simultaneously and independently constrained by observational adequacy and conservatism? There are, no doubt, lots of possible answers to this question; you will remember that I complained in the opening paragraph that teleological arguments have the form of affirmations of the consequent. Still, for what it's worth, *one* sort of architectural scheme that would work would be to modularize perception.

Roughly, the idea would be to make two estimates of levels of empirical confirmation in the course of hypothesis selection: First, decide which hypothesis you would accept given just the current evidence about the layout of local distal objects; then decide what hypothesis you would accept given this evidence plus solicitude for cognitive commitments previously undertaken. This procedure would have the desirable consequence of ensuring that both observational adequacy and conservatism have their voices heard in the course of belief fixation. Such a two-step approach to hypothesis selection would be supported by an architecture in which perceptual estimates of the local proximal layout are encapsulated, since encapsulated perception *just is* perception that's minimally varnished by conservatism. Conversely, the more cognitively penetrated perception is, the less it honors the injunction that rational confirmation should reconcile estimates of observational adequacy and conservatism that are *independently* arrived at.

So there's a teleological argument for modularity from plausible epistemological premises—for whatever teleological arguments may be worth. It bears emphasizing that this argument might hold even if the cost-accounting arguments don't. If the function of perception is its role in the fixation of true beliefs, then we would have epistemological reasons for wanting perception to be encapsulated *even if encapsulated perception is slow and expensive.*

Summary and Conclusion

In psychology—under the Bruner/New Look influence—teleological arguments about the design of perceptual mechanisms have generally assumed that the function of perception is to guide behavior. We have seen that such arguments are largely equivocal; whether penetrated or encapsulated systems would guide behavior most efficiently depends on empirical estimates that nobody knows how to make.

But why should we prefer the reflexological idea that the function of perception is to modulate action to the decision-theoretic idea that the function of perception is the fixation of belief? One needs, at this point, to resist the siren song of Pop-Darwinism. No doubt the cognitive architectures that survive are the ones that belong to the organisms that contrive to generate ecologically valid behaviors. No doubt the computational structure of our perceptual mechanism was shaped by selection processes that favor behavioral adaptivity. It would be perfectly natural to infer that the function which perceptual systems are designed to perform—the function for which perceptual systems are selected—is therefore the production of this self-same adaptive behavior. Perfectly natural, but utterly misled.

The inference involves a sort of distributive fallacy. To see just how utterly misled it is, consider, 'Selection pressures favor reproductive success; the design of the heart was shaped by selection pressures; so the function of the heart is to mediate reproductive successes'. Parallel arguments would show that the function of *all* organs is to mediate reproductive success; hence that all organs have the same function.

Poppycock! The function of the heart—*the function that its design reflects*—is to circulate the blood. There is no paradox in this, and nothing to affront Darwinian scruples. Animals that have good hearts are selected for their reproductive success as compared to animals that have less good hearts or no hearts at all. But their reproductive success is produced by a division of biological labor among their organs, and it's the function of the heart *relative to this division of labor*—viz. its function *as a pump*—that teleologically determines its design.

Analogously in the present case. It's entirely possible that the kind of mental architecture that maximizes behavioral adaptivity is one that institutes a computational division of labor: A perceptual mechanism that is specialized to report on how the world is provides input to a decision mechanism that is specialized to figure out how to get what you want in a world that is that way. If this is indeed the means that Nature uses to maximize the ecological validity of the behavior of higher primates, then the function that determines the design of perceptual mechanisms is their role in finding out how the world is. Specifically, what determines their design is their function in providing contingent premises for nondemonstrative inferences to true empirical conclusions.

Compare (and contrast) some recent comments by Patricia Churchland (1987): "There is a fatal tendency to think of the brain as essentially in the fact-finding business. . . . Looked at from an evolutionary point of view, the principle function of nervous systems is to enable the organism to move appropriately. . . . The principle chore of nervous system is to get the body parts where they should be in order that the organism may survive. . . . Truth, whatever that is, definitely takes the hindmost" (pp. 548–549). It looks as though

Churchland is arguing, 'Organisms get selected for getting their bodies to be where they should be; only nervous systems that belong to organisms that get selected survive; so the function of nervous systems—the function in virtue of which their design is teleologically intelligible—is not "fact-finding" but getting the bodies of organisms to where they should be'. But as we've just been seeing, that is a distributive fallacy, hence not a good way to argue; it overlooks the possibility that nervous systems get organisms to where they should be *by* fact-finding and acting upon the facts that they find.

Alternatively, it may be that Churchland is committing a version of the genetic fallacy against which Gould and Lewontin have recently warned us: "[There are cases where one finds] adaptation and selection, but the adaptation is a secondary utilization of parts present for reasons of architecture, development, or history. . . . If blushing turns out to be an adaptation affected by sexual selection in humans, it will not help us to understand why blood is red. The immediate utility of an organic structure often says nothing at all about the [original] reason for its being" (1979, p. 159). If this is true, it follows that the *current* function of an organ cannot be securely inferred from the function in virtue of which its possession initially bestowed selectional advantage. Apparently the original use of feathered wings was not flight but thermal insulation. Correspondingly, it may be that the original use of nervous systems was the integration of movements. Nothing would follow about what they are used for *now*.

It is, in short, unclear just what about "an evolutionary point of view" rules out the hypothesis that the way that nervous systems affect the ecologically appropriate disposition of the body parts of (anyhow, higher) organisms is by mediating the fixation of largely true beliefs and the integration of largely rational actions. *Thinking—* specifically, thinking *true thoughts*—is arguably the best way to achieve adaptivity that evolution has thus far devised.

On this story, the biological demands on perception are exactly analogous to the epistemological demands on scientific observation: In both cases, what's wanted is procedures that yield accurate data about local distal layouts. Correspondingly, the demands that cognition places on perception favor encapsulation for the same reason that rational scientific practice favors unbiased observation. In both cases, the goal of the exercise is to draw good inductive inferences; and good inductive inferences require independent estimates of conservatism and observational adequacy. The bottom line is that— unlike the teleological arguments from cost-accounting—teleological arguments from epistemology are reasonably univocal on the question of modularity. They suggest that perception ought to be encapsulated.

On the other hand, how many things have *you* heard of recently that are the way they ought to be?

Notes

1. For a recent attempt to understand cognition in terms of its phylogenetic connections to sensor-motor reflexes, see Linas, 1987.
2. I assume that it's a psychological law that, all else being equal, organisms that believe $P \rightarrow Q$ and P believe Q. The ceteris paribus clause constrains both the character of the beliefs (e.g., their complexity) and the values of 'performance' variables (e.g., motivation, attention, available memory, etc.).
3. I don't want to argue the very complicated question whether the states of sensory mechanisms should count as representing—as well as merely registering—their proximal causes (in the way that perceptual states surely do count as representing their *distal* causes). I don't for the life of me see why they shouldn't, and, given a good theory of representation, it may turn out that the options are forced. For example, theories that construe representation in terms of causal covariance would surely imply that states of the retina represent the properties of incident light by which they are lawfully determined; that states of the tympanic membrane represent the spectrographic properties of acoustic proximal stimuli, etc. (See, for example, Dretske, 1981, Stampe, 1977, Fodor, 1987.) But the issues about modularity are presumably independent of the issues about representation, so I propose to beg the latter in what follows.
4. What I'm calling the poverty of the stimulus argument isn't the one that Chomsky uses that term for, though the two arguments are structurally similar. Chomsky's poverty of the stimulus argument infers the top-downness of language learning from its underdetermination by data (specifically from the underdetermination of the child's grammar by his corpus); analogously, the present argument infers the top-downness of perception from its underdetermination by sensation. Both sorts of underdetermination raise the question where the added information comes from. In the perceptual case, the obvious candidate is the perceiver's cognitive background; in the learning case, the obvious candidate is the child's innate cognitive commitments. So Chomsky argues from underdetermination to innateness; he doesn't, however, offer underdetermination as an argument that learning is a species of inference. He just takes that for granted.
5. Or objects *parts of which* are at some spatial remove from the organism. I touch part of its surface and thereby acquire the belief that there's a table in the landscape.
6. This is different from saying that, in such cases, the thought that if A then B must mediate the causal relation between the thought that A and the thought that B. Any such requirement would lead to the well-known Lewis Carroll regress.
7. Since the inference is nondemonstrative, there is no promise that the canonical description of the speaker's communicative intention that it delivers will actually be *true* of him. It's another question whether you're guaranteed that it will be true of him *if he is obeying the linguistic conventions*. The answer to this question depends, of course, on what linguistic conventions are. I'm inclined to think that they are something like pairings of acoustic types with mental state types; they specify the acoustic properties of the noise you should make iff you intend to communicate

the belief that *P*. If that's right, then the inference from the acoustical properties of the utterance to the intentional state of the speaker *is* apodictic (subject to ambiguity, of course) when he observes the conventions.

8. For example, the elementary operations can often be larger in a dedicated processor than in a general-purpose one, thereby eliminating redundant computations. Since you always wear socks two at a time, it makes sense to buy and sell them in pairs. (Compare mix-and-match.)

9. Chomsky (1986, p.14) denies the algorithmic character of speech perception on the grounds that there are "garden-path" sentences which speakers regularly misparse; "the horse raced past the barn fell" is the classic example. I doubt, however, that such cases show the nonmechanical character of speech perception. Rather, they suggest that the class of structures that perceptual algorithms recover fails (slightly) to correspond to the class of well-formed sentences; there is a degree of mismatch between what one can parse and what the grammar of the language generates. Phenomonological (to say nothing of chronometric) considerations make it plausible that, when he encounters a garden-path sentence, the hearer goes over into a problem-solving mode of processing that is quite different from the usual smooth functioning of perceptual parsing.

10. I suppose this corresponds, roughly, to the distinction between the 'declarative' and the 'procedural' stage in problem solving (see Anderson, 1983, ch. 6); or, in a slightly older idiom, to the difference between formulating a plan and executing it (see Miller, Galanter, and Pribrum, 1960). I'm not, however, convinced that the psychological theorizing in this area has gotten much beyond Granny's common sense intuitions. Until it does, I propose to continue to talk in Granny's terms.

11. In these respects speech perception resembles other overlearned and routinized cognitive skills. For example, in solving physics problems, ". . . novices use painful means-end analyses, working with equations they hope are relevant to the problem. In contrast, experts apply correct equations in a forward direction, indicating that they have planned the whole solution before they begin. . . . The schemata in terms of which experts organize their knowledge . . . enable them to grasp the structure of problems in a way that novices cannot." (Carey, 1985, p.3, summarizing Larkin, 1983). This is not, however, to say that the mechanical character of speech perception is plausibly an effect of overlearning. So far as anybody knows, the ontogenesis of speech perception exhibits nothing comparable to the 'novice/expert' shift. In the exercise of their linguistic competences, children are never novices; all normal children behave like expert users of the characteristic dialect of their developmental stage. Thus, a four-year-old's prattling is nothing like a neophyte's hesitant grappling with a hard computational task. Analogous observations would appear to hold for the ontogenesis of other perceptual capacities like, for example, the visual detection of three-dimensional depth.

12. In fact, even in the linguistic case it's only roughly true that the connection between the psychophysical properties of utterances and the intentional properties of their mental causes is conventional. Part of the perceptual problem in decoding speech is to infer the speaker's phonetic intentions from a representation of the spectrographic structure of his utterance. Such inferences are reliable because phonetic intentions have regular acoustic consequences. But the regularity that connects phonetic intentions to types of sounds is not a convention but a law. The speaker realizes such intentions by activating his vocal tract, and the acoustic consequences of his doing so are determined by the physical structure of that organ.

13. More exactly, I argued that perception should exploit only such background as dedicated mechanisms require for algorithmic computations of very general properties of proximal-distal relations; see the preceding discussion.

14. At one point, Bruner remarks that ". . . the most appropriate pattern of readiness at any given moment would be that one which would lead, on the average, to the most veridical guess about the nature of the world around one at the moment. . . . And it follows from this that the most ready perceiver would then have the best chances of estimating situations most adequately and planning accordingly. It is in this general sense that the ready perceiver who can proceed with fairly minimal inputs is also in a position to use his cognitive readiness not only for perceiving what is before him but in foreseeing what is likely to be before him."(p.15). But having the most veridical guess *on average* doesn't, in fact, entail "having the best chances of estimating situations most adequately and planning accordingly" unless you're indifferent about how your right and wrong guesses are distributed. Most people would be prepared to trade lots of wrong guesses about the weather for just a few right ones about the stock market.

15. Notice how much accuracy is what we want even if accuracy costs a lot of money; notice how much we are often prepared to pay for sensitive instruments of scientific observation.

16. That a certain degree of theoretical bias is unavoidable in observational instruments is perhaps a moral of Duhemian philosophy of science (just as it is perhaps a moral of Kantian philosophy of mind that a certain amount of theoretical bias is unavoidable in perception). But an a priori argument that there *must* be penetration is quite a different thing from a teleological argument that there *ought* to be. And, of course, it's compatible with both Duhem and Kant that observation, though inevitably biased in some respects, should be neutral with respect to indefinitely many hypotheses that scientists investigate.

Chapter 10
Observation Reconsidered

Granny and I think that things have gone too far, what with relativism, idealism, and pragmatism at Harvard, graffiti in the subway stations, and Lord knows what all next. Granny and I have decided to put our feet down and dig our heels in. Granny is particularly aroused about people playing fast and loose with the observation/inference distinction, and when Granny is aroused, she is terrible. "We may not have prayers in the public schools," Granny says, "but by G-d, we will have a distinction between observation and inference."

The observation/inference distinction according to Granny:

"There are", Granny says, "two quite different routes to the fixation of belief. There is, on the one hand, belief fixation directly consequent upon the activation of the senses (belief fixation "by observation," as I shall say for short) and there is belief fixation via inference from beliefs previously held ("theoretical" inference, as I shall say for short). This taxonomy of the means of belief *fixation* implies, moreover, a corresponding taxonomy of *beliefs*. For, the character of an organism's sensory apparatus—and, more generally, the character of its perceptual psychology—may determine that certain beliefs, if acquired at all, must be inferential and cannot be attained by observation. It is, for example, an accident (of our geography) that our beliefs about Martian fauna are nonobservationally acquired. By contrast, it is *not* an accident that our beliefs about the doings of electromagnetic energy in the extreme ultraviolet are all inferential. If there are Martian fauna, then were we close enough, we could observe some (unless Martians are *very* small). But making observations in the extreme ultraviolet would require alteration of our sensory/perceptual mechanisms; beliefs about the extreme ultraviolet *must*, for us, all be inferential.

"Some beliefs are thus nonobservational in the nature of things. (To a first approximation, no beliefs are noninferential in the nature of things; any belief *could* be fixed by inference excepting, maybe, tricky ones of the 'I exist' variety.) Moreover, beliefs that are fixed by observation play an interesting and central role in the acquisition of knowledge. (Not, perhaps, so interesting and central as philosophers have sometimes supposed, but still. . . .) For one thing, observation-ally fixed beliefs tend, by and large, to be more reliable than infer-entially fixed beliefs. This is primarily because the etiological route from the fact that *P* to the belief that *P* is metaphorically—and maybe literally—*shorter* in observation than in inference; less is likely to go wrong because there's less that *can* go wrong. And, because beliefs that are fixed by observation tend to be relatively reliable, our rational confidence in our knowledge claims depends very largely on their ability to survive observational assessment.

"Second, the observational fixation of belief plays a special role in the adjudication and resolution of clashes of opinion. When obser-vation is *not* appealed to, attempts to settle disputes often take the form of a search for premises that the disputants share. There is, in general, no point to my convincing you that belief *B* is derivable from theory *T* unless *T* is a theory you endorse; otherwise, my argument will seem to you merely a reductio of its premises. This is a peculiarly nasty property of inferential belief fixation because it means that *the more we disagree about, the harder it will likely be to settle any of our disagreements.* None of this applies, however, when the beliefs at issue are observational. Since observation is not a process in which new beliefs are inferred from old ones, the use of obser-vation to resolve disputes does not depend on a prior consensus as to what premises may be assumed. The moral, children, is approxi-mately Baconian. Don't think; look. Try not to argue."

Also sprach Granny. Recent opinion, however, has tended to ignore these homely truths. In this paper, I want to claim that widely en-dorsed arguments against the possibility of drawing a principled observation/theory distinction have, in fact, been oversold. This does not amount quite to Granny's vindication, since I will not attempt to say in any detail what role the notion of observational belief fixation might come to play in a reasonably naturalized epistemology. Suffice it, for present purposes, to have cleared the way for such a reconstruction.

The claim, then, is that there is a class of beliefs that are typically fixed by sensory/perceptual processes, and that the fixation of beliefs in this class is, in a sense that wants spelling out, importantly theory neutral. As a first shot at what the theory neutrality of observation comes to: given the same stimulations, two organisms with the same sensory/perceptual psychology will quite generally observe the same things, and hence arrive at the same observational beliefs, *however much their theoretical commitments may differ.* This will get some pretty comprehensive refinement as we go along, but it's good enough to start from.

There are, as far as I know, three sorts of arguments that have been alleged to show that no serious observation/inference distinction can be drawn.[1] These are: ordinary language arguments, meaning holism arguments, and de facto psychological arguments. I propose to concentrate, in what follows, mostly on arguments of the third kind; I think that recent changes in the way (some) psychologists view sensory/perceptual processes have significant implications for the present philosophical issues. But it's worth a fast run-through to see why the first two sorts of arguments are also, to put it mildly, less than decisive.

The Ordinary Language Argument

The main contention of this chapter is that there is a theory-neutral observation/inference distinction; that the boundary between what can be observed and what must be inferred is largely determined by fixed architectural features of an organism's sensory/perceptual psychology. I'm prepared to concede, however, that this is *not* the doctrine that emerges from attention to the linguistic practices of working scientists. Scientists do have a use for a distinction between what is observed and what is inferred, but the distinction that they have in mind is typically relativized to the inquiry they have in hand. Roughly, so far as I can tell, what a working scientist counts as an experimental *observation* depends on what issue his experiment is designed to settle and what empirical assumptions the design of his experiment takes for granted. One speaks of telescopic observations—and of the telescope as an instrument of observation—because the functioning of the telescope is assumed in experimental designs that give us observations of celestial events. One speaks of observed reaction times because the operation of the clock is assumed in the design of experiments when reaction time is the dependent variable. If, by contrast, it begins to seem that perhaps the clock is broken, it then becomes an issue whether reaction times *are* observed when the experimenter reads the numerals that the clock displays.

That way of using the observation/inference distinction is, of course, responsive to an epistemically important fact: not all the empirical assumptions of an experiment can get tested in the same design; we can't test all of our beliefs at once. It is perfectly reasonable of working scientists to want to mark the distinction between what's foreground in an experiment and what is merely taken for granted, and it is again perfectly reasonable of them to do so by relativizing the notion of an observation to whatever experimental assumptions are operative. But, of course, if *that* is what one means by the observation/inference distinction, then there is no interesting issue about whether scientific observation can be theory neutral. Patently, on that construal, the theory of the experimental instruments and the (e.g., statistical) theory of the experimental design will be presupposed by the scientist's observational vocabulary, and what the scientist can (be said to) observe will change as these background theories mature. We can *now* observe craters on Venus (small differences in reaction times) because we now have powerful enough telescopes (accurate enough clocks). On this way of drawing it, the observation/inference distinction is inherently heuristic; it is relativized not just to the sensory/perceptual psychology of the observer, but also to the currently available armementarium of scientific theories and gadgets.

Much that is philosophically illuminating can, no doubt, be learned by careful attention to what working scientists use terms like 'observed' and 'inferred' to do; but naturalized epistemology is not, for all that, a merely sociolinguistic discipline. Though one of the things that these terms are used for is to mark a distinction that is beyond doubt theory-relative, that does *not* settle the case against Granny. For, it is open to Granny to argue like this:

"True, there is an epistemologically important distinction that it's reasonable to call 'the' observation/inference distinction, and that is theory-relative. And, also true, it is this theory-relative distinction that scientists usually use the terms 'observed' and 'inferred' to mark. But that is quite compatible with there being another distinction, which it is also reasonable to call 'the' observation/inference distinction, which is also of central significance to the epistemology of science, and which is *not* theory-relative. No linguistic considerations can decide this, and I therefore propose to ignore mere matters of vulgar dialectology henceforth."

In her advanced years, Granny has become quite bitter about ordinary language arguments.

Arguments from Meaning Holism

Think of a theory (or, mutatis mutandis, the system of beliefs a given person holds) as represented by an infinite, connected graph. The nodes of the graph correspond to the entailments of the theory, and the paths between the nodes correspond to a variety of semantically significant relations that hold among its theorems; inferential relations, evidence relations, and so forth. When the theory is tested, confirmation percolates from node to node along the connecting paths. When the theory is disturbed—e.g., by abandoning a postulate or a principle of inference—the local geometry of the graph is distorted, and the resulting strains are distributed throughout the network, sometimes showing up in unanticipated deformations of the structure of the graph far from the initial locus of the disturbance.

That sort of picture has done a lot of work for philosophers since Quine wrote "Two Dogmas." Most famously, skeptical work. Since, so the story goes, everything connects, the unit of meaning—the minimal context, so to speak, within which the meaning of a theoretical postulate is fixed—appears to be *the whole theory*. It is thus unclear how two theories could dispute the claim that P (since the claim that P means something different in a theory that entails that P than it does in, say, a theory that entails its denial). And, similarly, it is unclear how two belief systems that differ anywhere can help but differ everywhere (since a node is identified by its position in a graph, and since a graph is identified by the totality of its nodes and paths, it appears that only identical graphs can have any nodes in common).

It is, of course, possible to accept this sort of holism (as, by the way, Granny and I do not) and still acknowledge *some* sort of distinction between observation and inference; e.g., the distinction might be construed as epistemic rather than semantic. Suppose every sentence gets its *meaning* from its theoretical context; still, some sentences are closer to the 'edges' of the graph than others, and these might be supposed to depend more directly upon experience for their *confirmation* than sentences further inland do. Quine himself has some such tale to tell. However—and this is what bears on the present issues—the holism story does suggest that observation couldn't be *theory neutral* in the way that Granny and I think it is. On the holistic account, what you can observe is going to depend comprehensively upon what theories you hold because *what your observation sentences mean depends comprehensively on what theories you hold*.

This is precisely the moral that a number of philosophers have drawn from Quinean holism. For example, here are some quotations from Paul Churchland's *Scientific Realism and The Plasticity of Mind* (1979):

> The meaning of the relevant observation terms has nothing to do with the intrinsic qualitative identity of whatever sensations just happen to prompt their non-inferential application in sin-

gular empirical judgements. Rather, their position in semantic space appears to be determined by the network of sentences containing them accepted by the speakers who use them (p. 12).

. . . the view that the meaning of our common observation terms is given in, or determined by, sensation must be rejected outright, and as we saw, we are left with networks of belief as the bearers or determinants of understanding . . . (p. 13).

. . . a child's initial (stimulus-response) use of, say, 'white' as a response to the familiar kind of sensation, provides that term with no semantic identity. It acquires a semantic identity as, and only as, it comes to figure in a network of beliefs and a correlative pattern of inferences. Depending on what that acquired network happens to be, that term could come to mean *white* or *hot* . . ., or an infinity of other things (p. 14).

And so forth. So Churchland holds, on holistic grounds, that an observation sentence might mean *anything* depending upon theoretical context.

I emphasize that this conclusion is equivalent to the claim that *anything might be an observation sentence* depending upon theoretical context; or, material mode, that *anything might be observed* depending upon theoretical context. For Churchland—as, of course, for many other philosophers—*you can change your observational capacities by changing your theories.* Indeed, Churchland sees in this a program for educational reform. "If our perceptual judgements must be laden with theory in any case, then why not exchange the Neolithic legacy now in use for the conception of reality embodied in modern-era science?" (p. 35). Really well brought up children would not

. . . sit on the beach and listen to the steady roar of the pounding surf. They sit on the beach and listen to the aperiodic atmospheric compression waves produced as the coherent energy of the ocean waves is audibly redistributed in the chaotic turbulence of the shallows. . . . They do not observe the western sky redden as the Sun sets. They observe the wavelength distribution of incoming solar radiation shift towards the longer wavelengths . . . as the shorter are increasingly scattered away from the lengthening atmospheric path that they must take as terrestrial rotation turns us slowly away from their source. . . . They do not feel common objects grow cooler with the onset of darkness, nor observe the dew forming on every surface. They feel the molecular KE of common aggregates dwindle with the now uncompensated radiation of their energy starwards, and they observe the accretion of reassociated atmospheric H_2O molecules as their KE is lost to the now more quiescent aggregates with which they collide . . . (p. 30).

Oh brave new world/that has such children in it.

Once again: the moral that Churchland (and others) draw from holistic semantic doctrines about beliefs/theories is that an observation sentence can mean anything depending on theoretical context; hence that anything can *be* an observation sentence depending on theoretical context; hence that *there could not be a class of beliefs that must be inferential regardless of what theories the believer esouses.* Churchland's way of putting this is, perhaps, misleading. After all, if the gathering of the dew *is* the accretion of atmospheric H_2O molecules, then of course we do, right now and without technological retraining, observe the accretion of atmospheric H_2O molecules whenever we observe the gathering of the dew; 'observe' is transparent to the substitutivity of identicals. But I don't really think that Churchland (or anybody else party to the present controversy) is seriously confused about this, and I don't propose to carp about it. Indeed, it's easy to fix up. What Churchland must be claiming, on grounds of holism, is that what you can see things *as*—what you can *observe that things are* is comprehensively determined by theoretical context; so that, depending on context, you can, or can learn to, see anything as anything.

Granny and I doubt that you can learn to see anything as anything (that anything can be an observation sentence); but our reasons for doubting this will keep until section 3. For present purposes, suffice it to repeat the lesson that causal semantic theories have recently been teaching us, viz., that holism may not be true. Specifically, it may not be true that (all) the semantical properties of sentences (/beliefs) are determined by their location in the theoretical networks in which they are embedded; it may be that some of their semantic properties are determined by the character of their attachment to the world (e.g., by the character of the causal route from distal objects and events to the tokening of the sentence or the fixation of the belief.) The point is, of course, that their attachment to the world, unlike their inferential role, is something that symbols (/beliefs) can have *severally*; so that, when such attachments are at issue, the morals of holism need not apply.

At a minimum, this suggests a way out of Churchland's dilemma. It will have been clear from the fragments quoted above that Churchland's discussion relies heavily, if implicitly, on the following modus tollens: if the semantics of observation sentences is theory neutral, that must be because observation sentences get their meanings—somehow—from their connections with sensations. But we have good reason to deny that they get their semantics that way. The alternative is that observation sentences get their meanings from their theoretical contexts (from "networks of beliefs").

In fact, however, *neither* of these accounts of the semantics of observation sentences seems particularly attractive, least of all for color terms, although, as it happens, color terms are Churchland's favorite working examples. It tells against the first alternative that 'white' is typically used to refer to the color of objects, not to the color of sensations; and it tells against the second that the inferential roles of color terms tend to be isomorphic—hence inverted spectrum puzzles—so that color words provide the worst possible cases for 'functional role' theories of meaning. In fact, it looks as though the sensible thing to say about 'white' might be that it means what it does because of the special character of its association (not with a sensation or an inferential role but) *with white things*. To accept that, however, is to reject holism as, anyhow, the *whole* story about the semantics of color terms.

I don't suppose that there's anything much novel in this, and I certainly don't suppose it establishes that there *is* a viable, theory neutral, observation/inference distinction. The point I have been making is merely negative: meaning holism is unequivocally destructive of a theory-neutral notion of observation only if you suppose that *all* the semantic properties of sentences/beliefs are determined by their theoretical context; for, if some are not, then perhaps the essential semantic conditions for being observational can be framed in terms of these. The obvious suggestion would be, on the one hand, that what makes a term observational is that it denotes what is, by independent criteria, an observable property; and, on the other, that what a term denotes is nonholistically (perhaps causally) determined. In light of this, I propose simply not to grant that all the semantic properties of sentences/beliefs are determined by their theoretical context. And Granny proposes not to grant that too.

Psychological Arguments

Precisely parallel to the philosophical doctrine that there can be no principled distinction between *observation* and *inference* is the psychological doctrine that there can be no principled distinction between *perception* and *cognition*. The leading idea here is that "perception involves a kind of problem solving—a kind of intelligence" (Gregory 1970, p. 30). Perception, according to this account, is the process wherein an organism assigns probable distal causes to the proximal stimulations it encounters. What makes the solution of perceptual problems other than mere routine is the fact that, as a matter of principle, any given pattern of proximal stimulation is compatible with a great variety of distal causes; there are, if you like, many possible worlds that would project a given pattern of excitation onto the sensory mechanisms of an organism. To view the mental processes which mediate perception as inferences is thus necessarily to view them as *nondemonstrative* inferences. "We are forced . . . to suppose that perception involves betting on the most probable interpretation of sensory data, in terms of the world of objects" (Gregory 1970, p. 29). It is worth stressing the putative moral: what mediates perception is an inference from effects to causes. The sort of mentation required for perception is thus not different in *kind*—though no doubt it differs a lot in conscious accessability—from what goes on in Sherlock Holmes' head when he infers the identity of the criminal from a stray cigar band and a hair or two. If what Holmes does deserves to be called cognition, perception deserved to be called cognition too, or so, at least, some psychologists like to say.

Neither Granny nor I have heard of a serious alternative to this view of perception, so let's suppose, for purposes of argument at least, that these psychologists are right. It may then seem that the psychology of perception provides an argument—indeed, quite a direct argument—that observation can't be theory neutral. To see how such an argument might go, consider the following question: if, in general, there are many distal solutions compatible with the perceptual problem that a given sensory pattern poses, how is it possible that perception should ever manage to univocal (to say nothing of *veridical*)? Why, that is, doesn't the world look to be many ways ambiguous, with one 'reading' of the ambiguity corresponding to each distal layout that is compatible with the current sensory excitation; (as, indeed, a Necker cube *does* look to be several ways ambiguous, with one term of the ambiguity corresponding to each of the possible optical projections from a three-dimensional cube onto a two-dimensional surface). Assuming, in short, that perception is problem solving, how on earth do perceptual problems ever get solved? As Gregory comments, "it is surely remarkable that out of the infinity of possibilities the perceptual brain generally hits on just about the best one" (1970, p. 29).

All psychological theories that endorse the continuity of perception with problem solving offer much the same answer to this question: viz., that though perceptual analyses are underdetermined by sensory arrays, it does not follow that they are underdetermined *tout court.* For, perceptual analyses are constrained not just by the available sensory information, but also by such prior knowledge as the perceiver may bring to the task. What happens in perceptual processing, according to this account, is that sensory information is interpreted by reference to the perceiver's background theories, the latter serving, in effect, to rule out certain etiologies as implausible causal histories for the present sensory array. Only thus is sensory ambiguity resolved; and, if perception is typically veridical, that's because the background theories that organisms exploit in perceptual analysis are, for the most part, true.

Accepting this account of the perceptual reduction of sensory ambiguity is, of course, fully compatible with stressing the analogy between perception and problem solving. There are many, many ways that the hairs and the cigar band could have come to where Holmes found them; many projections, if you like, of possible criminals onto actual clues. How, then, it is possible—even in principle—that Holmes should solve the crime? Answer: Holmes knows about the clues, but he knows a lot more too; and his background knowledge comes into play when the clues get unravelled. Jones couldn't have left brown hairs because Jones is blond; Smith couldn't have left the cigar band because he only smokes iced tea. Bentley, however, has brown hair and his dog collects cigar bands; so Bentley and his dog it must have been. The clues underdetermine the criminal, but the clues plus background knowledge may be univocal up to a very high order of probability. The trick—the trick that problem solving *always* amounts to—is having the right background information and knowing when and how to apply it. So too in the case of perception, according to the cognitivists.

What has all this to do with reconsidering observation? The point is that, if the present story is right, then the appeal to a background theory is *inherent* in the process of perceptual analysis. Perception wouldn't work without it because the perceptual problem is the reduction of sensory ambiguity, and that problem is solved only when one's sensory information is interpreted in the light of one's prior beliefs. So, the one thing that perception *couldn't* be, on this account of how it works, is theory neutral. Indeed, this is precisely the moral that a number of philosophers have drawn from the psychological texts. Thus, Thomas Kuhn remarks that "the rich experimental literature [in psychology] . . . makes one suspect that something like a paradigm is prerequisite to perception itself. What a man sees depends both upon what he looks at and also upon what his previous visual-conceptual experience has taught him to see" (Kuhn 1962, p. 113). Kuhn clearly thinks that, among the "visual-conceptual experiences" that can work such alterations in perception is the assimilation of scientific doctrine: "Paradigm changes do cause scientists to see the world of their research-engagements differently. . . . It is as elementary prototypes for these transformations of the scientist's world view that the familiar demonstrations of a switch in visual gestalt prove so suggestive" (1962, p. 111). Nelson Goodman reads the experimental literature on perception in much the same way. "That we find what we are prepared to find (what we look for or what forcefully affronts our expectations), and that we are likely to be blind to what neither helps nor hinders our pursuits, are commonplaces . . . amply attested in the psychological laboratory" (Goodman 1978, p. 14. See also Goodman's *Languages of Art*, where this view of perceptual psychology is strikingly in evidence.)

In fact, however, it is unclear that that's what the psychological laboratory *does* attest, and thereby hangs a puzzle. For if we ought to be impressed by the degree to which perception is interpretive, contextually sensitive, labile, responsive to background knowledge, and all that, we surely ought also to be impressed by the degree to which it is often bullheaded and recalcitrant. In fact, many of the standard psychological demonstrations seem to point both morals at the same time. Consider the famous Muller-Lyer figures. The textbook story goes like this: when the arrow heads bend in (top) the figure is unconsciously interpreted in three-dimensional projection as a convex corner with its edge emerging toward the viewer from the picture plane. Conversely, when the arrow heads bend out (bottom) the figure is unconsciously interpreted in three-dimensional projection as a concave corner with its edge receding from the viewer. It follows that the center line is interpreted as *farther from the observer* in the upper figure than in the lower one. Since, however, the two center lines are in fact of the same length, their retinal projections are identical in size. This identity of retinal projection could be compatible with the three-dimensional interpretation of the figures only if the center line were longer in the upper figure than in the lower; two objects at different distances can have the same retinal projection only if the more distant object is larger. So size constancy operates (to compensate, as one might say, for what appears to be the apparent effect of distance) and the two lines are perceived as differing in length. See what a nice regard for consistency the unconscious has, Freud to the contrary notwithstanding. There is abundant empirical evidence for this explanation including, notably, the fact that children, having had less experience with edges and corners than adults, are correspondingly less susceptible to the illusion.

The Muller-Lyer illusion thus appears to be and is often cited as a prime example of how background information—in this case a complex of assumptions about the relations between three-dimensional objects and their two-dimensional projections—can affect the perceptual analysis of a sensory array. "What," one might ask, "could be clearer evidence of the penetration of perception by information that is *not* available at the retina?" On the other hand, there's this: The Muller-Lyer is a *familiar* illusion; the news has pretty well gotten around by now. So, it's part of the "background theory" of anybody who lives in this culture and is at all into pop psychology that displays like figure 10.1 are in fact misleading and that it always turns out, on measurement, that the center lines of the arrows are the same length. Query: *Why isn't perception penetrated by THAT piece of background theory?* Why, that is, doesn't *knowing* that the lines are the same length make it *look as though* the lines are the same length? (For that matter, since one knows perfectly well that figure 10.1 is a drawing in two dimensions, why doesn't *that* information penetrate perception, thereby blocking the three-dimensional interpretation and cancelling the illusion?) This sort of consideration doesn't make it seem at all as though perception is, as it's often said to be, saturated with cognition through and through. On the contrary, it suggests just the reverse: that how the world looks can be peculiarly unaffected by how one knows it to be. I pause to emphasize that the Muller-Lyer is by no means atypical in this respect. To the best of my knowledge, all the standard perceptual illusions exhibit this curiously refractory character: knowing that they *are* illusions doesn't make them go away.[2]

I hope that the polemical situation is beginning to seem a little queer. On the one hand, reflection upon the impoverishment and ambiguity of sensory information leads, by a plausible route, to the analysis of perception as a form of problem solving in which proximal stimulations are interpreted in light of some background theory accessible to the perceiver. This makes it seem that how the world is perceived to be ought to depend very largely on the perceiver's prior beliefs and expectations; hence the perceptual effects of cognitive set that psychologists of the "New Look" persuasion made a living by

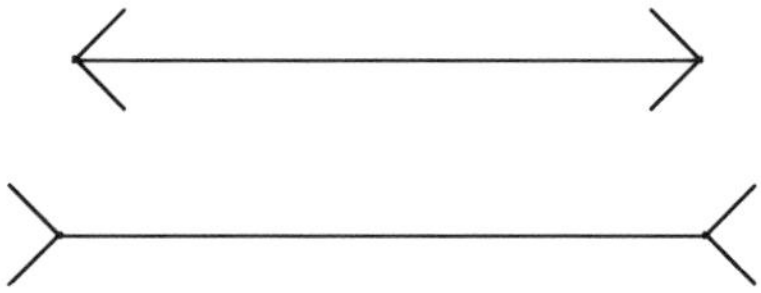

Figure 10.1.
The Muller-Lyer Illusion.

advertising. But, on the other hand, there are these curious and persuasive perceptual *im*plasticities, cases where knowing doesn't help seeing. It is, of course, reflection on examples of the second sort that keeps Granny going. These are the cases where the idea of theory-neutral observation can get a toehold. The problem is, which sort of cases ought we to believe? And, while we're at it, *how can a theory of perception accommodate the existence of both?*

We come to the main point at last. The New Look idea that perception is a kind of problem solving does not, all by itself, imply the theory dependence of observation. Philosophers who read that moral in the psychological texts read the texts too fast. (Granny says that a little psychology is a dangerous thing and inclineth a man to relativism.) To get from a cognitivist interpretation of perception to any epistemologically interesting version of the conclusion that observation is theory dependent, you need *not only the premise that perception is problem solving, but also the premise that perceptual problem solving has access to ALL (or, anyhow, arbitrarily much) of the background information at the perceiver's disposal.* Perceptual implasticities of the sorts we've just been noticing make it highly implausible, however, that this second premise is true.

All this suggests that we'd better distinguish between two questions that up until now we've been treating as the same: the question whether perception is a kind of problem solving (i.e., whether observation is inferential) and the question whether perception is comprehensively penetrated by background beliefs (i.e., whether observation can be theory-neutral). It is entirely possible—to put the point another way—to steer a middle course between Granny and Jerome Bruner: to agree with Bruner (as against Granny) that there is an important sense in which observation is a kind of inference, but also to agree with Granny (as against Harvard relativists) that there is, in perception, a radical isolation of how things look from the effects of much of what one believes.

Since it is the second issue rather than the first that raises all the epistemological questions, this seems to be a moral victory for Granny. If for example the inferential character of perception is, as I'm supposing, compatible with the theory neutrality of observation, then *nothing* follows from perceptual psychology about whether scientists who accept radically different theories can observe the same phenomena. In particular, on this view, it would *not* follow from the inferential character of perception that "the infant and the layman . . . cannot see what the physicist sees" (Hanson, 1961, p. 17), or that "[when the physicist looks at an X-ray tube] . . . he sees the instrument in terms of electrical circuit theory, thermodynamic theory, the theories of metal and glass structure, thermionic emission, optical transmission, refraction, diffraction, atomic theory, quantum theory and special relativity" (pp. 15–16). Similarly, on this account, the inferential character of perception leaves it open that the children whom Churchland wants to teach not to see the gathering of the dew might, thank God, see things much the same way after they've learned physics as they did before. The argument for the relativity of observation requires, to repeat, not just the inferential character of perception, but the idea that *all* your background knowledge, including especially your scientific theories, is accessible as premises for perceptual integration. By contrast, if you think that perception, though inferential, is nevertheless encapsulated from much of what the perceiver believes, the common epistemic situation of the scientist and the layman starts to show through. There is, perhaps, just one perceptual world, though the experts sometimes know more about it than the amateurs.

What might the psychology of perception look like if observation is *both* inferential and theory neutral? I'll say a word about this before returning to the epistemological issues.

The view that perception is problem solving, though it takes the distinction between perception and *cognition* as heuristic, takes quite seriously the distinction between perception and *sensation*. Sensory processes, according to this account, merely register such proximal stimulations as an organism's environment affords. It's left to cognitive processes—notably the perceptual ones—to interpret sensory states by assigning probably distal causes. So we have the following picture: sensation is responsive solely to the character of proximal stimulation and is noninferential. Perception is both inferential and responsive to the perceiver's background theories. It is not, of course, an accident that things are supposed to line up this way; inference requires premises. Perceptual processes *can* be inferential because the perceiver's background theory supplies the premises that the inferences run on. Sensory processes *can't* be inferential because they have, by assumption, no access to the background theories in light of which the distal causes of proximal stimulations are inferred. The moral is that, if you want to split the difference between Granny and the New Look, you need to postulate a *tertium quid*; a kind of psychological mechanism which is both encapsulated (like sensation) and inferential (like cognition). The apparent contradiction between inference and encapsulation is resolved by assuming that the access to background theory that such mechanisms have is sharply delimited; indeed, delimited by the intrinsic character of the mechanisms.

I won't say much about this here since I've set out the psychological story at some length in a previous study (see Fodor, 1983) and I'm anxious to return to the philosophical morals. Suffice it just to suggest, by way of a brief example, what the organization of such "modular" perceptual mechanisms might be like.

It's plausible to assume that the perceptual analysis of speech typically effects an assignment of sentence tokens to sentence types. One reason it's plausible to assume this is that it's obviously true. Another reason is that understanding what someone says typically requires knowing what form of words he uttered, and to assign an utterance to a form of words *is* to assign a token to a type. Cognitive psychology proceeds by diagnosing functions and postulating mechanisms to perform them; let's assume that there is some psychological mechanism—a *parser*, let's call it—whose function is this: it takes sensory (as it might be, acoustic) representations of utterances as inputs and produces representations of sentence types (as it might be, linguistic structural descriptions) as outputs. No doubt this way of setting up the problem assumes a lot that a lot of you won't want to grant—for example, that there are psychological mechanisms, and that they are properly viewed as functions from one sort of representations onto another. However, remember the context: we've been wondering what current psychological theory implies about the observation/inference distinction. And the sort of psychological theory that's current is the one I've just outlined.

There is abundant empirical evidence—with which, however, I won't bother you—that parsing has all the properties that make psychologists want to say that perception is inferential. All the indications are that the acoustic character of an utterance significantly underdetermines its structural description, so the parser—if it is to succeed in its function—will have to know a lot of background theory. This isn't, by the way, particularly mysterious. Consider the property of being a noun—a sort of property that some utterances surely have and that adequate structural descriptions of utterances must surely mark. Patently, that property has no sensory/acoustic correspondent; there's nothing that nouns qua nouns sound like, or look like on an oscilliscope. So a mechanism that can recognize utterances of nouns as such must know about something more than the acoustic/sensory properties of the tokens it classifies, in this case, something about the language that it parses; i.e., it has to know which words in the language are nouns.

Well, then, what would it be like for the parser to be a module? A simple story might go like this; a parser for *L* contains a grammar of *L*. What it does when it does its thing is, it infers from certain acoustic properties of a token to a characterization of certain of the distal causes of the token (e.g., to the speaker's intention that the utterance should be a token of a certain linguistic type). Premises of this inference can include whatever information about the acoustics of the token the mechanisms of sensory transduction provide, whatever information about the linguistic types in *L* the internally represented grammar provides, *and nothing else*. It is, of course, the closure condition that makes the parser modular.

Compare a New Look parser. In the extreme case, a New Look parser can bring to the process of assigning structural descriptions *anything that the organism knows* (or believes, or hopes, or expects, etc.). For example, a New Look parser knows how *very* unlikely it is that anyone would say, right smack in the course of a philosophical lecture on observation and inference, "Piglet gave Pooh a stiffening sort of nudge, and Pooh, who felt more and more that he was somewhere else, got up slowly and began to look for himself." So if someone *were* to say that, right smack in the middle of a philosophical lecture on observation and inference, a New Look parser would presumably have a lot of trouble understanding it; by definition, a New Look parser tends to hear just what it expects to hear. By the way, this example suggests one of the reasons why encapsulated perceptual modules might be quite a good thing for an organism to have: background beliefs, and the expectations that they engender, from time to time prove *not to be true*. That doesn't matter so much when they are background beliefs about observation and inference, or about Pooh and Piglet. When, however, they are background beliefs about Tigger, it's a different story. Tiggers bounce. And bite.

I won't try to convince you that the parser—or any other perceptual mechanism—actually *is* modular; what I want to urge, for present purposes, is just that *if* perception is modular (inferential but encapsulated), then that has serious implications for the putative psychological arguments against the theory neutrality of observation. I have a scattering of points to make about this.

First, and most important, if perceptual processes are modular, then, by definition, bodies of theory that are inaccessible to the modules *do not affect the way the perceiver sees the world*. Specifically, perceivers who differ profoundly in their background theories—scientists with quite different axes to grind, for example—might nevertheless see the world in *exactly* the same way, so long as the bodies of theory that they disagree about are inaccessible to their perceptual mechanisms.

Second, the modularity story suggests not only that something can be made of the notion of theory neutral observation, but also that something can be made of the notion of observation *language*; i.e., that—much current opinion to the contrary notwithstanding—there is a good sense in which some terms (like 'red', as it might be) are observational and others (like 'proton', as it might be) are not. Suppose that perceptual mechanisms are modular and that the body of background theory accessible to processes of perceptual integration is therefore rigidly fixed. By hypothesis, only those properties of the distal stimulus count as observable which terms in the *accessible* background theory denote. The point is, no doubt, entirely empirical, but I am willing to bet lots that 'red' will prove to be observational by this criterion and that 'proton' will not. This is, of course, just a way of betting that Hanson, Kuhn, Churchland, Goodman, and Co. are wrong; that physics doesn't belong to the accessible background.

There are other more exciting cases where we are already in a pretty good position to say which properties of distal objects will count as observable, hence which terms will count as observation vocabulary. The case of parsing is among these. This is because it is plausible to suppose that the background theory accessible to a modularized parser would have to be a grammar, and we know, more or less, what sorts of properties of sentences grammatical descriptions specify. So then, applying the present criterion to the present assumptions, the observable linguistic properties of utterances of sentences ought to include things like being an utterance of a sentence, being an utterance of a sentence that contains the word 'the', being an utterance of a sentence that contains a word that refers to trees, and so forth, depending on details of your views about what properties of sentences linguistic structural descriptions specify. By contrast, what would *not* count as observable on the current assumptions are such properties of sentences as being uttered with the intention of deceiving John, being ill-advised in the context, containing a word that is frequently used in restaurants where they sell hamburgers, and so forth. It should be noted in passing that this sort of account permits one to distinguish sharply between observable properties and *sensory* properties. If sensory properties are ones that *non*inferential psychological mechanisms respond to, then the sensory properties of utterances are plausibly all acoustic and almost all are inaccessible to consciousness.

Third point: what I've been saying about modularity so far is equivalent to the claim that perceptual processes are "synchronically" impenetrable by—insensitive to—much of the perceiver's background knowledge. Your current sophistication about the Muller-Lyer is inaccessible to the module that mediates visual form perception and does not, therefore, serve to dispel the illusion. But this leaves open the question whether perception may be "diachronically" penetrable; in effect, whether experience and training can affect the accessability of background theory to perceptual mechanisms.

To deny diachronic penetrability would be to claim, in effect, that *all* the background information that is accessible to modular perceptual systems is endogenously specified, and that is viewed as implausible even by mad-dog nativists like me. For example, parsing may be modular, but children must learn *something* about their language from the language that they hear; why else would children living in China so often grow up speaking Chinese? The point about the diachronic penetrability of perception is, however, just like the point about its synchronic penetrability: it offers an argument for the continuity of perception with cognition only if just any old learning or experience can affect the way you see, and there is no reason at all to suppose that that is so. Perhaps, on the contrary, perception is diachronically penetrable only within strictly—maybe endogenously—defined limits. Not only do your current Copernican prejudices fail to much dispel the apparent motion of the sun, it may be that there is *no* educational program that would do the trick; because it may be that the inaccessibility of astronomical background to the processes of visual perceptual integration is a consequence of innate and unalterable architecture features of our mental structure. In this case, our agreement on the general character of the perceptual world might transcend the particularities of our training and go as deep as our common humanity. Granny and I hope that this is so since common humanity is something that we favor.

I return now to more strictly epistemological concerns. Two points and I'll have done.

First, if Granny wants to appeal to modularity psychology as a way of holding onto theory-neutral observation, she is going to have to give a bit. In particular she is going to have to distinguish between *observation* and *the perceptual fixation of belief*. It is only for the former that claims for theory neutrality have any plausibility.

Thus far, I've been emphasizing that psychological sophistication doesn't change the way the Muller-Lyer *looks*. Knowing that it's an illusion—even knowing how the illusion works—doesn't make the effect go away. But if one side of perception is about the look of things, the other side is about how things are judged to be; and it bears emphasis that how the Muller-Lyer looks doesn't, in the case of a sophisticated audience, much affect the perceptual beliefs that its observers come to have. I assume, for example, that you're not remotely tempted to suppose that the center line in the lower figure actually is longer than the center line in the upper; and the reason you're not is that *the mechanisms of belief fixation, in contrast to the*

presumptive perceptual modules, ARE in contact with background theory.
Belief fixation, unlike the fixation of appearances—what I'm calling
observation—is a *conservative* process; to a first approximation, it uses
everything you know.

Here is one way to conceptualize the situation: the fixation of
perceptual belief effects a reconciliation between the character of
current sensory stimulation, as analyzed by modular processors, and
background theory. The modular systems might be thought of as
proposing hypotheses about the distal sources of sensory stimulation;
these hypotheses are couched in a restricted (viz., observational)
vocabulary and are predicated on a correspondingly restricted body
of information, viz., current sensory information together with whatever fragment of background theory the modules have access to. The
hypotheses that modular systems propose are then compared with
the rest of the organism's background theory, and the perceptual
fixation of belief is consequent upon this comparison.

So, to a first approximation, the activity of the modules determines
what you would believe if you were going on the appearances alone.
But, of course, this is *only* a first approximation since, as remarked
above, modules deal not only in a restricted body of background
knowledge, but also in a restricted conceptual repertoire. There are
some hypotheses that modules *never* offer because they have no
access to a vocabulary in which to express them: hypotheses about
the instantiation of nonobservable properties such as that what's
currently on view is a proton. So one might better put it that the
activity of modules determines what you would believe *about the
appearances* if you were going just on the appearances. Less gnomi-
cally: modules offer hypotheses about the instantiation of observable
properties of things, and the fixation of *perceptual belief* is the evaluation of such hypotheses in light of the totality of background theory.
According to this usage, what you observe is related to what you
believe in something like the way that what you want is related to
what you want on balance.

It should be clear from all this that even if Granny gets the theory-
neutrality of observation, she is unlikely to get anything remotely
like its infallibility. For starters, only a faculty of belief fixation can
be infallible and, according to the present story, the psychological
mechanisms that are informationally encapsulated do not, in and of
themselves, effect the fixation of belief. Anyhow—beside this somewhat legalistic consideration—the infallibility of observation would
presumably require the introspective availability of its deliverances;
and, though I suppose one usually knows how things look to one,
it seems to be empirically false that one always does. If, for example,

the story I told about the Muller-Lyer is true, then the existence of
the illusion turns on the fact that one sees the figures as three-
dimensional corners. But it is *not* introspectively obvious that one
sees them that way, and the psychologists who figured out the
illusion did so not by introspecting but by the usual route of theory
construction and experimentation. (Similarly, a crucial issue in the
history of the psychology of color perception was whether yellow
looks to be a mixed hue. It is *now*—post-theoretically—introspectively
obvious that it does not.)

"But look," you might say, growing by now understandably impatient, "if the notion of observation we're left with is as attenuated
as it now appears to be, what, epistemologically speaking, is it good
for? Haven't you and your Granny really given away everything that
the opposition ever wanted?"

I quote from Norwood Russell Hanson: "To say that Tycho and
Kepler, Simplicius and Galileo, Hooke and Newton, Priestly and
Lavoisier, Soddy and Einstein, De Broglie and Born, Heisenberg and
Bohm all make the same observations but use them differently is too
easy. This parallels the too-easy epistemological doctrine that all
normal observers see the same things in *x*, but interpret them differently. It does not explain controversy in research science" (Hanson
1961, p. 13. In Hanson's text, the second sentence appears as a
footnote at the point where I have inserted it.) Now, on the view of
science that Granny and I hold to, this is worse than the wrong
answer; it's the answer to the wrong question. It is no particular
puzzle, given the nondemonstrative character of empirical inference,
that there should be scientific controversy. Rather, as the skeptical
tradition in philosophy has made crystal clear, the epistemological
problem *par excellence* is *to explain scientific consensus*; to explain how
it is possible, given the vast and notorious underdetermination of
theory by data, that scientists should agree about so much so much
of the time.

What Granny and I think is that part of the story about scientific
consensus turns crucially on the theory neutrality of observation.
Because the way one sees the world is largely independent of one's
theoretical attachments, it is possible to see that the predictions—
even of theories that one likes a lot—aren't coming out. Because the
way one sees the world is largely independent of one's theoretical
attachments, it is often possible for scientists whose theoretical attachments differ to agree on what experiments would be relevant to
deciding between their views, and to agree on how to describe the
outcomes of the experiments once they've been run. We admit,
Granny and I do, that working scientists indulge in every conceivable

form of fudging, smoothing over, brow beating, false advertising, self-deception, and outright rat painting—all the intellectual ills that flesh is heir to. It is, indeed, a main moral of this paper that, in many important ways, *scientists are a lot like us.* Nevertheless, it is perfectly obviously true that scientific observations often turn up unexpected and unwelcome facts, that experiments often fail *and are often seen to do so,* in short that what scientists observe isn't determined solely, or even largely, by the theories that they endorse, still less by the hopes that they cherish. It's *these* facts that the theory neutrality of observation allows us to explain.

The thing is: if you don't think that theory-neutral observation can settle scientific disputes, you're likely to think that they are settled by appeals to coherence, or convention or—worse yet—by mere consensus. And Granny—who is a Realist down to her tennis sneakers—doesn't see how any of those could compel *rational* belief. Granny and I have become pretty hardened, in our respective old ages; but we're both still moved by the idea that belief in the best science is rational because it is objective, and that it is objective because the predictions of our best theories can be *observed to be true.* I'm less adamant than Granny is, but I don't find the arguments against the theory neutrality of observation persuasive, and I think that the theory neutrality of observation is a doctrine that Realists have got to hold onto. "Help stamp out creeping pluralism," Granny says; "give 'em an inch and they'll take a mile!" "Right on (with certain significant qualifications)!" say I.

Notes

1. Well, four really. But I shan't discuss *ontological* approaches that support a distinction between observation terms and others by claiming that only the former denote (e.g., because whatever is unobservable is ipso facto fictitious). That the assumptions of the present discussion are fully Realistic with respect to unobservables will become entirely apparent as we proceed.

2. Interestingly enough, Jerome Bruner, in his foundational New Look disquisition "On Perceptual Readiness," takes note of this point using, in fact, the same examples I have cited. But he makes nothing of it, remarking only that the persistence of illusions in face of contrary background knowledge, though it militates against the "utter indistinguishability of perceptual and more conceptual interferences . . . must not lead us to overlook the common feature of inference underlying so much of cognitive activity" (1973, p. 8). The issue, however, is not whether some inferences are "more conceptual" than others—whatever, precisely, that might mean— or even whether perception is in some important sense inferential. What's at issue is rather: how much of what you know actually does affect the way you see. Failing to distinguish among these questions was, in my view, the original sin of New Look psychological theorizing.

Appendix

A Reply to Churchland's "Perceptual Plasticity and Theoretical Neutrality"

I have it in mind one of these days to write a paper called "Modularity and Objectivity" (or maybe "Objectivity and Modularity"). This, however, isn't it. What I propose to do in this appendix is argue a *very* narrow case. Churchland (1988) offers a batch of considerations intended to convince us that the cognitive impenetrability of perception "does not establish a theory-neutral foundation for knowledge" and that my empirical "views on impenetrability are almost certainly false." I propose to go through these arguments and show, in some detail, that they are no good; i.e., that they are no good *whether or not their conclusions are true.*

Churchland's paper is mostly concerned with three topics: 1. What are the epistemological implications of perceptual encapsulation (assuming, for the moment, that perceptual processes are indeed encapsulated)? 2. Is the encapsulation thesis true? 3. Some semantical considerations that are supposed to show that the meaning of observation terms must be theory dependent even if the perceptual processes involved in observing things are encapsulated and theory neutral. I propose to discuss Churchland's arguments under these heads, but with a spare category inserted for miscellanea.

The Epistemological Implications of Encapsulation

Churchland: "Let us suppose . . . that our perceptual modules . . . embody a systematic set of . . . assumptions about the world, whose influence on perceptual processing is unaffected by further or contrary information . . . this may be a recipe for a certain limited *consensus* among human perceivers, but it is hardly a recipe for theoretical *neutrality*. . . . What we have is a universal dogmatism, not an innocent Eden of objectivity. . . . Encapsulation does nothing to insure the truth of our perceptual beliefs. . ." (p. 5)

Reply: Nobody was offering innocence or a guarantee of truth. The question at issue is, what are the psychological conditions under which differences among the theories that observers hold are *not* impediments to perceptual consensus among the observers? Cognitive encapsulation seems to be an empirically necessary condition for this, and one that is (contrary to New Look psychologizing) apparently satisfied.

However, if you consider the sort of background information that penetrates perception (according to modularity theory), it turns out that perception *is* neutral, de facto, *with respect to most of the scientific (and, for that matter, practical) disagreements that observation is called upon to resolve.* According to standard versions of modularity theory (including the version I set out in *The Modularity of Mind*) perceptual processing has access only to background information about certain pervasive features of the relations between distal layouts and their proximal projections. (Hardly surprising, since it is precisely the relation between proximal and distal stimuli that perceptual processes are required to compute.) Thus, in the case of vision, a good candidate for accessible background is information about the geometrical relations between three-dimensional objects and the two-dimensional images they project onto the surface of the retina. In the linguistic case, a good candidate for accessible background is information about the grammatical structures that inform the type/token relation for the speaker/hearer's dialect.

The point is that, in both cases, reliance on such information constitutes a perceptual bias; and in both cases it makes perception "inferential" in the required sense. But this bias leaves perception neutral with respect to *almost all* theoretical disputes, so it couldn't ground any *general* argument for the unreliability of observation. Contrary to Churchland, there seems no reason to doubt that this very restricted sort of bias might be compatible with more than enough perceptual neutrality to "ensure for us a theory-neutral foundation for knowledge." (p. 7) Indeed, it might leave us with enough theory-neutral observation to allow us *to discover, and correct for, our own perceptual biases.* We might do so by relying upon inferences from theories to the observational confirmation of which our perceptual biases are irrelevant. This sort of bootstrapping is complicated to describe but often routinely easy to perform.

By the way, the preceding is not me pulling in my horns after the fact. That the premises to which perceptual inferences can appeal are substantively restricted by the architecture of the mind is the *whole point* of modularity theory.

Churchland: "In any case, the consensus would last only until the first mutant or alien comes along, to confront us with a different perceptual point of view." (p. 7)

Reply: Churchland apparently wants a naturalistic account of scientific objectivity to supply a guarantee that an arbitrary collection of intelligent organisms (e.g., a collection consisting of some homo sapiens and some Martians) would satisfy the empirical conditions for constituting a scientific community. *Of course* there can be no such guarantee. Our dependence upon the reliability of our cognitive faculties—perceptual biases and all—is part of the inductive risk that makes scientific inference nondemonstrative. On the other hand, I once had a book that purported to divide all the possible worries into the Real and the Merely Baroque. Churchland's worry—that (unspecified) aliens might arrive at a science different from ours in virtue of (unspecified) differences between their perceptual biases and ours—belongs, it seems to me, to the second category.

Is the Encapsulation Thesis True?

Two preliminary points: First, modularity is an *empirical* thesis, so how it comes out depends largely on what the psychological data prove to be. Second, the epistemologically relevant question is not whether modules are perfectly encapsulated, but whether they are encapsulated enough to permit theory-neutral, observational resolution of scientific disputes. Now read on, s.v.p.

Ambiguity

Churchland: "Many illusions [show] that our visual modules are indeed penetrable by higher cognitive assumptions. . . . One learns very quickly to make the [ambiguous] figure flip back and forth at will . . . by changing one's assumptions about the nature of the object or about the conditions of viewing." (p. 8)

Reply: False. One doesn't get the duck-rabbit (or the Necker cube) to flip by "changing one's assumptions"; one does it by (e.g.) changing one's fixation point. Believing that it's a duck doesn't help you see it as one; wanting to see it as a duck doesn't help much either. But knowing where to fixate *can* help. Fixate there *and then the flipping is automatic.*

When one becomes sophisticated about the laws that govern the way things look, one can finagle the looks by playing the laws. In the most obvious cases: one squints to make things look sharper; one cups one's hand behind one's ear to make them sound louder, etc. It doesn't begin to follow that auditory and visual acuity are cognitively penetrable.

Exactly in the same way, one learns that one can get the figure to flip by altering one's fixation point (or, for that matter, by just *waiting*; eventually it will flip of its own accord). To confuse this with the penetration of perception by utilities is to make the following mistake:

(a) Heart rate is cognitively penetrable! I can choose the rate at which my heart beats.
(b) Remarkable; how do you do it?
(a) Well, when I want it to beat faster, I touch my toes a hundred times. When I want it to beat slower, I take a little nap.
(b) Oh.

Churchland has some further, rather complicated cases on offer in which the reversal of an ambiguous figure brings other perceptual effects automatically in train (e.g., if you see the figure as reversed in depth, its apparent surface illumination is also seen to change.) Churchland's conclusion seems to be: So I can see the surface illumination as I choose.

But these examples don't advance the argument; they rest on the same mistake just scouted—only, as it were, at one further remove. What is going on is: (i) there's a choice about how you see the shape-ambiguous figure; and (ii) there's a nomic connection between seeing the figure as having a certain shape and seeing it as having a certain surface illumination. So you get to see the illumination you want *by* choosing how you see the shape. (And you get to see the shape you want by, e.g., squinting, altering your fixation point, etc.) *It doesn't follow that you can choose how you see the illumination*; all that follows is that there are things you can do to get yourself to see the illumination one way or the other (cf. the heartbeat case). A fortiori, it doesn't follow that there are "a wide range of elements central to visual perception . . . all of which are cognitively penetrable" (p. 10). Indeed, so far we haven't seen *any*. It may be that you can resolve an ambiguous figure by deciding what to attend to. But (a) which figures are ambiguous is *not* something you can decide; (b) nor can you decide what the terms of the ambiguity are; (c) nor can you decide what further psychological consequences (e.g., consequences for apparent illumination) the resolution of the ambiguity will entrain. This all sounds pretty unpenetrated to me.

Attention is, in short, a wild-card in an account of observational neutrality; but it may well be that if you fix the perceptual apparatus and you fix the object of attention, then you fix the appearances for all normal observers *even in the case of ambiguous figures*. If this is true it's epistemologically interesting, since part of arriving at a consensus as to what experiment to perform to choose among rival theories is agreeing about *what part of the experimental environment to attend to.* "It's where the dial points to that matters, not the color of the numerals;" and so forth.

Final word about Necker cubes. Even if they showed that the perceptual analysis of structurally ambiguous figures is unencapsulated (which they don't), that mightn't matter much for the neutrality of observation at large since, patently, *most stimuli aren't structurally ambiguous.*

Synchronic and Diachronic Penetration

Churchland: The issue is "not whether visual processing is in general very *easily* or *quickly* penetrated by novel or contrary information; the issue is whether in general, it is penetrable at all [for example by] long regimes of determined training, practice or conditioning." (p. 11)

Reply: It looks to me as though there are several issues. Let's see where we are.

It used to be thought that there is lots of evidence for relatively short-term effects of beliefs and utilities on perception; perceptual effects of your expectations about the color/suit correlations of playing cards; perceptual effects of transient peer pressures, etc. This was the evidential stuff of which New Look perceptual theory was made. And it was worrying because insensitivity to local alterations in beliefs and utilities is, in any event, a *necessary* condition for the theory neutrality of observation.

But now it is conceded that there may, after all, be *no* such local effects. It is, perhaps, only "comprehensive and protracted kinds of pressures" (15) to which perceptual processing is plastic. (These might not even be perceptual effects of acquiring *beliefs*; perhaps they're perceptual effects of *having the experiences* in virtue of which the beliefs are acquired.)

How much would this matter? What degree of *diachronic* encapsulation would be required for the possibility of theory-neutral observational resolution of scientific disputes? Well, surely less than cast-iron insensitivity of perceptual processes to training. Rather, what seems to be required is just enough diachronic encapsulation to allow perceptual consensus to survive the effects of the kinds of differences of learning histories that observers actually exhibit. For example, if training affects perceptual acuity, then that would be a kind of failure of diachronic encapsulation; but it wouldn't be anything that an epistemologist need worry about since observational consensus doesn't generally depend on the observers all having perceptual acuity to the same degree.

Well, what's the evidence? Is there enough diachronic encapsulation for the purposes at hand?

Answer: moot. Naturalized epistemology awaits the empirical findings. Whereas there's a respectable empirical argument to be made for synchronic encapsulation, *nobody* knows what's going on in the diachronic case; the only point that is worth making is that *if* diachronic encapsulation proves to be pervasive, then we will be within hailing distance of a naturalistic account of how theory-neutral observation is possible.

In any event, the point of present concern is that the considerations Churchland raises as militating against diachronic encapsulation cut next to no ice at all. There are a number of these.

Inverting Lenses   It is, at first blush, a shock to modularity theory that people can adapt to such drastic affronts to their perceptual prejudices as the inversion of the retinal image. This really does suggest the sort of perceptual plasticity—the sort of penetration of perception by experience—that modularity theory says shouldn't be there.

That's first blush; second blush is much better. For there are, after all, good ecological reasons why you might expect plasticity of this sort. Viz., organisms *grow,* and as they grow they must recalibrate the perceptual/motor mechanisms that correlate bodily gestures with perceived spatial positions (paradigmatically, in the human case, the mechanisms of hand-eye coordination). That is, what needs to be kept open for recalibration is whatever mechanisms compute the appropriate motor commands for getting to (or pointing to, or grasping) a visible object on the basis of its perceived location. Adaptation to inverted (and otherwise spatially distorting) lenses is plausibly an extreme case of this sort of recalibration. Indeed, there is experimental evidence that this is so. It turns out that smooth adaptation occurs only when the subject is permitted to actively manipulate the environment. In particular, adaptation does *not* occur (much) in organisms that are, for example, passively wheeled around but deprived of perceptual-motor feedback. (See Held and Bossom, 1961.)

In short, the subject in an inverting lens experiment has to learn such things as to *grasp* down for what *looks* up and vice versa. And this sort of relearning is likely not different in kind from the corrections that have to be made for alterations in the angular relations between hand, eye, and distal object in consequence of growth. So it's plausible that there are specific mechanisms that function to effect the required visual-motor calibrations, and that it's these mechanisms that are engaged in adaptation to inverting lenses. The moral of the inverting lens experiment thus seems to be, you find specific perceptual plasticity pretty much where you'd expect to find it on specific ecological grounds. What Churchland needs to show—and doesn't— is that you *also* find perceptual plasticity where you *wouldn't* expect it on specific ecological grounds; e.g., that you can somehow reshape the perceptual field by learning physics. Churchland offers, however, no examples of this. I strongly suspect that's because there aren't any.

Reading Churchland: "In recent centuries [we] have learned to perceive speech, not just aurally, but visually: we have learned to read. . . . the eyes . . . were [not] evolved for the instantaneous perception of those complex structures originally found in auditory phenomena, but their acquired mastery here illustrates the highly sophisticated and super-normal capacities that learning can produce in them." (p. 16)

Impatient reply: In recent centuries we have learned to perceive automobiles (not just aurally, but visually). Now the eyes were not evolved for the instantaneous perception of those complex structures. So doesn't their acquired mastery illustrate the highly sophisticated and super-normal capacities that learning can produce in perception?

Fiddlesticks. Churchland needs, and doesn't have, an argument that the visual perceptual capacities of people who can read (or, mutatis mutandis, people who can automobile-spot) differ in any interesting way from the visual perceptual capacities of people who can't. In precisely what respects does he suppose illiterates to be *visually* incapacitated?

The old story is: you read (spot automobiles) by making educated inferences from properties of things that your visual system *was* evolved to detect; shape, form, color, sequence and the like. Churchland offers no evidence that educating the inferences alters the perceptual apparatus.

Neurological Data Churchland: There are lots of "descending pathways" from higher to perceptual centers. To be sure, "experimentation on their functional significance is so far sparse, but . . ." (17)

Reply: None required. Heaven knows what psychological function "descending pathways" subserve. (Heaven knows what psychological function 98.769 percent of known neuroanatomical structures subserve, for that matter). One thing *is* clear: if there is no cognitive penetration of perception, then at least "descending pathways" aren't for *that*.

Perceptual Learning   Churchland: Someone musically sophisticated "perceives, in any composition whether great or mundane, a structure, development and rationale that is lost on the untrained ear." (20)

Reply: This merely begs the question, which is whether the effects of musical training are, in fact, perceptual. Churchland adds that one can "just as easily learn to recognize sounds under their dominant *frequency* description [or] under their *wavelength* description" (p. 20), but again no argument is provided that someone who has learned this has learned to perceive differently (as opposed to having learned a different way of labelling his perceptions and a different theory about what his perceptions are perceptions *of*; see below).

What Churchland has to show is, first, that *perceptual* capacities are altered by learning musical theory (as opposed to the truism that learning musical theory alters what you know about music;) second, that it's learning the theory (as opposed to just listening to lots of music) that alters the perception; and third that perception is altered in some different way if you learn not musical theory but acoustics. Churchland doesn't show any of these things—he doesn't even bother to *argue* for any of them—and I doubt that any of them are true. (Attempts to make a case for the corresponding phenomena in color perception have not fared well; see the recent experimental literature on the "Whorf hypothesis.") In any event, you don't refuse modularity theory by the unsupported assertion that it is contrary to the facts.

Miscellaneous: Two Digressions

The Argument about Caloric
I am not at all clear how Churchland thinks this argument goes. I paraphrase under correction.

Churchland: Somebody who describes his heat experiences in terms of caloric theory could insist upon the cognitive impenetrability of 'caloric illusions' (e.g., of the two-bucket illusion) with the absurd consequence that "our perceptual judgments about the caloric fluid pressures of common objects are in an important sense theory neutral." (p. 25)

Reply: What on earth does Churchland suppose that this observation shows? The theory neutrality of perception isn't about the impact of one's beliefs upon how one *describes* one's experiences; it's about the impact of one's beliefs upon one's experiences. It is thus perfectly true, and perfectly harmless, that our perceptual judgments about the caloric fluid pressures of common objects are in an important sense theory neutral; i.e., they are theory neutral qua perceptual judgments, but not qua judgments about caloric fluid pressures. Thus, if we changed theories, then we would no longer describe the illusion in term of the apparent caloric pressures in the two buckets; perhaps we'd describe it in terms of the apparent mmke. But, to repeat, the encapsulation thesis isn't that changing a guy's beliefs leaves his *descriptions* of his experiences intact; it's that it leaves *the experiences themselves* intact; in the present case, changing from the caloric theory to the mmke story *doesn't make the illusion go away*.

I do not wish to harp on this, but *really*! The "false" conclusion of which the thought experiment is supposed to be a reductio is that "the theories we embrace have no effect on caloric perception, and all humans with normal perceptual systems will thus perceive the world in exactly the same way" (25). Now, (a) the first conjunct is surely true; since there is no such thing as caloric, there is no such thing as caloric perception. What theories one holds doesn't change that, so the theories we embrace have no effect on caloric perception. And (b) the second conjunct *may* be false, but it's not shown to be by remarking that if you think there is caloric and you don't think there is mmke, then if you have a heat illusion you will describe it as a caloric illusion and you won't describe it as an mmke illusion. It's not only not *shown*; the observation doesn't even *bear*.

If you experience a perceptual phenomenon and you happen to think it's the sort of perceptual phenomenon that Granny is always experiencing, then you will perhaps describe it as a Granny phenomenon. And if you then happen to stop thinking that it is the sort of phenomenon that Granny is always experiencing, you will then perhaps stop describing it as a Granny phenomenon. These truisms do *not* tend to substantiate the hypothesis that your perceptual phenomena are penetrated by your beliefs about Granny. (Or, for that matter, to substantiate its denial).

It may be that Churchland has in mind an argument that goes like this: Our theories change the way we *describe* our experiences. But establishing a scientific consensus requires that there be some descriptions of perception that are theory neutral (e.g., the dial is pointing to the seven, the fluid has turned pink, etc.). So even if our *experiences* are theory neutral, that's not enough for theory-neutral observational validation of our theories; not, at least, if observational validation is something that scientific *communities* do.

Reply: The thought experiment about caloric shows that *some* of the ways we describe our experiences change with changes in theory (so does the thought about Granny); but what Churchland needs is that *all* of the ways we describe our experiences are (in principle) theory sensitive. In effect, he needs to argue that there can be no theory-neutral observation vocabulary even if there is theory-neutral observation. This seems to me, to put it mildly, less than self-evident. In any event, it surely doesn't not follow from the thought experiments. Or from any other argument that Churchland offers, so far as I can tell.

Digression on Sensations
Churchland: "If rigidity in the character of our sensations is all Fodor is concerned to defend, then I do not understand his objection to and dismissal of . . . alternative perceptual possibilities [that make] no assumptions about the plasticity of our sensations." (p. 30)

Reply: Churchland constructs a sensation/judgment dilemma, and then proposes that I impale myself on one of the horns. No thanks. There may be some nontruthvaluable (purely sensory) states involved in perception, but they aren't the output states of modules. To a first approximation, the outputs of modules are judgments about how things appear; judgments which are then up for being corrected by reference to background beliefs in the course of "higher" cognitive processing. The idea is that there are two sorts of judgmental processes (perceptual and higher cognitive), one but not the other of which is encapsulated. This idea is *neutral* on the issue of whether there is also some *non*judgmental process whose encapsulation might follow (perhaps trivially) from its nonjudgementalness. Modularity theory is neutral on all of this, and so am I.

Semantics

Churchland: If you accept a "conceptual role" story about meaning, then it will probably follow that what theory you hold determines what your observation statements mean.

Reply: So much the worse for conceptual role stories about meaning. So much the worse for use theories in general, for that matter; I wouldn't have one at a discount.

Churchland: You had better accept a conceptual role story about meaning, because "If a term 'F' is to be a meaningful observation term, then it's predication 'Fa' must have some material *consequences*: it must imply some further sentences . . . But if 'F' figures in no . . . background beliefs or assumptions whatever, then 'Fa' will be entirely without consequence or significance for anything . . . it will be a wheel that turns nothing. . . . Meaningful observation terms therefore will always be embedded within some set of assumptions. And since there is no analytic/synthetic distinction, these assumptions will always be speculative and corrigible." (p. 28)

Reply: (a) From the fact that meaningful observation (or other) terms are always embedded in a theory, it does not follow that the theory that a term is embedded in contributes to determining what it means. (b) The observation sentence 'Fa' is true iff *a* is *F*. So, by assumption, 'Fa' has a truth condition and is a fortiori significant. It would appear that this is so *whether or not* 'F' "figures in background beliefs or assumptions," so I'm at a loss to imagine what argument Churchland thinks he has given for a conceptual-role theory of meaning. (Of course, Churchland might claim that 'Fa' *couldn't* have a truth condition *unless* 'F' figures in background beliefs; but that would be to beg the question and establish conceptual role semantics by fiat.) For discussion of what appears to be a similar bad argument that turns up in Dennett's "Intentional Systems", see Fodor, 1987, p. 89.

Coda

Churchland: Must the journey end here? . . . The long awakening is potentially endless. The human spirit will continue its breathtaking adventure of self-reconstruction, and its perceptual and motor capacities will continue to develop as an integral part of its self-reconstruction" (p. 35).

Reply: An endless awakening sounds like not all that much fun, come to think of it: I, for one, am simply unable to self-reconstruct until I've had my morning coffee. Actually, theories come and theories go and people don't really change very much; or so it seems to me. That's probably just as well; if we *become* our theories, how are they to "die in our stead"?

References

Anderson, J. 1983. *The Architecture of Cognition*. Cambridge, MA: Harvard University Press.

Baker, Lynne. Forthcoming. "On a Causal Theory of Content," in *Philosophical Perspectives*.

Barwise, J., and J. Perry. 1983. *Situations and Attitudes*. Cambridge, MA: MIT Press.

Boghossian, P. 1989. "Review of Colin McGinn's *Wittgenstein on Meaning*," *Philosophical Review* 1, 83–84.

Bruner, J. 1957. "On Perceptual Readiness," *Psychological Review* 65, 14–21. Reprinted in J. Anglin, ed., *Beyond The Information Given*. New York: W.W. Norton, 1973.

Carey, S. 1985. *Conceptual Change in Childhood*. Cambridge, MA: MIT Press.

Chomsky, N. 1959. "A Review of B.F. Skinner's Verbal Behavior," *Language* 35, 1, 26–58.

Chomsky, N. 1986. *Knowledge of Language*. New York: Praeger.

Churchland, Patricia. 1987. "Epistemology in the Age of Neuroscience," *Journal of Philosophy* 84, 10, 544–555.

Churchland, Paul. 1979. *Scientific Realism and The Plasticity of Mind*. Cambridge: Cambridge University Press.

Churchland, Paul. 1981. "Eliminative Materialism and Propositional Attitudes," *Journal of Philosophy* 78, 2, 67–90.

Churchland, Paul. 1988. "Perceptual Plasticity and Theoretical Neutrality," *Philosophy of Science* 55, 2, 167–187.

Cummins, R. 1983. *The Nature of Psychological Explanation*. Cambridge, MA: MIT Press.

Cummins, R. 1989. "Representation and Covariaton," in S. Silvers, ed., *Representation* 40 (*Philosophical Study Series*, Dodrecht: Kluwer).

Dennett, D. 1978a. *Brainstorms*. Cambridge, MA: Bradford Books.

Dennett, D. 1978b. "A Cure for the Common Code?" in Dennett, *Brainstorms*, q.v.

Dennett, D. 1978c. "Intentional Systems," in Dennett, *Brainstorms*, q.v.

Dennett, D. 1981. "True Believers: The Intentional Stance and Why It Works," in A.F. Heath, ed., *Scientific Explanation: Papers Based on Herbert Spencer Lectures Given in the University of Oxford*. Oxford: Clarendon Press.

Dennett, D. 1987. *The Intentional Stance*. Cambridge, MA: MIT Press.

Dretske, F. 1981. *Knowledge and the Flow of Information*. Cambridge, MA: MIT Press

Dretske, F. 1983a. "The Epistemology of Belief," *Synthese* 55, 3–19.

Dretske, F. 1983b. "Précis of *Knowledge and the Flow of Information*," *The Behavioral and Brain Sciences* 6, 55–90.

Dreyfus, H. 1979. *What Computers Can't Do*. New York: Harper & Row.

Field, H. 1978. "Mental Representation," *Erkenntnis* 13; also in N. Block, ed., *Readings in Philosophy of Psychology* 2. Cambridge, MA: Harvard University Press.

Fodor, J. Forthcoming. "Information and Representation," in P. Hanson, ed., Information, Language, and Cognition, Vancouver: University of British Columbia Press.

Fodor, J. Unpublished. "Psychosemantics, Or Where Do Truth Conditions Come From." Unpublished manuscript.

Fodor, J. 1975. *The Language of Thought.* New York: Thomas Y. Crowell, Co. Reprinted by Harvard University Press, 1979.

Fodor, J. 1978. "Propositional Attitudes," *The Monist* 61, 4, 501–523. Reprinted in Fodor, J., *Representations*, q.v.

Fodor, J. 1981a. "The Mind-Body Problem" *Scientific American* 244, 515–531.

Fodor, J. 1981b. "Methodological Solipsism," *The Behavioral and Brain Sciences* 3, 1980; reprinted in Fodor, J., *Representations*. q.v.

Fodor, J. 1981c. *Representations.* Cambridge, MA: MIT Press.

Fodor, J. 1981d. "The Current Status of The Innateness Controversy," in Fodor, *Representations*, q.v.

Fodor, J. 1983. *The Modularity of Mind.* Cambridge, MA: MIT Press.

Fodor, J. 1984. "Semantics, Wisconsin Style." *Synthese* 59, 231–250. Reprinted in this volume.

Fodor, J. 1985. "Banish Discontent," in J. Butterfield, ed., *Language Mind and Logic,* Cambridge: Cambridge University Press.

Fodor, J. 1987. *Psychosemantics; The Problem of Meaning in the Philosophy of Mind.* Cambridge, MA: MIT Press.

Fodor, J., T. Bever, and M. Garrett. 1974. *The Psychology of Language.* New York: McGraw Hill.

Fodor, J., and Z. Pylyshyn. 1988. "Connectionism and Cognitive Architecture," *Cognition* 28, 3–71.

Fodor, J., and B. McLaughlin, 1989. "Connectionism and the Problem of Systematicity; Why Smolensky's Solution Doesn't Work," forthcoming in *Cognition.*

Glymour, C. 1987. "Android Epistemology and the Frame Problem," in Z. Pylyshyn, ed., *The Robot's Dilemma,* Ontario:

Goodman, N. 1978. *Ways of Worldmaking.* Indianapolis: Hackett Publishing Company.

Gould, S. J., and R. C. Lewontin, 1979. "The Spandrels of San Marco and the Panglossian Paradigm: A Critique of the Adaptationist Program," *Proceedings of the Royal Society of London,* B 205, 581–598.

Gregory, R. 1970. *The Intelligent Eye.* New York: McGraw-Hill Book Company.

Hanson, N. 1961. *Patterns of Discovery.* Cambridge: Cambridge University Press.

Haugeland, J. 1981. "The Nature and Plausibility of Cognitivism," *The Behavioral and Brain Sciences* 2, 215–260.

Held, R., and Bossom, J. 1961. "Neonatal Deprivation and Adult Rearrangement: Complementary Techniques for Analyzing Plastic Sensory-Motor Coordinations," *Journal of Comparative and Physiological Psychology* 56, 872–876.

Hornstein, N. 1988. "The Heartbreak of Semantics," *Mind and Language* 3, 9–27.

Israel, D. 1987. *The Role of Propositional Objects of Belief in Action,* CSLI Monograph Report No. CSLI-87-72. Palo Alto: Stanford University.

Jackendoff, R. 1972. *Semantic Interpretations in Generative Grammar.* Cambridge, MA: MIT Press.

Kripke, S. 1979. "A Puzzle about Belief," in A. Margalit, ed., *Meaning and Use,* Dordrecht: Reidel.

Kripke, S. 1982. *Wittgenstein on Rules and Private Language.* Cambridge, MA: Harvard University Press.

Kuhn, T. 1962. *The Structure of Scientific Revolutions*. Chicago: The University of Chicago Press.

Larkin, J. 1987. "The Role of Problem Representation in Physics," in D. Gentner and A. Stevens, eds., *Mental Models*. New York: Lawrence Erlbaum.

Lepore, E., and B. Loewer. 1987. "Mind Matters," *Journal of Philosophy* 84, 11, 630–642.

Linas, R. 1987. 'Mindedness' as a Functional State of the Brain," in C. Blakemore, ed., *Mindwaves*, Oxford: Basil Blackwell, Ltd.

Loar, B. 1981. *Mind and Meaning*. Cambridge: Cambridge University Press.

Marslen-Wilson, W., and L. Tyhler. 1987. "Against Modularity," in J.L. Garfield, ed., *Modularity in Knowledge Representation and Natural Language Understanding*. Cambridge, MA: MIT Press.

Mates, B. 1952. "Synonymity," in L. Linsky, ed., Semantics and the Philosophy of Language, Urbana: University of Illinois Press.

Matthews, R. 1984. "Troubles with Representationalism," *Social Research* 51, 4, 1065–1097.

MacCorquodale, K. 1970. "On Chomsky's Review of Skinner's *Verbal Behavior*," *Journal of The Experimental Analysis of Behavior* 13, 1, 83–99.

McLaughlin, B. Unpublished. "Type Epiphenomenalism, Type Dualism, and the Causal Priority of the Physical." (manuscript).

Miller, G., E. Galanter, and K. Pribram, 1960. *Plans and The Structure of Behavior*. New York: Holt, Reinhart, and Winston.

Millikan, R. 1984. *Language, Thought and Other Biological Categories*. Cambridge, MA: MIT Press.

Millikan, R. 1986. "Thoughts without Laws: Cognitive Science without Content," *Philosophical Review* 95, 47–80.

Papineau, D. 1988 *Reality and Representation*. Oxford: Basil Blackwell, Ltd.

Putnam, H. 1983. "Computational Psychology and Interpretation Theory," in *Philosophical Papers III: Realism and Reason*. Cambridge: Cambridge University Press.

Putnam, H. 1986. "Meaning Holism," in L. Hahn and P. Schilpp, eds., *The Philosophy of W.V. Quine (The Library of Living Philosophers, vol. 18)*. La Salle, IL: Open Court Publishers.

Putnam, H. 1988. *Representation and Reality*. Cambridge, MA: MIT Press.

Pylyshyn, Z. 1984. *Computation and Cognition*. Cambridge, MA: MIT Press.

Rey, G. Unpublished. "Concepts, Stereotypes and Individual Psychology; Sketch of A Framework." (ms)

Rock, I. 1983. *The Logic of Perception*, Cambridge, MA: MIT Press.

Ross, W. 1975. *Sail Power*. New York: Alfred A. Knopf.

Searle, J. 1980. "Minds, Brains and Programs," *The Behavioral and Brain Sciences* 3, 417–424.

Skinner, B.F. 1957. *Verbal Behavior*. New York: Appleton-Century-Crofts.

Stabler, E. 1983. "How are Grammars Represented?" *The Behavioral and Brain Sciences* 6, 391–402.

Stalnaker, R. 1984. *Inquiry*. Cambridge, MA: MIT Press.

Shiffer, S. 1987. *Remnants of Meaning*, Cambridge, MA: MIT Press.

Stampe, D. 1975. "Show and Tell," in B. Freed, A. Marras, and P. Maynard, eds., *Forms of Representation*. New York: American Elsevier Publishing Company, Inc.

Stampe, D. 1977. "Towards a Causal Theory of Linguistic Representation," in P.

French, T. Euhling, and H. Wettstein, eds., *Midwest Studies in Philosophy* 2, 42–63. Minneapolis: University of Minneapolis Press.

Stich, S. 1983. *From Folk Psychology to Cognitive Science*. Cambridge, MA: MIT Press.

Vendler, Z. 1983. *Res Cogitans*. Ithaca, NY: Cornell University Press.

Wagner, S. Unpublished. "Theories of Mental Representation," (ms).

Wittgenstein, L. 1953. *Philosophical Investigations*. New York: Macmillan.

Index of Names